Joanne Woodward

ALSO BY PETER SHELLEY
AND FROM MCFARLAND

Gene Hackman: The Life and Work (2019)

Philip Seymour Hoffman: The Life and Work (2017)

Anne Bancroft: The Life and Work (2017)

*Neil Simon on Screen: Adaptations and Original Scripts
for Film and Television* (2015)

Gwen Verdon: A Life on Stage and Screen (2015)

Sandy Dennis: The Life and Films (2014)

Australian Horror Films, 1973–2010 (2012)

Jules Dassin: The Life and Films (2011)

Frances Farmer: The Life and Films of a Troubled Star (2011)

*Grande Dame Guignol Cinema: A History of Hag Horror
from* Baby Jane *to* Mother (2009)

Joanne Woodward

Her Life and Career

Peter Shelley

McFarland & Company, Inc., Publishers
Jefferson, North Carolina

Acknowledgments

Continued thanks are offered to
Kath Perry and Barry Lowe
for their encouragement.

ISBN (print) 978-1-4766-7580-0 ∞
ISBN (ebook) 978-1-4766-3697-9

LIBRARY OF CONGRESS CATALOGUING DATA ARE AVAILABLE

BRITISH LIBRARY CATALOGUING DATA ARE AVAILABLE

Front cover: Joanne Woodward (Photofest)

Printed in the United States of America

*McFarland & Company, Inc., Publishers
Box 611, Jefferson, North Carolina 28640
www.mcfarlandpub.com*

Table of Contents

Preface

I think I first saw Joanne Woodward in the film *Rachel, Rachel* (1969) where she gave a remarkable performance, expanding the cliché of the virgin old maid to incorporate nobility, a wistful lyricism, intelligence and wit. She was Oscar-nominated but that year the Academy featured four other remarkable female performances, resulting in an unprecedented tie for the award by Katharine Hepburn and Barbra Streisand. Woodward had already won the Best Actress Oscar for *The Three Faces of Eve* (1957), but while that seemed to be a triumph of technique, with *Rachel, Rachel* she achieved real screen transparency. As far as we knew, this was the real Woodward and not just an aspiring actress facing the challenge of portraying a woman with three personalities.

Her greatest strengths as a performer were her pragmatism and likability. Pauline Kael wrote that Woodward had a trouper quality: a briny actress with solidity, great audience rapport and a wide streak of humor about herself. It seemed no coincidence that she was Oscar-nominated two more times for playing inhibited conventional women with those qualities in *Summer Wishes, Winter Dreams* (1973) and *Mr. & Mrs. Bridge* (1990). Even on the rare occasions when Woodward played dragon ladies, she made you understand their nastiness: the rich bitch in *From the Terrace* (1960) and the crazy rabbit-killer in *The Effect of Gamma Rays on Man-in-the Moon Marigolds* (1972), perhaps the actress's most provocative role. She had the range to do other kinds of parts, in dramas and comedies, and even sang, though it did not get her cast in musicals. Woodward's expression of anger was nearly always funny, though in her comedies with Paul Newman—*Rally 'Round the Flag, Boys!* (1958) and *A New Kind of Love* (1963)—she lacked his lightness of touch. The latter title was particularly bizarre in that her character transformed from male drag to female drag, both equally unamusing. The comedy *A Fine Madness* (1966) saw the actress give her only bad performance where her playing was too broad. The attempts at sexpot roles, like *The Stripper* (1963), were equally problematic since she was not the Marilyn Monroe type.

Woodward also played a prostitute, in *WUSA* (1970), though one with a facial scarring that added something different to the canon. And she was miscast as the slatternly and sloppy Lola in TV's *Come Back Little Sheba* (1977). Newman reported that in *The Shadow Box* (1980), his wife played closest to her real personality, though the extrovert character was also a drunk.

Woodward's training with the Neighborhood Playhouse and the Actors Studio had her perceived as a Method actress. In her book *From Reverence to Rape: The Treatment of Women in the Movies*, Molly Haskell describes her as one of the serious-artist actresses in black-and-white film, like Anne Bancroft, Julie Harris, Kim Stanley and Barbara Bel

1

Geddes. These women emerged in Hollywood movies of the 1950s, but were not personality actresses, movie-movie stars in living Technicolor like Marilyn Monroe, Elizabeth Taylor and Grace Kelly. Haskell seemed to have a point about Woodward, since in the black-and-white *The Three Faces of Eve* she didn't give a movie star performance. Her Method origins were also evident in actor mannerisms, though she used them in real life when interviewed as well. They may have been choices made to express realism but her self-conscious self-touching read as fiddling, and her pursed and twisted mouth was inexplicable. The mannerisms were not as extreme and annoying as Method alumni Sandy Dennis and Geraldine Page, but they could draw unnecessary focus and undermine the actress' work. She also had trouble with tears, since though Woodward could cry, tears were not visible. She could do accents, and though the actress had learned to neutralize her own Southern accent, it could still be heard in the pronunciation of some words when she wasn't playing a Southerner. For parts, Woodward changed her hair color and style, used wigs and wore glasses.

She played leading roles in five films as well as a number of supporting ones, but as she aged and got better at her craft, the parts dried up. This led her back to the stage (where she had dabbled before) and to television, where she had the leading role in a series of quality projects. The actress also produced and directed, the latter mostly for the stage, though there was a short film entitled *Come Along with Me* that was broadcast on television in 1982. Woodward's mature years also saw her support of the Westport Country Playhouse intensify when she took on its artistic leadership from 2000 to 2005.

This is the first book to span the actress's solo career. There have been three prior biographies of the Newmans—the out-of-print 1975 *Joanne Woodward and Paul Newman: Their Lives Together (and Apart)* by Gene Shalit, the 1988 *Paul and Joanne* by Joe Morella and Edward Z. Epstein, and the 1989 *Paul Newman and Joanne Woodward* by Susan Netter. Her life and career were also covered in Newman biographies by Elena Oumano (1989), Eric Lax (1996), Daniel O'Brien (2004), Shawn Levy (2009), Lawrence J. Quirk (2009) and Darwin Porter (2009). The Porter book in particular explored the rumor that the Newmans had a lavender marriage and named many male stars that he had allegedly had affairs with, though no females were named as being lovers of the actress. This gossip is only mentioned since Joanne Woodward herself commented on it to the press, denouncing the rumors as fiction. But while her husband was undoubtedly the greater movie star, Woodward was considered the greater actor and therefore her work was deserving of individual attention.

This book cannot be considered the definitive coverage of her career since some of her television work is not available for viewing. My biggest regrets are not being able to see the cable version of the stage hit *Candida* and the episode on Woodward in *Inside the Actors Studio*. In these cases, as much information as possible has been provided. Accessing the aforementioned sources and any associated biographies and books on co-workers allowed me to consider differing views of some of the events in her life and to highlight any apparent inaccuracies. My research had me review the available interviews that the actress gave for newspapers and magazines, with the archives of *The New York Times* and the Internet Movie Database's Related News being particularly helpful. YouTube was also invaluable in sourcing interviews, as was the Getty Images website with their record of her public attendances.

The book is written as a biography, with Woodward's career presented in the context of her life. I have not made new chapters for each film, television appearance or stage show. Rather they are mixed into the biography, with work listed chronologically according to when they were made as opposed to when they were first seen. I have given an analysis of the work when possible, positioning the actress' place in the project, commenting on her look and performance, and quoting any comments I have found by Woodward as well as those about her by director and co-stars. I have also given the critical reaction that the work received and information about any awards it earned. To complement the text, I have supplied stills from some of the films. Additionally, the book comes with an appendix of work and a bibliography of reference sources.

1

Beginning

Joanne Gignilliat Trimmier Woodward was a winter baby, born on February 27, 1930, in the small town of Thomasville in southern Georgia. The blonde-haired, green-eyed child was the second of Wade Woodward (December 24, 1900–December 16, 1976) from Georgia and Elinor Gasque Gignilliat *née* Trimmier Woodward (July 3, 1903–September 8, 1992) from South Carolina, their first being Wade Jr. The names Gignilliat and Trimmier were of Huguenot origin. Wade Sr., a graduate of Clemson College, was a school system administrator; he started off as a teacher, then became a principal in another school and a superintendent in another. Elinor was the prototypical Southern belle, raised an Episcopalian, and the family lived in modest circumstances.

Located about ten miles from the Florida border, Thomasville had once flourished as a winter resort but there was little culture in the town. Elinor was an avid moviegoer, naming her daughter after Joan Crawford having nearly given birth to her the middle of the Crawford MGM comedy film *Our Modern Maidens* (1929). She took her daughter to the movies from an early age so that they made a great impression on her. Woodward said in an October 6, 1957, *New York Times* interview that she wanted to be an actress from the age of three.

Her favorite was Bette Davis, though one source claims that seeing Greer Garson in the MGM biopic *Madame Curie* (1943) made such an impression on the girl that she initially wanted to be a doctor. Woodward herself reported that another early ambition was to be an opera singer. She became devoted to light opera after someone gave her a recording of *Carmen*; the young girl adored it and sang along. She also loved the recordings of Nelson Eddy and Jeanette MacDonald. But Woodward didn't pursue singing because there wasn't much of an opportunity to advance an operatic career where she lived.

When she was two, her older brother was supposed to do the Pledge of Allegiance at the movie house, but he got the measles, so Joanne did it instead since she had learned it. After the girl spoke, the audience applauded, partly because she was really cute with her Shirley Temple curls. Hearing the applause, she ran back on stage and said it again, and the audience applauded again. One source claims there was an attempt at a third rendition but her mother finally dragged her off the stage. To show she was her own person, Woodward reported that she was actually interested in pigtails rather than curls and snipped off the ringlets on her Shirley Temple doll.

Childhood had given her what would become a lifelong love of needlepoint but at the age of 12 she also kept a list on her bedside table of "How to Be a Fascinating Woman." The items included pausing in doorways when entering a room, being well-read, talking very little but speaking in a low voice, and being a good listener. It was reported that Woodward earned money when she was five after swiping jonquils from her mother's backyard garden and selling them in the front yard to neighbors. This tale could have been apocryphal, from a 20th Century–Fox publicity handout around the time of her Oscar nomination for *The Three Faces of Eve*. At age six she directed and starred in front-porch shows, dragging people off the street and charging them a nickel apiece to watch her playing all the leading roles herself. She also had piano and ballet lessons, and read books and plays to further her interest in acting.

Because of Wade's work, the family moved around for several years, leaving Thomasville when Joanne was in the second grade and relocating to Blakely and Thomaston before settling in Marietta, Georgia, where she attended Marietta High School. Marietta was located about 15 miles from Atlanta and her mother took her to the premiere of *Gone with the Wind* in December 1939 when she was nine. They had seen the romance *Wuthering Heights* (1939) and she had fallen madly in love with Laurence Olivier, who attended the *Gone with the Wind* event with his wife, Vivien Leigh, and Joanne saw them. One source has Woodward running from the crowd lining the streets to catch a glimpse, shrieking hysterically. Another claims she had convinced her mother to wait outside the hotel where Olivier was staying with Leigh. Woodward then leapt into their limousine when the door opened and landed smack on Olivier and told him he was her favorite actor. Her mother also reported that Woodward was so excited when they watched the film that she kept jumping up and down in her seat whenever Leigh was on the screen. The girl pointed to the actress and whispered to her mother that one day she (Joanne) would be a great actress. Her mother said that her daughter was so convincing that she believed her.

The family moved once again when Woodward was a junior in high school after her parents divorced, and settled in Greenville, South Carolina. Woodward was said to have an I.Q. of 135 and her mother claimed that the girl memorized parts of the *Encyclopædia Britannica*. Woodward claimed that was something her mother made up, though she admitted to reading the encyclopedia. She did well at school, graduating from Greenville High School in 1947. Her father had become associated with the Macmillan Publishing Company, and joined Charles Scribner's Sons in New York where he was a publishing executive. Woodward later said that it was too bad she didn't want to be a writer because her father became vice-president of the company, a position he retired from in 1966. But although her parents were no longer together, Wade remained involved in the lives of his children. Woodward never felt

A 1950 portrait of Joanne Woodward.

close to her father, since it appeared he favored her brother. Later she admitted to having therapy as an adult to help her come to terms with what the actress saw as his loss.

With the encouragement of her mother who considered her daughter the prettiest girl in town, the girl entered beauty contests and won. At this time, Woodward was little over 5'4", weighed 117 pounds and sported a petite but curvaceous figure, described as 34–24–34. She reportedly attracted a lot of male attention but she did not allow herself to be diverted from her love of acting. Her goal was to go to Hollywood or New York.

In high school, she appeared in theatrical productions, including a memorable role as Lady Make-Believe, an animated doll. She impressed her drama teacher, who felt the girl's future was in New York. Her father did not agree, wanting Woodward to go to college. After he convinced Joanne and her mother, she was enrolled at Louisiana State University in Baton Rouge, with a major in drama. There Woodward was an initiate of Chi Omega sorority, and studied classical theater. She played Ophelia, complete with a Southern drawl. The actress felt she was awful and vowed never to play Shakespeare again until she could speak the language. Woodward was in nearly every play at LSU but also darkly neurotic, wearing black sweaters and rather pretentiously carrying around a copy of *Ulysses*. Another possibly fanciful Fox studio publicity tale was that in high school and college, the girl modeled for a dollar an hour, and between classes held rummage sales on the street corner; she used the pin money to buy chocolates.

She dropped out of LSU after two years, never completing her studies. Woodward had the opportunity to go to New York and drama school. She worked as a secretary in Greenville for a few months, then appeared in several productions at Greenville's Little Theatre. Her father saw her in *The Glass Menagerie*, where she played Laura, and was so impressed that he agreed to her going to New York. Before she left, Woodward spent a season in summer stock in Chatham, Massachusetts, playing starring roles in *Liliom, All My Sons* and *Ten Little Indians*.

The aspiring 21-year-old actress arrived in New York by train. She lived in a barren cold-water apartment at 72nd Street and York Avenue but her basic expenses were covered by an allowance from her father of $60 a month. The apartment had a little gas oven, but also cockroaches and a horrible old male neighbor who used to peek out at the girls. Breakfast was hot dogs, bought from street wagons.

Woodward spent her days trudging to modeling agencies, and worked for a few months for the John Robert Powers agency. She also did the rounds of casting offices, bought standing-room tickets for Broadway shows, and had coffees and beers in the luncheonettes and bars that aspiring performers frequented. She spent hours at the Commodore Drug Store, sipping coffee with Rod Steiger and James Dean, though when they raised the minimum to 50 cents most actors couldn't go in anymore. She almost became a tour guide. Woodward had a crush on Ezio Pinza, who was starring in the musical *South Pacific* on Broadway. She bought a standing-room ticket to see him and used to haunt the Astor Pharmacy to get a glimpse of him on the way to the Majestic Theatre.

The actress enrolled in the Neighborhood Playhouse (54th Street off First Avenue), studying with Sanford Meisner. He practiced the Stanislavsky acting theory and system distinct from that of Lee Strasberg and the Actors Studio. She was surprised to be accepted into the school, because they turned down a lot of people. At first Woodward hated Meisner though she later called him the greatest dramatic coach in the world. On her first day, the actress had to stand up and give her name and say where she came from, and the whole class laughed at her Southern accent. Woodward learned that she would have to lose it since speech was the actor's stock-in-trade, and having a regional accent would limit her opportunities to plays by Tennessee Williams. It took the actress six months of hard work to learn "theater English."

She was also aware that her looks were not the type that was then fashionable—even at the Playhouse. Woodward acquired the belief that she was not attractive, since the type in favor was little dark neurotic girls from the wrong side of the tracks. The boys at the Playhouse wouldn't date anybody else so Woodward tried to turn herself into the type, but it didn't work. She and her roommate, Rawn Harding, used to compete to see who was more neurotic, since they wanted to be the worst neurotic.

At the Playhouse, there were two acting classes a day, dance classes taught by Martha Graham, and classes in speech, singing, and theater history. Graham felt that everything came from the body, and that the body moved because of emotion. It was either Graham or Louis Horst who taught a class called Pre-Classic Dance Forms, teaching students how to move. Woodward discovered that there was no easy way to learn her craft. Meisner told her at an early stage that she was a character actress, which was a shock to her, because Woodward thought of herself as an ingénue. He refused to give her anything but character parts, which she hated. For two years, Woodward said she was slapped down, torn apart, and taught to act by Meisner. The student was determined to show her teacher that she could be a good actress, whether she ever became a star or not. One day she was doing an improv scene in which she had to ask another actor for $200 for an abortion, after his brother had knocked her up. The actress was off stage, terrified, and then went in, staggering, and said, "You have to give me $200 because I'm, I'm, I'm…" and she couldn't get the word pregnant out of her mouth. The other actor looked at her and started to laugh, and Woodward just felt terrible. She started to cry and ran out of the room. Finally, Meisner sent someone to drag her back and Woodward stood there quaking. Then he said to her, "Well, Joanne, that's the best thing you've done in six months." She found other Meisner methods useful, like daydreaming about a part in pre-rehearsal and creating an image of the character. He believed acting was playing and having a wonderful time, and the actress would employ these techniques in her work.

In her second year in New York, 1952, an MCA agency representative saw her perform at the Playhouse. He placed Woodward under contract, and she reported that this led her to get her first professional work two weeks after graduating. John Foreman at MCA was handling the television careers of new actors and brought the actress to the attention of Robert Montgomery, who was producing a dramatic television anthology series for NBC entitled *Robert Montgomery Presents*. She had to audition for the teleplay writer Emily Kimbrough and was cast in the episode "Penny," which was shot in New York and broadcast on June 9, 1952. Woodward played the title character, a 15-year-old whose trials and tribulations have to be understood by her father (Walter Abel).

One source claims that the actress was cast in the CBS *Studio One* production "The Kill" (September 22, 1952). This had a teleplay by Reginald Rose, based on the novel by Cameron Owen, and was directed by Franklin Schaffner. However, it appears Woodward was not in this show. She was in the CBS live historical anthology television series *Omnibus* in the five-part episode "Mr. Lincoln" a.k.a. "Abraham Lincoln." The five episodes aired on November 16 and 30 and December 14, 1952, and January 11 and February 8, 1953. The show was shot in New York, written by James Agee and directed by Norman Lloyd. The title character was played by Royal Dano and Joanne played Ann

Rutledge, Lincoln's fiancée when he lived in New Salem, Illinois, between 1831 and 1835. The show was broadcast over six hours but the available copy is an edited version at 72 minutes. In this, Woodward only appears in Parts 2 and 3, and is billed 13th. Her hair is worn shoulder-length, parted in the middle, and she wears period clothes including a full-length skirt, shawl and bonnet. Regrettably for the actress, Ann's death occurs off-screen. Her best scene is perhaps when Ann listens to Abe as he tells her that he cannot marry her because he wants a career in politics.

She was next in the ABC horror-mystery anthology television series *Tales of Tomorrow* episode "The Bitter Storm" (December 26, 1952). Scripted by A. Aulicino and directed by Don Medford, it centered on Prof. Leland Russell (Arnold Moss), a scientist living on an island who invents a machine which picks up and recaptures sounds from the past. Woodward played Pat, Leland's niece, a supporting role. She wears her shoulder-length blonde hair in a middle part. The role has Pat speak Aramaic. The actress' best moment is perhaps when Pat expresses to Leland her emotional concern over Steve (Phillip Pine) being out in the storm.

Some of her television work was shot in Hollywood. She was happy to go there, though she didn't have enough money to rent a car in California. The actress considered her television experience marvelous days.

She worked on the 1952 presidential campaign for Adlai Stevenson, standing around on street corners passing out leaflets.

Woodward met Paul Newman one day at MCA, though sources differ as to who it was that introduced them. The actress said she was introduced by agent Maynard Morris, while another said it was John Foreman, who kept her waiting when his meeting with Newman went long. Aspiring actor Newman was at MCA making the rounds of agents hoping to get a job. He thought that she was an extraordinarily pretty girl, and he said hello, though another source claims he was not bowled over by her. Woodward was unimpressed, hating him on sight. She said Newman was pretty and neat like an Arrow Collar ad. To her, he looked like a snobby college boy type in an unimpressive seersucker suit, the kind insurance salesmen wore in summer in her native Georgia. She also hated him because he was funny.

The couple met again when both were cast by director Joshua Logan in his Broadway production of the William Inge play *Picnic*. Woodward had attended a cattle call for the new show, which was originally titled *Front Porch* and set a small town in Kansas, in the backyard shared by Flo Owens and Helen Potts. She was then summoned to appear before Logan, who asked her to read a scene from the new play. He liked Woodward's reading and hired her as the understudy for two parts: Madge Owens, the prettiest girl in town, and her younger sister Millie. Madge would be played by Janice Rule and Millie by Kim Stanley. John Foreman reported that Logan said the actress wasn't pretty enough for Madge and much too pretty for Millie. The director himself commented that she saved the production a lot of money by being able to play both parts. Woodward said that she would have probably also agreed to go on for Elizabeth Wilson who played the school-teacher Christine Schoenwalder, though Wilson was a lot taller than she was. Logan commented that Newman was cast as a wisecracking paperboy who appears to have been initially named Jockset, then Joker, but was later known as Bomber.

When Woodward reported for work the next day, Logan introduced her to Newman, and she commented that they had met before. He didn't remember meeting her at the MCA office, because the actor said he met so many aspiring actresses. This comment didn't endear him to Woodward and seemed to confirm her initial impression that he was a conceited snob. Newman confided to Rod Steiger that he had all the lovers he could handle at the time and he wasn't about to take on another, even though he could tell that Woodward was attracted to him. The actor already had a wife and child, with another on the way. He had married actress Jacqueline "Jackie" Emily Witte, who somewhat resembled Woodward, on December 27, 1949. She had their son Scott on September 23, 1950; their second child Susan, born February 21, 1953, would be born after the Broadway run of the play had opened.

Picnic premiered at the Hartman Theater in Columbus, Ohio, then moved to William Inge's hometown of St. Louis, the Hanna Theater in Cleveland, Boston and then Broadway. Woodward was called in to fill for Rule and Stanley during the out-of-town tryouts though Logan said he missed her performances because they were having such trouble with other parts of the play that he spent a lot of time with Inge. She forgave him but the director thought she didn't really. The try-outs also saw Newman recast as Alan Seymour, the wealthy guy who loses the girl, and as the understudy for the sexually magnetic vagrant Hal (played by Ralph Meeker).

Woodward reportedly didn't think much of Newman when she first saw him perform, feeling he was just a pretty face and had no craft. (The pretty face reminded her of a Botticelli angel.) But doing the show on the road made the actress realize he wasn't conceited at all. In fact, she found him rather modest for such a good-looking boy. The actress said he had a protective wall around him when they met, but deep down Newman was a sensitive man with the soul of an artist. He just didn't want to world to know that.

Their relationship developed as they dated in a casual way. They often had lunch or dinner together before or after their performances, sometimes not leaving each other until two in the morning. The couple talked about the play and its weaknesses, particularly the third act which Logan and Inge were fighting about being rewritten. They talked about books they read, Method acting, movies or plays they'd seen. They sometimes took in a film or a play, often to see the work of someone they knew or admired. Newman claimed that in the beginning he did not view Woodward as a romantic partner but just a good like-minded friend. Kim Stanley commented that she had no doubt the couple were sexually attracted to each other but they weren't admitting it, not even to themselves. Logan didn't know if Newman was paying secret visits to Woodward's hotel room, but he predicted that the actor soon would be.

He considered her modern and independent, and himself a bit shy and conservative, so it took him a long time to persuade her that he wasn't as dull as he looked. They found themselves compatible in every way, both hating social occasions like cocktail parties, though the couple enjoyed late night gatherings of actor and writers. They felt they could tell each other anything without fear of rejection or ridicule. The actors also both vowed not to go to Hollywood to make movies, after they had supposedly received offers.

Woodward may have been offered the part of Edie Doyle in Elia Kazan's crime drama *On the Waterfront* (1954). She was reportedly considered before offers were made to others and Eva Marie Saint was signed. According to Kazan, Woodward and Newman prepared a scene for the consideration of Sam Spiegel, since the producer was also considering casting him as the ex-prizefighter turned longshoreman Terry Molloy, but the initial casting of Frank Sinatra as Molloy intervened. One source claims that Kazan had asked Karl Malden, who would play the part of Father Barry in the film, to coach Newman for a screen test, and Malden asked Woodward to work with him. She accepted and

Malden said that there was a definite chemistry between the two. Malden worked with them not in a scene from the screenplay but a scene from Ferenc Molnar's play *Liliom* as a sample until he felt they were camera-ready. Then he called Kazan and told him the film's stars had been found, predicting the couple would sizzle on the screen. The test was shot and Kazan was pleased, but Sam Spiegel was not.

Things advanced further when the pair worked together on *Picnic,* with Newman rehearsing as Hal and dancing to the song "Moonglow" with Woodward playing Madge. After they went through the routine three times, Logan was not pleased. He said with Ralph Meeker and Janice Rule there was sizzle; with Newman and Woodward it was fizzle. The actor still wasn't giving the director what he wanted, even after Logan put his hands on Newman's buttocks and moved them in rhythm to the music, wanting him to wiggle more. Then, when Logan had almost given up, all of a sudden the pair got it, moving into each other like some sort of erotic mating dance. Logan said that after the dance that afternoon, Jackie had lost her husband. The director reported that over a drink that night, Woodward confessed that she had set her sights on Newman. Married or not, the actress was going to get him. This was a notion that Eileen Heckart, who played the schoolteacher Rosemary Sydney in the production, confirmed. She said they all suspected that something was happening between the pair, and that Woodward, in her little assertive way, had quite a lot of steel.

The play opened on Broadway at the Music Box Theatre on February 19, 1953, and was a hit, running until April 10, 1954. It was praised by Brooks Atkinson in *The New York Times*, and earned a Tony for Best Director for Logan and the Pulitzer Prize for Drama for Inge. The play would also be adapted into a film released in 1955 that Logan also directed. Neither Newman nor Woodward were cast in it, though he screen-tested for it.

During the production's season, she was called in 50 times. Logan described the actress as a brilliant girl in her own way, one who made you notice her somehow. He felt she had a great talent, personality and drive. Logan also said that Woodward was like Newman in that both had a certain discipline about their lives that made them into the stars and the great people they would become.

When John Foreman came to see them essay the play's leads at a Saturday matinee, he said their electric performances told him that the actors were in love. They said they fought their attraction to each other but it was not an easy situation because the couple were at the theater every night and for day matinees for a year. Newman told the other cast members that he and Woodward were just friends but apparently no one believed it. The pair took classes together but it was also suspected that Newman had occasional sleepovers at Woodward's new apartment on 56th Street and Madison Avenue. This was a five-story walk-up which had one large room and a tiny kitchen. A female cast member reported that one day when she dropped in, the pair were both stark naked and painting the walls and ceiling, with Woodward wearing a shower cap to protect her hair. Newman supposedly hurried into the bathroom for his clothes, and the actress explained that they were naked because they didn't want to ruin their clothes with spilled paint. In her new place, Woodward did her own laundry, including sheets, in a bathtub and then hung it over the shower rod. The actress said that she was so grateful for being poor because the experience taught her never to take money for granted.

On television, Woodward was in the *Philco Television Playhouse* drama "A Young Lady of Property" which was broadcast on NBC on April 5, 1953. The teleplay was by

Horton Foote and the director was Vincent J. Donehue. The story centered on Wilma Thompson (Kim Stanley) a 15-year-old who has dreams of becoming a movie star. After her mother's death, she is sent to live with her aunt (Margaret Barker). Woodward played the part of Arabella Cuckenboo, Wilma's tagalong friend. The show was praised by *Variety*.

Next was the drama series *Goodyear Television Playhouse* episode "The Young and the Fair," broadcast on NBC on July 26, 1953, and shot in New York. The teleplay by N. Richard Nash was an adaptation of his Broadway play. The play had run from November 22 to December 11, 1948, at the Fullon Theatre and from December 26, 1948, to January at the International Theatre and was directed by Harold Clurman. It was set in a fashionable junior college for young women, where a sincere and intelligent alumna returns to her alma mater with her idealistic younger sister, who enters as a student.

Woodward also became a member of the Actors Studio, after Newman was admitted. Jack Garfein, a young director there, judged her audition, saying though he knew she was understudying in *Picnic* he didn't know how good she was. Garfein knew the actress in civilian life and considered her a very quiet, inward person. When he saw her name on the audition sheet, he assumed that she would do a scene as a sensitive, introverted girl. He was in for a surprise: Woodward played with a sharp edge. Her seven-minute scene went over the strict five-minute audition rule but Garfein let her go on. He also broke the other rule—that actors could not be told whether they had passed or not. Garfein said he was so excited that he could not resist telling her how good she was. The whole time in the Studio, Woodward wore no makeup (believing that good actresses didn't), an indication of how wide-eyed she was about the profession.

She and Newman did a joint screen test for the Warner Bros. war movie–romance *Battle Cry* (1955), about World War II Marines. William Orr, the son-in-law of Jack Warner, conducted the test and said they came in with a preconceived idea of what they wanted to do. First the couple rolled around on a mattress on the floor, then they jumped up and engaged in a boxing match, then rolled around on a blanket. Orr said it had to be the worst screen test in the history of motion pictures and he suggested to Warner that the part Newman was up for—the young soldier Danny Forrester—should be given to James Dean. Tab Hunter was cast instead and Dorothy Malone was cast as the love-hungry Navy wife role that Woodward hoped for.

The actress next appeared on the drama television series *Danger* in the episode "In Line of Duty" (a.k.a. "In the Line of Duty"), broadcast on CBS on February 9, 1954. The show was shot in New York and directed by Mel Goldberg. She returned to the *Philco Television Playhouse* for the episode "The Dancers," broadcast on NBC on March 7, 1954. The teleplay was by Horton Foote and the director was Vincent Donehue. James Broderick played Horace, a meek young boy who visits his sister in a small town. Woodward played Emily, the town's prettiest and most popular girl, whom Horace asks to a school dance.

She next appeared on CBS's *Studio One* in the episode "Stir Mugs" (April 5, 1954). Scripted by Robert R. Presnell Sr. and directed by Paul Nickell, it centered on parolees in war service who decide to escape on the night of V-J Day rather than return home. Woodward played Lisa Molloy. On April 29, 1954, she was on ABC's dramatic anthology television series *Kraft Television Theatre* in the episode "Unequal Contest." Shot in New York, it had a teleplay by Abby Mann based on his play.

In May 1954, Woodward screen-tested for director Elia Kazan for the part of Abra in the Warner Bros. drama *East of Eden* (1955), but Julie Harris was cast instead.

The relationship between the actress and Newman might have been changed had he been allowed to go on the national tour of *Picnic*, taking over the role of Hal, but Joshua Logan didn't believe the actor had the requisite sexual threat for the part. Though Woodward claimed that the pair had spent their time running away from each other, she described Newman as her closest friend, though the actress dated other men.

Funnily enough, he introduced her to the playwright and actor James Costigan. He and Newman appeared together in the July 19, 1953, episode of CBS's live dramatic anthology television series *The Web*, "The Bells of Damon." Newman supposedly told Costigan that he could get him a date with a "wonderful girl" that he was not sleeping with. Woodward would announce her engagement to Costigan, saying that all Southern girls like to get engaged even when they weren't ready to get married, with the actress's reluctance to marry also perhaps influenced by her parents' marital discord. Costigan said that he came into Woodward's life when she was dating Newman on the sly. He claimed that the actress was never in love with him and he certainly wasn't in love with her. She was just using him and felt that, by going out with Costigan, Woodward would make Newman jealous. Costigan said she had commented, "Surely he'll come to his senses and divorce Jackie and marry me. She's all wrong for him. I'm Miss Right. I could make him happy." Costigan said that in many respects, what Woodward said was true, something which time proved right. He and the actress both got a chuckle out of the press printing the rumors of their engagement and said that all the talk that Costigan and Newman were fighting over her was moronic. Costigan said that ever since *Picnic*, she was determined to get Newman one way or the other. Woodward had heard that Jackie was prettier and sexier than she was, and it infuriated her. The actress was quoted as saying, "That one trapped Paul, first with her good looks and then with all those babies." Woodward said Newman was her best friend and she couldn't stand to see him so miserable. The actress knew that it was going to be hard but she would prevail. Woodward wanted him and when a Georgia girl like her went after a man, she usually got him.

Writer Gore Vidal was another beau, and the actress announced that she was engaged to *him* too. He had met her in 1952 or 1953 (sources differ) at a Manhattan party. Vidal said that he had hardly any recollection of that meeting, but Woodward thought him handsome, almost beautiful, and was deeply impressed with his accomplishments as a writer. Vidal would know the actress more when he began to write for television in 1954, and dubbed her "The Dixie Duse." He said he liked Woodward because he found her intelligent, a trait that he did not normally associate with actresses, and he would teach her words. The writer confirmed that the idea that they were engaged was a piece of fiction, given his homosexual preference, and he claimed it was a blatant ploy by her to push Newman into getting a divorce. She would also visit Vidal at Edgewater House (in New York's Hudson Valley), which he owned from 1950 to 1969. The actress said that it was *the* hangout and it was wonderful.

She also dated Marlon Brando for a month, which was seen as another ploy to enrage Newman. Brando had the career that Newman envied, being considered the star of the Actors Studio and a major movie star after the success of *A Streetcar Named Desire* (1951). Brando was also a notorious womanizer and supposedly didn't take his relationship with Woodward seriously. But apparently neither did she.

A source claims that the actress wanted to distance herself from Newman, so she decided to take a vacation in Hollywood and bought a round-trip tourist ticket. Woodward worked hard, doing seven television shows in seven weeks in New York, then spent three months in Hollywood, but they would be lonely, bitter months. When she heard that Newman was coming to Hollywood in June 1954 to make the drama *The Silver Chalice* for Warner Bros., the actress moved back to New York.

When he finished the film in August, he went back to New York and *she* went back to Hollywood. Newman was ashamed of *The Silver Chalice* and refused to see himself in it, but Woodward must have seen it because she commented that it was the only time that an actor played a role without lifting his head. Woodward claimed that you couldn't even see Newman's blue eyes, though a viewing of the film shows this to be untrue. Despite her avoidance tactics, one source claims that she still corresponded with Newman, and promised to join him soon in Hollywood.

The actress next appeared on CBS's historical re-enactment dramatic television series *You Are There* in the episode "The Oklahoma Land Rush (April 22, 1889)," broadcast on September 12, 1954. The show had a teleplay by Kate Nickerson. She appeared on the same network's *The Web* in the episode "Welcome Home" (September 26, 1954), shot in New York.

Next was the comedy-drama anthology television series *Singer Four Star Playhouse* episode "Interlude," broadcast on CBS October 14, 1954. The show was shot in Hollywood, with a teleplay by Frederick J. Lipp based on his story and directed by Roy Kellino. Woodward stars as a student at the Lowell Hall School for Girls boarding school. Neglected by her family, she befriends Chris (Dick Powell), a divorced vacationing newspaper correspondent 20 years her elder. In the show's end credits, the actress is billed after Powell, who was also the producer. Her character wears glasses and has shoulder-length hair which she favors wearing tied back with bangs. Woodward's fashions are by Ohrbach's. The role allows her to use a fishing rod and the actress' delicate performance has her fingering a necklace which has context for the self-conscious character. Woodward's best scene is perhaps when Vicki expresses her disappointment when she is told by Chris that he is unable to attend her graduating ceremony.

2

20th Century-Fox

Dick Powell was so impressed with Woodward that he sent a print of the show to 20th Century–Fox production executive Buddy Adler, who was being groomed to succeed Darryl F. Zanuck as head of production. Adler wanted to sign the actress but Zanuck didn't think she had possibilities, supposedly saying, "No tits, no talent, no looks, and no tail." He had heard that she would not put out and only dated "fags" like Newman and Vidal. Zanuck said Adler could sign her, but he would be to blame if Woodward lost the studio money.

Woodward was in New York when she heard from MCA about the offer. The actress flew to Hollywood to meet with Adler. Her agent then negotiated the deal and she became part of Fox's Young Actors Program which groomed people for stardom. Woodward signed a seven-year contract with an option that the studio had every year to continue or not. The actress also set some precedents, working out her salary so that she was paid for the standard 46 weeks out of the 52 a year but got a weekly paycheck year-round at an adjusted rate. She also had a clause that allowed her to appear on television for no more than six shows a year. The actress had it stipulated that she could live in New York, since at the time all contracts stated that one could not go more than 50 miles from Beverly Hills or Hollywood without permission from the studio. Fox agreed on the condition that Woodward paid her own way traveling back and forth between coasts.

One source claims that the studio had nothing to offer her at the time, though another says they made offers, which she rejected, since she wanted to wait for something she knew she was right for. Woodward was also reportedly adamant about the way in which her career should be managed, refusing to do publicity as a starlet or pin-up. This might have caused her to be labeled difficult or a troublemaker but, again, she seemed to get her way. In the meantime, Woodward availed herself of the clause to continue to work in television, commuting back and forth between Hollywood and New York where the jobs were.

At this time, Newman reportedly discussed his personal life with actress Geraldine Page after a class at the Actors Studio in New York. He told her he was in love with Woodward but couldn't leave Jackie now that she was pregnant with their third child. Newman also supposedly admitted that his love for Woodward didn't help him be faithful to her, which Page considered typical of an actor. Newman assured Jackie he had given up Woodward, but when Page later saw how miserable the actor was, she urged him to divorce and marry his love or otherwise he would self-destruct.

Woodward was next on the comedy-drama television anthology series *The Ford Television Theatre* in the 30-minute episode "Segment," broadcast on NBC on October 21, 1954. It was shot in Hollywood and directed by Fred F. Sears. The teleplay was by Michael Kraike, based on a television play by David Swift, which had been previously produced by *The Philco Television Playhouse* under the same title as a 60-minute drama and broadcast on January 27, 1952. The Ledbetter family comes to a New York hotel from Chicago for a vacation. When Mildred (Rosemary De Camp) tells Carl (William Bendix) that she plans to reveal to their daughter June (Woodward) that she was adopted, he threatens to kill her with a segment of smashed bathroom mirror. Woodward is fourth-billed with her hair worn in a shoulder-length style with ponytail and bangs. In her best scene, she is told on the phone by Carl of his murderous intention, and June reacts emotionally.

The actress appeared in the television anthology series *The Elgin Hour* in the episode "High Man," shot in New York and broadcast on ABC on November 2, 1954. The teleplay was by David Davidson and the director was Donald Richardson. Woodward played the part of Nancy.

She was next on the live comedy-drama television anthology series *Lux Video Theatre* in the 60-minute episode "Five Star Final," broadcast on NBC on November 11, 1954. Shot in Hollywood, it was written by S.H. Barnett based on a play by Louis Weitzenhorn, which had been made as a crime drama film with the same title by Warner Bros. in 1931. The show's director was Earl Eby. Randall (Edmond O'Brien), city editor of a sleazy tabloid, goes against his own journalistic ethics to resurrect a 20-year-old murder case—with tragic results. Woodward played Jenny Townsend, the daughter of Nancy Voorhees Townsend (Mae Clarke), who was accused of the murder.

Woodward returned to NBC's *Robert Montgomery Presents* for "Homecoming" broadcast on November 22, 1954. Written by Noel B. Gerson, the story centered on Mark Pine (Don Taylor), a college football star who on the weekend of the big homecoming game plans for an improved future with the rich coed he's dating. Woodward played the part of Elsie.

The actress appeared on NBC's dramatic television anthology *Armstrong Circle Theatre* in "Brink of Disaster" (November 23, 1954). In Jay Presson Allen's teleplay, a family man (Ed Begley) who is tired of dealing with his immature wife and her family reaches his breaking point.

In order to get the actress working, Buddy Adler loaned her out to Columbia for what he considered a small movie. In November 1954, Woodward was cast by director George Sherman in the color western *Count Three and Pray* (1955), which had the working title *The Calico Pony*. Scripted by Herb Meadow, it began production in late January 1955 and finished in mid–February, shot on location at the North Ranch in Agoura Hills, California. Luke Fargo (Van Heflin), a pastor, returns to the town of Winchester after serving in the Civil War. Second-billed Woodward played Lissy, a teenage orphan hillbilly who is squatting in the burned-out parsonage. Her hair by Helen Hunt is worn in a blonde short style with bangs, and she has two costumes by Jean Louis: a flesh-colored shirt with gray-blue pants and a black feathered long dress with a matching red-feathered black hat, red underskirt and red choker. The role allows the actress to use a Southern accent, fire guns, smoke a cigar, be forcibly washed by Luke, ride a horse, sit in a tree, shave Luke's neck with a razor, and cry. Lissy gets some funny lines when she tells Luke she can skin a squirrel with her teeth, and she says of Yancy Huggins (Raymond Burr), "Bet he'd squish just like a watermelon if someone stepped on him." Woodward uses some over-gesturing in her performance. In her best scene, Lissy asks Luke if he could like her.

The film premiered in Greenville, South Carolina, at the Paris Theatre, and was released in October 1955 with the taglines "Luke Fargo was through with sin ... but sin wasn't through with Luke Fargo!," "A whip-wielding woman ... a gun-toting girl ... and a hate-loaded town!" and "The rowdy, rousing, rollicking story of Luke Fargo ... and his three women!"

Woodward was recommended for her role by Richard Quine, a man she had never met. The actress was in New York when producer Ted Richmond sent her the script. After reading one paragraph, she decided to do it. Woodward described it as a lovely thing about a wistful waif who went barefoot and she got to wear funny clothes and cut her hair. At the age of 24, the actress didn't think in terms of the significance of the film, she just considered it a helluva good part. Woodward

Woodward as Lissy in *Count Three and Pray* (1955).

would later say that this was the only movie she really liked and enjoyed making. The actress adored working with Heflin and George Sherman. Heflin was pleasantly surprised at the ability and honesty of the newcomer to films, and he said she seemed remarkably free of pretension and nonsense.

The actress complained about the studio system after having been under contract for a year. They had failed to find what Fox considered a suitable role for her and she wondered if this was because Woodward was definitely not the glamor type. But she didn't want to be a glamor girl and rejected their attempts to mold her into a femme fatale.

Woodward returned to television in the dramatic anthology series *The Star and the Story* in the episode "Dark Stranger" (January 8, 1955). It was shot in Hollywood; the teleplay was by Betty Ulius and Joel Murcott, based on a story by Ulius, and the director was Arthur Ripley. It told the story of Ray Ericson (Edmond O'Brien), a novelist who believes the heroine of his new book, Jill Andrews (second-billed Woodward), has come to life as a professional model. Jill is seen on the cover of Ray's book and in head shots. The actress wears her hair in a shoulder-length style with bangs. The role gives her a death scene. While Woodward's performance is sometimes mannered, she plays both the superficiality of a model and the mysteriousness of an imaginary person. Her best scene is perhaps when Jill tells Ray that she loves him, though director Ripley presents the actress in an unflattering angle when she hugs O'Brien.

Woodward reportedly visited Newman when he appeared on Broadway in the Joseph Hayes melodrama *The Desperate Hours*, which ran from February 10 to August 13, 1955, at the Ethel Barrymore Theatre.

Woodward was next on the dramatic anthology series *Star Tonight* in the March 31, 1955, episode "Death of a Stranger," shot in New York. The teleplay was by Rupert Brooks, based on his play. She was back on ABC's *Kraft Television Theatre* for the episode "Cynara" (May 12, 1955), shot in New York. The teleplay was by R.F. Gore-Brown, based on his novel. The story involved a London attorney who, though married, becomes tragically involved with a shop girl.

Her next film was the United Artists crime mystery *A Kiss Before Dying* (1956). The screenplay was by Lawrence Roman based on the novel by Ira Levin, and the director was Gerd Oswald. Bud Corliss (Robert Wagner), a ruthless student at Lupton's Stoddard State University, resorts to murder to avoid marrying copper heiress Dorothy Kingship (fourth-billed Woodward), whom he has made pregnant. The film was shot from early June to July 7, 1955, at the RKO-Pathe Studios and on location in Arizona and California. Woodward's blonde short-cropped hair is by Kay Shea and her wardrobe by Henry Helfman and Evelyn Carruth. She is heard sobbing before being seen and Oswald obscures our view of her face in her first scene. The role allows the actress to drive a car, tumble down the stairway of the college stadium bleachers, and have a death scene being pushed off the roof of the municipal building by Bud. The latter two actions are apparently not performed by her, since her face is seen in neither. (It appears to be a dummy falling from the roof.) Her best scene is perhaps when Dorothy tells Bud how she wants to get married despite his objections.

The film was released on June 12, 1956, with the tagline "Some secrets can't be kept … they have to be buried!" *Variety* praised the film and noted that Woodward was particularly good. A box office success, it was remade in 1991 by director James Deardon with Sean Young playing Woodward's old role.

Although Fox had bought to the rights to the novel in 1953, the film was distributed by United Artists, which meant that the actress was on loan-out. She tried to give a certain depth and texture to her character and made no attempt to glamorize herself. Woodward described the film as the worst ever made in Hollywood and only did it because she wanted to work. The actress was unhappy in Hollywood, since one film every few months was not enough activity to keep her interested when in New York she could have done a dozen or more television shows.

Robert Wagner was said to have been under consideration for the part of Bud from 1953, but both Montgomery Clift and Newman had passed on it. In his book *I Loved Her in the Movies: Memories of Hollywood's Legendary Actresses*, Wagner wrote that he didn't really know what to expect from Woodward. He knew she followed the Method, which Wagner said didn't particularly work for him, and in between scenes the actress would sit and knit and think about her character. She never tried to convince anyone else that hers was the best way. Although the film was only the second she made, the actress was incredibly centered—she was already an old soul.

She was considered for the part of wheelchair-bound Zosh in the United Artists crime drama *The Man with the Golden Arm* (1955) but director Otto Preminger cast Eleanor Parker instead. The actress returned to CBS's Four Star Playhouse (now known as *Star Performance*) for the episode "Full Circle" (October 27, 1955), shot in Hollywood. The teleplay was by Herman J. Epstein based on his story, and the director was Harry

Horner. Terry (Woodward), a Broadway actress, gets a particularly bad review for her performance in the play *Geraldine's Necklace* and schemes to humiliate the drama critic Howard Maxwell (David Niven). She was billed second after Niven, who was also the show's producer, but has more scenes than he does. Her hair is short, blonde and wavy with bangs. The actress' hands are seen before her face and the role allows Woodward to act the role of an actress. Playing an actress is a tricky role and this one adds another layer because of Terry's duplicity. She is funny when she reads the bad review and, despite her mannerisms, convincing. The actress underplays in the scene when Terry tells Maxwell she loves him, and her best scene is perhaps when Terry reveals her agenda since she uses a mix of pride, anger and pain.

On the set of *A Kiss Before Dying* **(1956) with Robert Wagner.**

Woodward appeared in the dramatic anthology television series *The 20th Century–Fox Hour* in the episode "The Late George Apley," shot at Fox in Hollywood and broadcast on CBS on November 16, 1955. The teleplay was by Edward Hope and John P. Marquand and based on Marquand's novel which had previously been made as a 1947 Fox film by Joseph L. Mankiewicz. The show's director was Jules Bricken. Eleanor Apley (Woodward), daughter of a socially prominent family, rebels against the snobbery of her father George (Raymond Massey) when he opposes her marriage to a young man from the wrong side of the tracks. Eleanor was played by Peggy Cummins in the film.

Woodward wanted to take a principal role in Leslie Stevens' 12th-century drama *The Lovers*, to open on Broadway the next March with rehearsals to begin in late November under director Michael Gordon. The play dealt with the tragic effects of an ancient law permitting a warlord to pre-empt the bride of one of his vassals. So keen was Woodward that in order to do the play, she was willing to break her Fox contract, but the studio allowed her to return to Broadway to play the medieval peasant bride Douane.

In late November 1955, Newman came back to Hollywood to make the war drama *The Rack* (1956) for MGM. He and Woodward ran into each other on a sound stage, and he noticed that she had slimmed down to 108 pounds and looked svelte and sophisticated in a Hollywood wardrobe. Seeing her, Newman supposedly knew she was the only girl he would ever love. Again the couple tried to keep away from each other, though this time in the same town.

The actress was next on CBS's live comedy-drama television anthology series *The United States Steel Hour* in the episode "White Gloves" (December 21, 1955), shot in New York. The teleplay was by her friend James Costigan. Ellen (Joan Blondell), a middle-aged actress, is visited by her grown-up son and his new wife Rocky (Woodward). *The New York Times* wrote that the actress appeared to best advantage in the final showdown scene with her new mother-in-law but otherwise gave the impression of being a chuckle-headed bobby-soxer.

She was back on NBC's *Kraft Television Theatre* in the episode "Eleven O'Clock Flight" (December 28, 1955), also shot in New York. The teleplay was by Jerry de Bono and the director was George Roy Hill. The story centered on a woman, in love with a young sailor, who is confronted by her ex-husband. Next she starred in CBS's anthology series *General Electric Theater* episode "Prologue to Glory," shot at the Republic Studios in Hollywood and broadcast live on February 12, 1956. The play by E.P. Conkle was a Federal Theatre Project in 1939 and ran on Broadway for a year. The teleplay was also by Conkle and the director was Don Medford. The show was a dramatization of the supposed romance between Abraham Lincoln (John Ireland) and Ann Rutledge (Woodward) when they lived in New Salem, Illinois, in the mid–1830s. Woodward had previously played the character on *Omnibus*.

The actress was reportedly on the set of the MGM biographical sports drama *Somebody Up There Likes Me* (1956) which starred Newman. The bulk of the film had been shot on location in New York from January 26 to March 1956 by director Robert Wise, but the production moved to Los Angeles Olympic Stadium in April to film the Yankee Stadium prizefighting scene. Woodward was spotted by Newman's co-star Pier Angeli; Angeli was upset by the way that Woodward kept staring at her. Angeli asked Wise to ask Woodward to stand out of her sight line. Angeli guessed that Woodward was there because she feared her boyfriend might be stolen. Around this time, Newman confided to Janice Rule that he was in love with Woodward and when he was with her he forgot all those other lovesick puppies.

The Lovers opened on May 10 at the Martin Beck Theatre. Although Michael Gordon was the credited director, the staging was actually done by Arthur Penn. The show was praised by *The New York Times'* Brooks Atkinson, who described the actress' performance as artless and lovely. It ran only four performances.

She was next on the live dramatic anthology television series *Westinghouse Studio One* a.k.a. *Studio One* in the episode "Family Protection," shot in New York and broadcast on CBS on May 28, 1956. The teleplay was by Palmer Thompson and the director was Franklin J. Schaffner. Mike Hudson (Everett Sloane) robs the Suburban Bank & Trust Company of $200,000 and makes an agreement with Eddie Gilmer (Corey Allen) and his wife Daisy (Woodward) to play house, so as not to give Mike up to the police. Woodward is billed second. Her hair reads as more brunette here and she wears it in a shoulder-length style with a side part. The actress is heard singing before she is seen. Daisy is initially shown to be loose by constantly chewing gum and the role also allows her to dance. Her best scene is perhaps when Daisy tells Mike that she has never been so happy.

The actress was back on *Four Star Playhouse*, a.k.a. *Star Performance*, in the episode "Watch the Sunset" (June 7, 1956), filmed in Hollywood. The teleplay was by James Bloodworth, based on the *Redbook* story by Jean C. Clark, and the director was Richard Kinon. Sales manager Philip Benton's (Dick Powell) wife Ann (Woodward) has been in a mental institution for five years, and he is contemplating starting a new relationship with his secretary Carol (Maxine Cooper). Woodward is billed sixth with a "with" credit. The actress' hair color is a darker brown and she wears it shoulder-length and off her forehead. Her wardrobe includes a notably ugly polka-dot skirt. Ann is first seen in a photograph in Philip's office. Woodward's mannerisms and stammering nicely fit her nervous and insane character. She gets a line about her mind being "like a telephone switchboard with some of the plugs pulled out" in regards to lost memories, and her best scene is when Ann listens to Philip talk about marriage. She tells him that because of their separation, "all promises are automatically cancelled," and stands suddenly

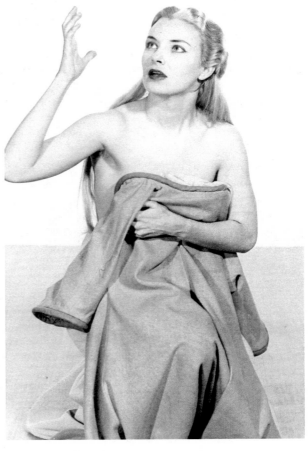

A publicity portrait of Woodward for *The Lovers*, which ran on Broadway May 10–12, 1956.

with an odd look on her face which plays against Philip's proclamation of love and Ann's own.

Woodward claimed she didn't want to present herself as glamorous. But when she arrived in New York to publicize *A Kiss Before Dying*, she posed for photographers wearing a tight-fitting sleeveless dress and sat on top of her luggage with legs crossed in quintessential pin-up style. She was in New York to do more television, being booked for *Kraft* and *The Alcoa Hour*.

Woodward met with the Broadway-Hollywood columnist Earl Wilson at the Russian Tea Room. She amazed him, he wrote, being so absurdly worldly at her age. Wilson asked her about James Dean, who had recently died. The actress felt he was sitting somewhere in hysterics over the whole excitement about him. She reported that her cold-water flat days were behind her and she now had a heated apartment, though you had to walk up five flights. Woodward was doing more television because she was willing to tackle any role as long as it was good. After one TV performance, a top Hollywood director told the actress that she was another Bette Davis. But Woodward would rather have been the first Joanne Woodward than a second Bette Davis, and she was sure Davis felt the same way when the older actress was getting started. Another director had said of her that all Woodward delivered was talent. No particular glamor, not publicity—just talent.

She was next on the CBS television series *Alfred Hitchcock Presents* in the episode "Momentum" (June 24, 1956), shot in Hollywood. The teleplay was by Francis Cockrell based on a story by Cornell Woolrich and the director was Robert Stevens. In the story, Dick Paine (Skip Homeier) decides to steal the $450 that his boss A.T. Burroughs (Ken Christy) has owed him for months. Second billed Woodward played Paine's wife Beth. She wears her brown hair in a short bob with a side part. Her performance is free of mannerism and she is believable in her desire for her husband, and fear of being left without him.

The actress was back on *Kraft Television Theatre* for the episode "Starfish" (June 27, 1956), shot in New York. The teleplay was by William Noble and the director was Marc Daniels. The story involved a young woman who hides from life because of a starfish-shaped scar on her face.

At this time Newman was reportedly drinking as a way to cope with his personal situation, despite his professional success. He wanted to leave his wife to be with Woodward but Jackie refused to give him a divorce. One source claims that Newman did leave his wife for Woodward but then, guilt-ridden, returned to his family. He and Woodward had reportedly spent time together when they were both in New York, in the early months of 1956. A friend said anyone who was around them could tell the pair were crazy about each other. One favorite thing was to find a restaurant somewhere up the coast that overlooked the ocean, preferably with a beach and fishing. They spent the afternoon palling around and couldn't keep their eyes and hands off each other. They didn't flaunt it—they just felt it. But after a few months, the couple had to come back to reality and despite Newman being in love, he didn't want to be the philandering type. In New York, it was easier to fight the attraction because his family was there, but in Hollywood he was alone and the temptation was stronger.

Things came to a head when on July 7 he was arrested on a traffic charge. Newman and a party had gone to the Jolly Fisherman, a Roslyn, Long Island, restaurant, to celebrate the success of *Somebody Up There Likes Me*. After midnight, the bartender Thomas Hutchek complained to the police that the actor's car had knocked down some shrubbery. Another report said he also knocked over or dented a fire hydrant on Roslyn's Main Street and ran a red light on Northern Boulevard. Police said that Newman was driving his Volkswagen under the influence of alcohol. Hutchek had given them the actor's license number. He was taken to the Mineola police station and charged with leaving the scene of an accident and running a red light.

Woodward reportedly also suffered because of the relationship, with their romance described as more of an ordeal than a courtship. She apparently was friendly with Jackie and didn't want to be a homewrecker for Newman's family, which now extended to a third child, Stephanie, born in the spring of 1955. The actress was particularly concerned over the plight of the children since she knew from personal experience how those of a broken family felt. She and Newman decided to end their relationship, with Newman to go back to his wife and family in New York.

Woodward was next on NBC's live dramatic anthology television series *The Alcoa Hour* in the episode "The Girl in Chapter One" (September 2, 1956), shot in New York. In Elihu Winer's teleplay, Vernon Elder (James Daly), a Pulitzer Prize novelist whose talent has faded, returns to his small hometown. Woodward played Margaret Spencer, the young girl whom Vernon wants to make his fourth wife until he learns that she is the daughter of the woman he jilted 20 years ago. Although Jack Gould in *The New York Times* described the show as unsubstantial, he wrote that Woodward's performance was luminous.

Woodward was back on *Studio One* for "A Man's World" (October 1, 1956), shot in New York. The teleplay was by Howard Rodman based on the novel by Douglas Fairbairn, and the director was Karl Genus. The story concerned a cabin boy on an American yacht who finds love in the French port of Cannes. She played the part of Christina.

On October 10, the actress was Dennis Hopper's date for the New York premiere of Warner Brothers' *Giant* (1956), in which he had a supporting part. The studio had demanded he take Natalie Wood and, though the couple are seen kissing in the premiere newsreel, Hopper had the hots for Woodward. It was the first film premiere the actress had attended. The actor claimed that nobody had then heard of her and the press thought she was his secretary. After the film, the couple went to the Copacabana nightclub and sat at Jack Warner's table where all the attention was focused on Elizabeth Taylor. Hopper told Woodward not to worry about being ignored since the ones doing the ignoring were a bunch of phonies. She was irritated that he kept leaving her to look for Taylor on behalf of Mike Todd after Taylor left the table to flit around the room. Fed up, Woodward asked Hopper to take her home but there, he tried to sweet-talk his way through the door of the apartment. When she barred him with her arm, Hopper wouldn't budge so the actress had no choice but to physically throw him down the stairs. He didn't know that Newman was waiting behind the door, and the couple had a good laugh about the incident. She would comment that when Hopper was in his twenties, he was a genius, though Woodward wasn't sure of what and it certainly wasn't acting. His May 29, 2010, *New York Times* obituary claimed that Hopper and the actress were linked romantically in the 1950s. His biographies claim that she was only a friend, to whom he also sold some of his painted canvasses. One reports that the pair's friendship also saw her grab a silver tray at a dinner party and smack him on the top of his head as hard as she could. Woodward was hoping to knock some sense into the actor, having become impatient with his moaning drivel about cutting Hollywood down to size.

The actress next appeared on the December 6 episode of the CBS anthology television series *Climax!,* "Savage Portrait." She played Katherine, a young girl who is carried away when a profile about her is published in a magazine. The show's teleplay was by Robert Bloomfield and the director was Buzz Kulik. It was shot in Hollywood.

In late 1956, Jackie Witte agreed to a separation from Newman. He and Woodward took a house in Malibu with Gore Vidal and his longtime companion Howard Austen. Another source claims they had a rented apartment in New York, though yet another source says *that* took place in late July 1957. The house at 38 Malibu Colony belonged to Shirley MacLaine. Vidal and Austen contributed to the rent of $1500 a week. Woodward's Fox salary was $500 a week. Newman earned $1000 a week from Warner Bros., but much of it went to child support. The couple shared a room, as did Vidal and Austen, and there were two small rooms in the back for guests. The writer said the house was big enough so that the couples could keep out of each other's way. Newman said there were a lot of linoleum floors which Woodward would start mopping at seven in the morning and finish at eight at night. He found the lifestyle pretty carefree, with a lot of outdoor cooking on a grill, but she became exasperated. The actress rebelled against what she called being the mother of them all and behaved like a virago who would storm around. Everybody was traipsing sand onto the white floors and Woodward did nothing but mop and wash everybody's underwear. Vidal described life on the beach as idyllic and marvelous. He teased the couple by calling them "Miss Georgia and Mr. Shaker Heights," since Newman was born in Shaker Heights. On the weekend there were parties, often with the house full of people who were unknown to any of the residents. She said they had one long party and everybody invited everybody. They had the most extraordinary people—everybody who was anybody came because Vidal knew everybody. Visitors included Claire Bloom, Christopher Isherwood and Don Bachardy, Romain Gary and his wife Leslie Blanche, and Anaïs Nin, the American diarist, essayist, novelist and writer of short stories and erotica. When Nin was introduced to Newman and Woodward, she reportedly dismissed them as "starlets." Nin said the actress was a Southern belle lacking in grace and charm, the very antithesis of Tennessee Williams' Blanche DuBois. She would have been more appropriately cast as a gum-chewing waitress at a burger drive-in, one on roller skates carrying trays of milkshakes. Nin accompanied the foursome to the Mocambo to see Edith Piaf, and after the show Piaf joined them at their table.

The couple also lived briefly at the Chateau Marmont with Vidal and Austen. One source claims this occurred in August 1955. Woodward commented that life at the Marmont was dark and strange and the four were closeted in together because they were all from New York. She said it was wonderful for Vidal to have found in Austen the person in his life who fulfilled that which was needed. The quartet was known in Hollywood as "The Unholy Four" and they were the hottest topic of gossip in town. All sorts of kinky rumors abounded about what they were actually doing after midnight, with news of the shack-up kept from the general public because of the damage it could have done to both actors' promising careers. Columnist Hedda Hopper was aware of the situation, something she reportedly told Newman when he met with her at her home for a chat and interview that had been arranged by the Warner Bros. publicity department. She offered not to spill the beans if the actor gave her some good copy. He promised to give her, and not her rival Louella Parsons, the scoop if he married Woodward.

In the mornings, Woodward would go to Fox and Newman would go to Warner Bros. In their free time, they read Vidal's novels around the pool of the hotel. Vidal reported that the actress insisted that they leaked to the press the idea that she was engaged to him, but the living arrangement was based entirely on her passion for Newman. Woodward spent time with the writer having intense discussions about the future of his race for presidency of the United States. It was thought that perhaps the idea of their engagement came from her as a means to help Vidal's campaign, since he might need a cover for his homosexual lifestyle. The actress quipped that she wouldn't have minded playing the role of First Lady, since it was a hell of a lot better than the part in *A Kiss Before Dying*. It would have also been more interesting than sitting around the pool waiting for Newman to make up his mind to divorce Jackie and marry her. Woodward apparently was serious about the marriage proposal to Vidal, and might have done it because she was so fond of him. The actress knew that many people had that sort of marriage but she couldn't have imagined how long it would have lasted. Woodward felt she would have driven him crazy or he would have done the same to her.

Her next film was to be the Fox drama *The Wayward Bus* (1957) which was to start shooting at the studio after the beginning of 1957. In 1952, Jennifer Jones had been announced to star with George Stevens directing at the Sam Goldwyn Studios. Then in September 1955, Susan Hayward and Gene Tierney were being considered for the leads with Henry Hathaway to direct. The new director was Victor Vicas. But the day before Woodward was scheduled to leave for California, she supposedly received a telephone call from her mother that changed things. She had read in the newspaper columns how the book *Three Faces of Eve* was to be made into a film. Rumor had it that Judy Garland was being considered for the leading role, but Woodward's mother told her daughter that she should do it. The actress doubted that was possible because the studio would want a star.

3

The Three Faces of Eve

Fox had reportedly had trouble with the film version of *The Three Faces of Eve*, which was first called *The Woman with Three Lives*. One problem was casting, since it was hard to find an actress capable of playing the title character who suffered from Multiple Personality Disorder. In 1956, writer-director Nunnally Johnson offered the part to Lana Turner, Olivia de Havilland, Doris Day, Jean Simmons and Carroll Baker, who all declined. Johnson suggested Marilyn Monroe, whom he knew after he had produced and written the screenplay for Fox's romantic comedy *How to Marry a Millionaire* (1953). She was making *Bus Stop* at the time, and when Johnson asked her about the part, the actress told him that she didn't want to do anything tragic. June Allyson said that she was offered it but her husband, Dick Powell, talked her out of it, thinking her miscast. The June 29, 1956, *New York Times* reported that Susan Hayward was negotiating with Johnson for the role, though another source claims that he went to Hayward after Judy Garland.

Johnson had talked to Garland and had decided she would be perfect after she had proven her dramatic skills in the Warner Bros. musical romance *A Star Is Born* (1954). He felt she would understand the part and sent her the script in Las Vegas where she was then performing at the New Frontier Hotel. Garland didn't quite understand the script, feeling it came across more as a domestic comedy than a dramatic piece. Johnson decided to go to Vegas and see her, and brought with him film made by doctors of the actual Eve being questioned and going in and out of her personalities. This convinced Garland, who said she and Johnson had to cut their wrists and mingle their blood and swear she would play the part.

Another source had Newman visiting Garland in her Hollywood home, where he was introduced to Johnson as he was leaving. There she showed him the script because the actress wanted him to play her husband. The actor borrowed the script, but not to show Woodward, who was attached to *The Wayward Bus*. Rather he wanted Vidal to read it, partly to have the husband part beefed up, so that Newman could take these revisions to the director if he was offered it. Vidal believed the part could be a star vehicle for Woodward. She was shown the script, though she believed Fox would want Susan Hayward. The actor told her about the offer to Garland. Woodward commented that Garland could probably do it if she could hold herself together, and quipped that the film would have to be renamed *The Five Faces of Eve*.

Garland changed her mind about the film. One source claims she got cold feet. According to another source, her husband Sid Luft felt it was a bad choice, describing it as a tacky little film noir that no one would see. Luft said Garland could instead break records in Vegas and make tons of money. The actress supposedly told Newman she feared she had all of Eve's characteristics but playing her could tip her over the deep edge. The role terrified her because she identified so strongly with her. Plus, there were no songs to sing, and Fox wanted her to lose 30 pounds which was something she was not sure could be done. Garland also had another project (a new version of *Alice Adams* to be made by RKO) in which she would play Alice. A third source claims that Johnson moved on from Garland after having concerns about her behavior on *A Star Is Born*, her reluctance to commit to or complete a project, and not hearing back further from the actress. He told the press that "clouds got in her way" and that Garland would rather get laryngitis in the dry desert air of Vegas than play Eve. Others stated that Garland ultimately decided that her performing schedule would not allow her to do the role, and she sent Johnson a nice note of apology. *The New York Times* of September 14 reported that Garland had opted to do a stage show at the Palace in New York and this run would last from September 26, 1956, to January 8, 1957. The *Times* also said that the actress and Luft, in association with a major studio, were to produce a film of the Margaret Echard novel *Born in Wedlock*, with her to star.

Newman decided not to tell Woodward that the part of Eve was now available, because he apparently thought she might wonder how he knew so much about it. And he also didn't want her to know that he intended to sabotage Johnson's next choice, Susan Hayward. The actor supposedly visited Hayward and told her he knew about Johnson's offer. She guessed that he wanted to play opposite her. The actress would only do the film if it was shot in color so that her red hair could be appreciated (she had vowed not to make another film in black and white). The pair read the script together and Hayward said she could do something with the part, but she was worried about the tremendous commitment required. The actress had done this for the MGM musical biography *I'll Cry Tomorrow* (1955) and had worked herself into a nervous breakdown, becoming suicidal, and she didn't want to go through that hell again. Newman agreed it wasn't worth taking that chance because it could cost Hayward her life. He also said that playing three different women all in one body was hard to pull off and could invite ridicule. Hayward had another script—the crime biography *I Want to Live!*—and after reading it, she said no one else but her could play it and it had Oscar written all over it. The actress called Nunnally Johnson to tell him that she was much too fragile to take on the challenging role of Eve. Hayward made *I Want to Live!* (1958) and won the Best Actress Oscar for her performance.

Newman now thought that the way was clear for Woodward but Johnson sent the script to Jennifer Jones. She declined the part. A source claims that Johnson and Buddy Adler now had the idea to use a newcomer instead of an established star. Johnson had apparently seen Woodward in a Dick Powell television drama and had been impressed. He said when he finished the screenplay for the film, Johnson had her in the back of his mind. Another source says that someone suggested the actress to him and he thought that she had done enough acting, especially on television, to give her the skill for the part. But despite Johnson and Adler being interested, apparently the people in Fox's New York office still believed that they needed a star. Woodward said she only got the part because Fox couldn't get any of the actresses they really wanted and by the process of elimination. Johnson and Adler battled the New York office objections and won.

The actress was traveling to California on the Broadway Limited from New York to start work on *The Wayward Bus* to play the role of stripper Camille Oakes, with the script for *The Three Faces of Eve*. After reading it, she got off the train at Chicago and called her agent, but with bad news. Woodward didn't want to do the film because she had no idea what it was about. The actress preferred *The Wayward Bus*, which was to co-star her friend and fellow Fox contract player Joan Collins, and continued on to California. But Fox told Woodward that *The Three Faces of Eve was* the film she was doing, and she was replaced by Jayne Mansfield in *The Wayward Bus*.

A limousine took her to meet with Johnson, a new luxury the studio provided. The actress was afraid she couldn't make the role believable, playing three different characters in the same role. But it was a starring role and Woodward knew she needed something big for her career. The real Eve came from Georgia, as did both the actress and Johnson, so his fears about a phony Southern accent were dispelled. After the time spent losing her accent, she now had to slip back into it. Fellow Georgians Woodward and Johnson hit it off.

Woodward asked that the film be shot in sequence to help her with the character transitions. She and Lee J. Cobb (who played Eve's doctor Curtis B. Luther) saw the film of the real Eve, which had been made for the American Psychiatric Association. The woman changed personalities very rapidly, and the actress felt to do it that way would seem funny. So they decided it was better to have Eve's personality changes manifest more gradually, especially at the beginning. As the film went on, the changes could be faster and that is how the device of the lowering of the head (signaling a personality change) came to be.

On January 9, 1957, it was announced that Woodward was to appear in the film with Fox giving their contract player an opportunity to achieve recognition as a star. The actress would play the heroine of a psychological study of a woman with three distinct personalities. Filming was due to start on January 28. She had been under contract to the studio for two years without having made a film for them. The screenplay by director Johnson was adapted from a manuscript by Dr. Corbett H. Thigpen and Dr. Hervey M. Clackley, which they had presented in 1953 at the convention of the American Psychiatric Association. Fox had decided to delay the start date in the wake of a rival multiple personality film. This was the MGM drama *Lizzie* (1957), based on the Shirley Jackson novel *The Bird's Nest*. That film was shot from September to October 1956 and released on March 15, 1957.

Woodward prepared the characterizations by exploring how each personality moved, using her body and voice to distinguish them. She said it was a frightening challenge but a great opportunity for any actress, and drew upon her Neighborhood Playhouse training with Martha Graham. The actress decided the "defeated wife" Eve White sat slumping inward and it gave her a different way of talking which affected everything else. She also held her bag in her lap and that was all about containment and self-protection. The "rollicking and irresponsible playgirl" Eve Black's posture was quite different and she let the bag hang off her arm. But Woodward was never happy with how she played the "pleasant young woman with no memory," Jane. The actress never liked that personality very much, finding her a little priggish and too nice, and wished she could have found something to make her a little more real.

Costumes also helped with the personalities. The dress that Eve White wore the first time she visited Luther was designed by Renie from crepe and was very staid and proper with a little round collar. As Woodward became Eve Black, she unbuttoned the top, took the hat off to let her hair loose, and leaned back in the chair, and the way the dress changed helped the actress become the character. When Eve Black went out on the town, she wore a red velvet dress with sequins, and open down the back.

The hardest scene was the last long one with eight pages of dialogue, where Eve had all three personalities emerge to Dr. Luther and she kept changing back and forth. It was shot in one take, since Woodward and Cobb decided it would be a lot easier to sustain the emotional ups and downs that way. She said Johnson was wonderful about letting them rehearse it as much as they needed before it was shot. After the take was done, the actress was devastated and a wreck. Then the cameraman said there was a hair in the aperture and they would have to do it again. She burst into tears. Cobb sat her down and told her that if she could do it once, she could do it again. There was another take, and Woodward admitted this time was better, though she certainly didn't want to try for a third time.

The actress recalled the grind and frustrations of moviemaking, as opposed to the fast-paced production of live television and the more leisurely building of character through rehearsals for the stage. She got up at 5:30 a.m. to be at the studio at 6:30. Her hair was washed and makeup applied so that the actress was on the set at 8:30 ready to act. Woodward wasn't even awake but was supposed to give a level of performance of four pages of dialogue she had just learned the night before, and wasn't sure she knew. Rehearsal was interrupted by the cameraman saying they couldn't stand where they were because the lights wouldn't hit them there, so they had to trip over cables, and avoid

Poster for *The Three Faces of Eve* (1957).

things that people dropped around their heads. The actress was never hit but there were some awfully narrow misses, and she was in constant terror of all the lights overhead. Fox executives were happy with the daily rushes they viewed, feeling that Woodward was delivering a unique performance.

The black and white mystery centered on Luther (Cobb), who treated the woman known as Eve "Evie" White, Eve Black and Jane a.k.a. Janey (Woodward) for two years. The film went into production on February 5, 1957, and shooting continued until March 25, with additional scenes shot on April 26. Woodward's blonde-brown shoulder length hair is by Helen Turpin, worn with a side part, sometimes tied back, sometimes loose, sometimes up in curls with flowers, and sometimes up without. Costumes are by Renie, with a notable black spangly dress with spaghetti straps and a leg split. The actress differentiates the three personalities by voice and posture. Woodward also employs what would become another mannerism: a pursed and oddly twisted mouth. Eve White has a soft Southern accent with the awkward body language of an inhibited person. Eve Black has a more pronounced Southern accent, speaks in a more familiar way with Dr. Luther, has a looser, more seductive posture, uses makeup and wears more provocative clothes. Jane has no accent with a voice probably the closest to Woodward's own. Her body language included self-conscious fiddling with a chair arm. The role allows the actress to sing and dance, operate the Hill Brothers switchboard, and be hypnotized, cry and scream. She makes Eve Black funny in her dislike of Ralph (David Wayne), and gets a funny line when Luther asks if Ralph has ever made love to her: "Boy, I'd like to see him try!" Director Johnson provides an extreme closeup of Woodward's eyes. Her best scene is perhaps the 20-minute climax of the film which allows her to transition between all personalities.

Before the film was released, on March 27, 1956, *New York Times* article reported that Johnson had allowed a finished sequence to be viewed, showing her transforming from Eve White into Eve Black. The *Times* said that the actress displayed considerable acting talent to go with her good looks. Woodward said that she knew it may be a long time before she got another role with such dimension, and she was enjoying it threefold.

The film was previewed at Grauman's Chinese Theatre in Hollywood in August; Woodward attended with Newman. Columnist Sidney Skolsky approached the couple and told her she was certain to get an Oscar nomination, and could win. The actress replied, "Aren't you sweet? I sure wish I could agree with you. And I'm not being coy. I'm not the coy type." Skolsky then bet her that she would win the Oscar. Woodward told him that she didn't want to take advantage but bet three dollars she *wouldn't* get a nomination. She had never won a bet in her life and said it would be awful if this spoiled her record.

The film had a premiere in Milan, Italy, on September 12, 1957, and then opened in the United States on September 23, with the taglines "The strangest true experience a young girl in love ever lived!" and "All true and utterly fantastic—The story of the most completely documented case of multiple personality in history!" Woodward did not attend the Hollywood premiere as she was busy filming the Fox drama *The Long, Hot Summer* (1958) in Louisiana but she thanked the audience in a pre-recorded segment that was shown before the movie. According to *Variety*, the film was notable for the performance of Woodward. Bosley Crowther of *The New York Times* said that she played with superlative flexibility and emotional power. The film was a box office success and earned Woodward a Best Actress Academy Award nomination.

Thirty minutes were cut from the film's running time, including some of her scenes. These included Eve and Ralph quarrelling about how to raise their four-and-a-half-year-old daughter Bonnie (Terry Ann Ross), the couple expressing their loss of sexual interest in each other in a scene that the censors would not approve, Eve and Ralph leaving Bonnie with her mother (Nancy Kulp), Eve visiting her parents and talking about her treatment, and Eve seeing Bonnie, who tells her, "Don't come back that other way."

The actress said she cried when she saw a rough cut of the film, thinking that her career was ruined. Newman was also invited to see the cut and told Gore Vidal that Woodward breathed life into all three women. He thought each gal had a distinct personality, and his favorite was Eve Black, whom she played as a whore. The actor predicted she would get the Oscar based on merit, though Vidal felt they didn't work that way because if they did, Newman would have got one for *Somebody Up There Likes Me*.

Woodward said she and Cobb had a good relationship. He epitomized everything the actress loved about the theater and everything she wanted to be. Woodward felt thoroughly comfortable trusting him as both her character and as an actress.

Nunnally Johnson did not use the techniques of dissolves over makeup changes though there are cutaways to indicate Eve's change of personalities in a scene with Luther when she is observed by Ralph. He said Woodward's performance was aided by the films made of Eve and the detailed case history she had to study which noted every motion, posture and inflection Eve made. Johnson said she was very easy to direct, and in fact could have almost directed herself because she was so knowledgeable about the part.

Johnson was so impressed by her performance that he quipped that it could have won her three Academy Awards.

Woodward was chosen for a lead role in the black and white Fox comic drama *No Down Payment* (1957), initially titled *Down Payment*, shot at the Fox studios and on locations in Los Angeles from mid–April to early June 1957. The screenplay was by Philip Yordan fronting for the blacklisted Ben Maddow, based on a novel by John McPartland. The director was Martin Ritt; he was replaced for the last two days of shooting because he refused to do the film's happy ending.

The story involved the marital difficulties of four couples living in the California housing development Sunrise Hills Estates. Woodward is billed first, although in terms of her number of scenes, she has a supporting role to Jeffrey Hunter who plays the electronic engineer David Martin. The actress plays the part of Leola Boone, the housewife of service station man-

A portrait for *No Down Payment* (1957).

ager Troy (Cameron Mitchell). Her hair by Helen Turpin is shoulder-length blonde, worn with a side part and bangs, and clothes by Mary Wills include a gauche flowered cap and fox fur piece. She uses a Southern accent since the Boones come from Tennessee, and the role allows Woodward to cook pancakes and gargle. Leola has funny lines. At a party when Troy comments that she is "stinko," she replies, "Oh, I do love a refined man who uses elegant words like stinko." Leola continues to drink, saying, "I might as well be bad now because I'm sure gonna get punished when I get home." Her best scene is perhaps the long party scene where she drunkenly flirts with David and cries over her lost baby.

Newman reportedly visited the set during production. The film was released on October 30, 1957, with the tagline "John McPartland's explosive novel that tell-tales on young married America!" *The New York Times* called Woodward eminently believable. The film was a box office success.

The actress said Martin Ritt insisted on having rehearsals, a practice that was not generally common at that time in Hollywood, and he also allowed the actors to improvise from time to time. For one scene he allowed her to improvise before rolling the camera—a practice that was said to have mesmerized the cameraman—like starting a scene off-stage and coming in with something. Woodward felt it was fascinating and she was one of the only ones who had done anything like it previously. The actress found Ritt to be a doll, feeling he was going to be an important director, and he could direct her in every film she did. Ritt could not recall when he first met the actress, but felt it could have been on the television series *Danger* (although he did not direct her 1954 episode of the show).

She and Newman had decided to wait before being seen out in public at a party and be known as an item. In all this time, they had not allowed themselves to be photographed together until they knew that his wife would file for a divorce. However in the summer, they were photographed dining out and attending premieres, and also spoke to the press. When asked if they were a couple, the actor said there had been too much talk about the subject which brought questions about their relationship status to an end. Jackie was still unwilling to agree to a divorce with the Newmans said to have reached a miserable stand-off.

Woodward was to be part of the cast of Fox's World War II drama *The Young Lions* (1958), an adaptation of the Irwin Shaw novel. The actress was cast as Hope Plowman but left the production (Hope Lange replaced her) to appear in Fox's *The Long, Hot Summer*, which would begin shooting in late September.

Newman was loaned to Fox from Warner Bros. and reportedly danced a jig of joy when he heard he would be co-starring with Woodward. He called Jackie to tell her he would be traveling to Louisiana two weeks before shooting was to begin, and with her deciding to take their children to live with her parents in Wisconsin, he knew his marriage was finally over. Newman told Woodward. Without her, he boarded a plane for New Orleans, deciding he didn't want to be photographed with her because of his pending divorce. In Hollywood, she faced questions from reporters, since rumors of her getting an Oscar nomination for *The Three Faces of Eve* had heightened her visibility. Asked if there were plans to marry Newman, Woodward always maintained that if a marriage didn't work out, divorce was inevitable. She was living with a girlfriend (Victor Saville's secretary) in the San Fernando Valley and was too busy to move into town but would be looking for an apartment to share with Joan Collins.

The Long, Hot Summer had a screenplay by Irving Ravetch and Harriet Frank, Jr., and it was based in part on three Faulkner works: the 1931 novella *Spotted Horses*, the 1939 short story "Barn Burning" and the 1940 novel *The Hamlet*. The director was Martin Ritt. Filming took place on the Fox studio backlot and it was completed on November 21 with a final sequence shot on December 6. The story centered on barn burner and farmer Ben Quick (Paul Newman), a con man who arrives in the town of Frenchmen's Bend, Mississippi, and ingratiates himself with its richest family, the Varners. Second billed after Newman, Woodward played 23-year-old Clara Varner, the schoolteacher daughter of farmer Will Varner (Orson Welles). Her shoulder-length blonde hair is by Helen Turpin and mostly worn tied back with bangs. Her clothes by Adele Palmer favor pastel colors with matching hair ribbons, with glasses when she is seen at school. The actress uses a Southern accent. She is first seen with the back of her head to the camera, and the role sees her driving a car. Clara gets some funny lines, including one she says to her friend Agnes Stewart (Sarah Marshall): When they are talking about being anxious about their love lives, Clara says, "Well, don't throw in the towel yet, Agnes dear. Those tranquilizers may see us through yet." Woodward's scenes with Newman are exciting, and her best is perhaps when Clara's beau, Alan, asks why he has never told her he loves her and her telling him how ashamed she felt "moonin' and dreamin'" over him.

The film premiered on March 5, 1958, in Baton Rouge, Louisiana, with the actress in attendance. She received an award from the lieutenant governor and was given a bouquet by the Lions Club president. It was released in New York on April 3, 1958, with the taglines "The red-hot lowdown on a southern family … that people talked about in whispers!" and "Adapted from the sensational novel by William Faulkner." Bosley Crowther in *The New York Times* wrote that Woodward was excellent. A box office success, it was remade as an ABC television series that ran only one season from 1965 to 1966 and had Nancy Malone as Clara, and as an NBC made-for-TV movie broadcast on October 6, 1985, with Clara renamed Noel and played by Judith Ivey.

Woodward said it was a very romantic film, describing Faulkner as juicy language, and thought that the screenwriters had captured it consistently. She could also easily relate to the role because the actress knew what it meant in the South to be 23 and not even engaged. While Newman commented that in their scenes together they were both fighting for their own closeup, Woodward reported that they had a close relationship and got along and that's what emerged in the film. During production she became pregnant with his child. One observer noted that everybody knew better than to knock on the door of whichever trailer the couple was in at the time. Newman supposedly once grabbed the collar of the assistant director and told him if the trailer's rockin', don't bother knockin'! An alternate version of this story is that the actor reportedly told Ritt, "If my dressing room is rock 'n' rolling, take the advice of that Marilyn Monroe film, *Don't Bother to Knock*." On weekends, Newman took the actress to nearby New Orleans, where in an antique store they came upon a large brass bed salvaged from a local bordello. He reported that three could sleep in it comfortably, which is why it had been in a bordello because there was no other reason to make a bed that big. She had to have it. When a hurricane hit and production was shut down, the couple holed up for five days and nights, with Ritt saying the actor didn't come up for a breath of fresh air. His having come early on location paid off for his relationship, since some of the fellas he had befriended were handy to have around since he was a married man working with his girlfriend and trying to keep that fact out of the papers. When a big-city journalist visited the set to pry into the romance, it was made clear to him that it wasn't a healthy line of inquiry, and the reporter left town. Anthony Franciosa, who played Jody Varner, joked that he thought they were already married being so obviously together and so beautifully close. They even allowed the set photographer to take candid photos of them in the town center, reading the newspaper and eating picnic lunches between takes.

Woodward commented that Ritt was very brave to direct Orson Welles. Although the director admired the actor, he also knew that Welles was intimated by all of the Method actors in the cast and a Method director who all thought they were so great because they came from New York. Welles was one of the most fun people she had ever worked with, once the actress caught on how to work with him. Ritt had originally wanted to cast Marlon Brando and Eva Marie Saint in the film, so that they would be reuniting after *On the Waterfront*. But Brando declined and Newman became Ritt's third choice after Robert Mitchum also turned down the role of Ben. Saint withdrew when she became pregnant and Woodward was cast. Ritt chose her because he had just done *No Down Payment* with her though there was some resistance from the studio. He said Woodward was a very good actress and although *The Three Faces of Eve* had yet to be released, there was strong word of mouth at Fox about it. When Ritt saw the first rushes of her and New-

A publicity portrait with Paul Newman for *The Long, Hot Summer* (1958).

man together, he was thrilled. It was not movie acting but bona fide passion and the director wired Fox executives with the news. She had reportedly told Ritt that she couldn't live without Newman.

Angela Lansbury, who played Minnie Littlejohn, commented that Newman and Woodward together made a wonderful duo and that's what made the relationship so exciting and very sexy. They seemed to have such a total understanding of each other that they were able to work in scenes where they were at each other's throats or falling under each other's spell. She also recalled that the couple spent most of their off-camera time alone and away from the other cast members.

After filming was completed, Woodward and Newman made a trip to Mexico. One source claims this was to allow him to arrange his divorce, though another says this did not happen until January when he went to Mexico alone before joining her in Vegas. Jackie was given a life-long financial settlement and agreed the children should live with her but have weekends and summers with their father. The actor said his children never lost the pain of the divorce, especially Scott. The boy seemed to almost hate his father for what he saw as deserting his mother.

Fox publicity said Woodward was getting the star build-up though they also disseminated inaccurate information about her. They proclaimed that when Woodward was in New York she had experienced the heartbreak that accompanied the business of twiddling one's thumbs, though the actress was actually working steadily. She disapproved of this approach and became more wary of the press. It didn't help that part of the publicity about Woodward and Newman was about their personal life. She said Hollywood had a small town mentality where everybody had to know everybody else's business and this was something the actress had spent her life trying to get away from.

Producer Jerry Wald hoped to reunite her with the other *No Down Payment* actresses in *The World of Crime*, based on another John McPartland novel. Filming was tentatively scheduled for February. The story dealt with young adults in the underworld. This film was never made.

Woodward said that her situation was a case of "reverse English" where the Southern accent she had worked to overcome had rewarded her with six leading roles in four films. But it was a coincidence since the producers didn't even know she could speak Southern until she demonstrated it. However, after un-learning the accent it didn't come naturally to her. She didn't want to be a stereotypical Hollywood star, just a competent actress. So many of those who found success discovered that it was only temporary, since when they started to age, they seemed to fade from the screen. Woodward didn't want that. She wanted to be a trifle familiar to people and not a household word, a comment the actress later considered pretentious and probably in line with how she belonged more to New York than Hollywood. A good role was more important than advancement in Hollywood and Woodward preferred a small role that she felt would be good for her than star in an unsuitable part. The actress would even risk studio suspension to turn down something not right for her, though she would never be suspended. Woodward believed you could turn down a part morally, if not legally.

Fox touted her for an Oscar nomination but she was reluctant to make the publicity rounds. The actress tried to play the game but often her answers to quote-seeking reporters on various subjects were unorthodox. She didn't diet and had nervous indigestion from being in Hollywood where you had to be nice to the right people, something Woodward had never been able to do then. She was the new breed of actor who had different goals, no longer stereotyped and wanting to play parts they liked. They had an artistic drive, rather than a commercial drive. The actress preferred New York and only went to Hollywood to make a name for herself in films. She didn't like California's legendary weather, preferring horrible weather because she was raised on *Wuthering Heights*. Woodward did her commuting between coasts by train because she hated flying after a bad experience, and rail travel permitted her to sit reading science fiction and knit. The actress preferred the television work she did in New York. She didn't know when she would marry Newman, but she was in no hurry. There were too many divorces among her friends, and because of the divorce of her parents, Woodward was being more than careful about getting married.

The actress appeared on the December 27 episode of CBS's documentary news television series *Person to Person*, directed by Franklin J. Schaffner. Woodward told Edward R. Murrow that the best gift she received for Christmas was a set of carriage lamps from

Newman, whom she described as a friend who knew her very well. In December, *The New York Post* ran a photo of the actress and Newman with a caption implying a wedding was impending.

The couple appeared together on the January 16, 1958, episode of CBS's 90-minute anthology series *Playhouse 90*, "The 80 Yard Run," shot in Hollywood. The teleplay was by David Shae based on a story by Irwin Shaw, and the director was Franklin Schaffner. Newman played Christian Darling, a college freshman who at his first football practice broke loose for an 80-yard touchdown run. Woodward played his girlfriend Louise Darling, the campus beauty queen, who becomes a fast-rising star on a fashion magazine. The actress criticized the script for being contrived and dramatically thin, and said its running time was better suited to 30 minutes. According to *The New York Times*, her performance was sensitive and effective. Another critic indicated that she employed her mannerisms since it is said for one scene Louise tapped concert tickets on her chin anxiously as she waited for a date, and nibbled her lower lip as she picked up Christian. She was described as the more accomplished actor though lacking in Newman's indelible star power.

The *Times* of January 26 included her among new actors to capture the public's imagination and draw millions back into movie houses, and said she had come along outstandingly in the last year.

Press photograph of the Newman-Woodward marriage on January 29, 1958.

Woodward told the press that she would soon be traveling to Europe with her mother, and that she was going to marry Newman. He felt guilty about leaving his first marriage and family and he would carry that guilt for the rest of his life, but without Woodward, he would be nowhere and nothing. She caught the train alone to Vegas and met him there for their wedding at the El Rancho Hotel and Casino on January 29, 1958. The tackiness of the locale was said to have fit the couple's sense of humor. Newman arrived via plane from Mexico around suppertime with his best man, Stewart Stern. A marriage license was acquired and Newman telephoned Hedda Hopper to report that he and Woodward were to be wed. He apologized to Hopper for keeping her in the dark until the last minute, not knowing when he would arrive and not wanting to keep his bride waiting at the church. The ceremony was executed by District Judge Frank McNamee in the bungalow of the resort owner, Beldon

Katleman. Also in attendance was Woodward's manager Ina Bernstein as the maid of honor, her agent Jay Kantor and his wife Judy Balaban, Steve Lawrence and Eydie Gorme, and Sophie Tucker and Joe E. Lewis, who were performing at the hotel and part of the Gorme-Lawrence party, since the singers were next in line to be married. Newman was 33 and Woodward was 27. He gave his bride an inscribed silver sherry cup. She was dressed in a light-colored long-sleeved suit with a pilgrim collar, her hair worn in a tied-back style with bangs, and she held a bouquet. There is also newsreel footage of the marriage in Newman's *A&E Biography*. Studio publicists had told newspapers that they decided to get married while making *Playhouse 90*.

Newman and Woodward were witnesses for the Gorme-Lawrence wedding. The Newmans later went to dinner at the Vegas club with Jay Kantor to see Joe E. Lewis' act. He told the audience to welcome a nice young couple who had just got married: Paul Newman and "Joan Woodbury." The actress said Kantor almost died, though there was a Joan Woodbury who did horror movies and had black hair and bangs.

They checked into a small Greenwich Village hotel for several days. Woodward said that they liked Greenwich Village but they were not village characters. The couple were seen in coffeehouses and bars. They planned to go to Paris but instead flew to London, where she had her first fur coat. It was an Alaskan seal, not mink because the actress wanted to be different. The couple met Gore Vidal and Howard Austen at the Connaught Hotel in Mayfair. They gave interviews and permitted photographers into their honeymoon suite where the couple were photographed fully clothed in the bedroom. Woodward said that she was delighted that they had had an intimate wedding. Fox and MGM sent flowers, arranged a car, and took care of theater tickets. Newspapers ran follow-up stories on the couple's romance, saying that they had tried desperately to fight their attraction to each other through the years, since both were determined to keep their careers free of emotional involvement.

Vidal was their guide to London, showing them Hampton Court and telling all sorts of juicy tidbits about past scandals. They visited pubs and restaurants, and he hosted a party for friends Peter Ustinov, Kenneth Tynan, Claire Bloom, Laurence Olivier, Ralph Richardson and John Gielgud. Woodward spent most of the party talking with Bloom and a new friendship developed. One night the couple went to the Salisbury pub near Leicester Square that attracted English stage stars. They rented a car to explore the English countryside but got lost and checked into an inn at nightfall. Newman said that after all the anxiety and secrecy surrounding the romance and the divorce, the ability to walk around freely as man and wife was intoxicating. They traveled to France and Switzerland and then returned to London to stay with Vidal and Austen at Chesham Place, a mews house according to one source and a flat according to another. There was a spooky English butler named Tattersall whom the actress thought looked like a man who had just stepped out of a Dickens novel. The pair also traveled to Scotland, staying in a small village where they went for walks in the cold weather, and frequented watering holes drinking mugs of stout and spending hours talking to the locals.

Back at Chesham Place, Woodward complained of stomach pains so Vidal summoned a doctor, who said that she was having a miscarriage. Taken to St. George's Hospital, the actress lost the child and remained there to recover from her ordeal. Claire Bloom visited Woodward every day and brought flowers. Then she was put on a plane and sent home. The miscarriage occurred in February according to some sources and March according to others.

4

Oscar

Joanne Woodward was listed as one of the year's "outstanding new personalities" by *Photoplay* magazine. On February 17, 1958, it was reported that she had been nominated for the Best Actress Academy Award for her performance in *The Three Faces of Eve*. Woodward didn't think her performance had been that good and she said her vote would be for Deborah Kerr for the Fox action adventure *Heaven Knows, Mr. Allison* (1957); Kerr was seen as the favorite to win. Woodward thought the Oscar shouldn't be given for a single role but rather based on continued excellence, and didn't care if she won. She also said she should probably stop giving interviews so as not to say the wrong thing. However the actress intended to pursue her career because she was not the domestic type. There would be babies but Woodward wasn't going to sit home and just be a mother. Her attitude enchanted many columnists but made others wonder why it seemed she had a compulsion to destroy herself. On February 26, she won the Best Dramatic Actress Golden Globe for *The Three Faces of Eve*.

Newman had to return to Hollywood to begin work on the MGM drama *Cat on a Hot Tin Roof* (1958), which went into production on March 6. Vidal and Austen left for New York, and Woodward was recalled to Hollywood to campaign for the Academy Award.

The Newmans rented a house on a lot in Laurel Canyon in Hollywood. The tiny place was described by Hedda Hopper as a glorified shanty, and it lacked the swimming pool that most movie star homes featured. They used rental cars instead of having their own limo and chauffeur and the place allowed them to live quietly. When Newman's children visited, they called the actress "Auntie Joanne." He read scripts every night and she thought Newman was going to wind up a director. Woodward feared that she would never be anything *but* an actor. She reported that when her husband was working, he was totally dedicated and did not talk to her. If it was a terribly difficult part, she didn't see him at all because the actor was off inside his head somewhere.

The actress spoke about her marriage and the commitment she had made. Woodward had been raised 1940s style to believe that a woman should be both wife and mistress to her husband, and only in that could she find her true fulfillment. This philosophy caused her grief because it was entangled with the actress's ambivalence about her career. She had always acted and had always wanted to be a star but there must have been something wrong with her for wanting more. Woodward had to learn more about herself and recommended analysis, which helped with the issue of her attractiveness. She also wasn't in her mind a movie star, someone people recognized on the street and went to see their movies whether the reviews were good or not. The actress had once said she hoped to marry an actor, and she had made good on that. What she really wanted was to have a life with no children, but she was raised in a generation that taught otherwise. She felt very torn, lured away by the satisfaction of acting, which was a worthy thing, and by her own sense of ambition, which was not. Fox spent hundreds of thousands of dollars but it seemed she was managing to offend the entire movie colony *and* her studio. But Woodward believed in the truth and not telling it would destroy her as a person and her integrity as an actress. She was pleased about winning the National Board of Review Best Actress award; Woodward respected them.

She received an offer from John Houseman to perform Shakespeare in Connecticut but this time Fox wouldn't let her have the time off. The actress now told her agent that she would only accept films shooting close to Newman's locations.

Woodward was cast in two Tennessee Williams plays to be presented on *Kraft Television Theatre* on April 16. They were "Mooney's Kids Don't Cry" and "This Property Is Condemned," to be directed by Sidney Lumet. She did not end up in this show which was entitled "Three Plays by Tennessee Williams" with the third play being "The Last of My Solid Gold Watches," a.k.a. "The Last of the Solid Gold Watches," shot live in New York and broadcast by NBC. She was replaced by Lee Grant in the first and by Zine Bethune in the second.

The Newmans attended the Academy Awards ceremony with their friend Joan Collins on March 26, 1958, at the RKO Hollywood Pantages Theater in Hollywood. The television broadcast directed by Alan Handley was on NBC. On the red carpet, Woodward predicted that Deborah Kerr would win the Best Actress Oscar, and announced that the dress she wore was homemade. It was described by some as a hand appliqued satin emerald green strapless gown with velvet bouffant skirt, and by others as being made of taffeta. The dress cost her $120, not counting her labor. The actress wore her hair off her forehead and tied up at the back.

She was both a nominee for Best Actress and a presenter (with Newman) of the Best Film Editing Award to Peter Taylor for the war adventure *The Bridge on the River Kwai* (1957). The couple were introduced by co-host David Niven as "an exciting new star and her recently acquired personal leading man." Woodward wore a matching cape over her dress with white gloves for the presentation, and Newman referred to her as "Mrs. Newman." She gave him the envelope to announce the winner, saying she was too nervous. They then returned to their seats in the audience, with Woodward sitting in the aisle seat. When John Wayne announced her as the Best Actress, she ran down the aisle to collect her award. In her acceptance speech, the actress reported she had been daydreaming about this moment since she was nine years old. She thanked Nunnally Johnson, who had more faith in her than she thought anybody could have.

Backstage after the broadcast, Newman embraced Woodward as she held her Oscar. At the post-ceremony party at the Beverly Hills Hotel, there were congratulatory telegrams. One was from Deborah Kerr offering congratulations and writing, "Here I go again. Always the bridesmaid, never the bride" referring to her additional previous three Best Actress losses. Although Woodward was complimented as one of the best-dressed movie queens of the night, the Paris-couture–looking dress caused some ire in the Hollywood community. Joan Crawford griped that the actress was setting the cause of Hollywood glamour back 20 years by making her own clothes. Woodward explained that she was the most parsimonious soul in the world, never throwing anything away, knowing more ways of using leftovers than anybody else she knew, and rarely buying clothes. A museum in Georgia asked for the dress, and she refused. She had bought the material, designed it, and worked on for two weeks, and was almost as proud of the dress as she was of her Oscar. Her exhilaration only lasted about nine minutes. Woodward felt acclaim was the fake aspect of the job, which screwed you up. You started to need it, like a drug, and in the final analysis, what did it all mean? Sitting in bed afterward and drinking her Ovaltine, she asked Newman, "Is that it?"

The attention the award gave the actress also evinced comment on her marriage, with Joan Crawford saying Newman could have shacked up with some of the biggest names in Hollywood but preferred "this Georgian redneck and her feedsack dress." The actor called his wife "The Last of the Great Broads," and famously asked, "Why go out for hamburger when you've got steak at home!" She chastised him for this comment, not liking being referred to as "Paul Newman's meat." Later he changed the comparison to "a classy '62 full-bodied burgundy and a cocktail," then changed the year of the Bordeaux to '59 because that aged well in the bottle. Susan Hayward reportedly also had a reaction, accusing Newman of tricking her because he wanted the part for his "ugly little girlfriend." The actor himself had an odd reaction to his wife's win. Newman posed with her Oscar in a gag photo, eyeing it enviously. He would have to wait until 1987 to receive his own for Best Actor for the sports drama *The Color of Money* (1986). Woodward's pals from the Neighborhood Playhouse, like Patrick O'Neal, were stunned the morning after.

The actress had observed in Hollywood that the big producers, directors and stars banded together, the lesser ones banded together, and the strugglers banded together. Because of her New York connection, Woodward was always relegated to a lower tier. But when she won her Academy Award, she became acceptable on a very false level. She had become a property. Woodward appeared to have made it but nothing was really different. You never really made it once and for all since with every new part and new picture, you had to make it all over again.

The Newmans rented an apartment in an old building on the Upper East Side of Manhattan. The place was large enough to accommodate his three children when they came to visit, and it also had its own study, library and maid's quarters. It was done in a comfortable rather than a lavish style, with a few really fine pieces of furniture, including the brass bed they had bought in New Orleans. Newman said that they were pretty self-sufficient and enjoyed being alone together. Despite both actors still being on salary from their respective studios, one source claims money was tight, since a lot of his income went to Jackie for child support and alimony. Jackie moved the family into a home in the San Fernando Valley. Newman's son Scott still resented Woodward, supposedly referring to her as "that Southern magnolia."

The couple were the subject of the April 27 episode of the NBC-TV documentary series *Wide Wide World*. "A Star's Story" focused on Hollywood's star system, its origins, growth and contemporary status and included footage of the New York Neighborhood Playhouse where Woodward trained. She demonstrated her preparation for *The Three Faces of Eve*, and Buddy Alder and Nunnally Johnson were interviewed on the subject of stardom.

The actress did her first sitting for the famed Hollywood photographer John Engstead. He recalled that she had not mastered the posing techniques for stills but found her a non-egotistical, intelligent lady. Engstead wanted to photograph Woodward's own particular aura and he felt they turned out beautifully. She would pose for him many times over the next few years.

The actress was sought by Fox producer Jerry Wald for one of the roles in his production of *The Best of Everything*, a film based on the novel by Rona Jaffe about five college girls in the business world. But she would not appear in the 1959 romance, with Hope Lange cast in the lead role of Caroline Bender that Woodward was presumably considered for. Wald also hoped to cast her in another Fox film, *The Story on Page One*, a new screenplay being written by Clifford Odets which dealt with circumstantial evidence. Filming was planned to begin in September with Odets having the option of also directing. Rita Hayworth was cast in the lead female role of Josephine Brown Morris in the drama. A part the actress declined was prostitute Ginny Moorehead in the MGM romance *Some Came Running* (1958), a role taken by Shirley MacLaine which earned her a Best Actress Oscar nomination. Woodward said she didn't want to work with Frank Sinatra, who played the lead. The actress had heard of his reputation for coming in late, shooting a scene just once, then running out, and she didn't want to work that way. Despite being anxious to go back to work, all these lost opportunities made Woodward the hottest unemployed actress in town.

The couple returned to Hollywood on May 23 to begin work on their new film together, the comedy *Rally 'Round the Flag, Boys!* (1958). It was shot on location in Connecticut and at the Fox studios from mid–June to mid–August 1958, with Woodward reported to have completed her scenes by August 15. The screenplay was by Claude Binyon and Leo McCarey, with uncredited work by George Axelrod, from the novel by Max Shulman, and the director was McCarey. The story centered on the citizens of Putnam's Landing on Long Island Sound and their reactions to an army missile base in their backyard. She played the part of Grace *née* Oglethorpe Bannerman, the activist wife of public relations executive Harry Bannerman (Newman). Her costumes by Charles LeMaire include glasses, a harem girl outfit with a bare midriff, and a soldier's greens. Her hair by Helen Turpin is blonde and sculptured, worn shorter and thick and off her forehead, and in one scene it is in curlers. The part sees the actress hang Grace's son Danny (an uncredited Ralph Osborn III) upside down after he has swallowed his allowance, cry, narrate the town's Fourth of July Pageant, jump into a bay, and share a scene with a chimpanzee who hugs her. She uses broad body language including overgesturing which perhaps has context for comedy, despite lacking Newman's lightness of touch. But Woodward has some funny moments, with her best being her reaction to a black cat walking in front of her. The actress' best scene is perhaps Grace's first with Harry, since it is a long one that shows her range from complaining to crying to romance.

The film was to be screened at the San Francisco International Film Festival which ran from October 29 to November 11 with Woodward to attend. But then it was withdrawn because a print was not ready for the festival's opening date. It was released on December 23, 1958, with the Newmans attending a screening. Taglines included "20th Century–Fox hilariously declares a national laugh holiday … as the cast of the year brings the #1 fun best-seller howlingly alive!," and "You'll Hang from the Rafters with Laughter.… It's That Funny!" It was praised by *Variety*, Bosley Crowther in *The New York Times*, and Tony Thomas and Aubrey Solomon in *The Films of 20th Century-Fox*. Crowther wrote that with all the odds against her, Woodward made a cheerful farceuse, on the order of the late Carole Lombard. The film was a box office disappointment.

Variety had reported in March 1958 that Buddy Adler was to produce the film and Deborah Kerr would be playing Grace. But that changed when Leo McCarey came on board as producer. The part of Angela Hoffa was originally intended for Jayne Mansfield, mainly because McCarey believed that blondes were funny. After intense lobbying from the Newmans, she was replaced with the brunette Joan Collins. Collins reported that they had insisted that Mansfield was far too tarty and obvious for the part, which needed a touch of class and an impish sense of humor. She considered the Newmans good friends and appreciated their loyalty. Newman had reportedly met Collins before Woodward but he told McCarey that his wife's friendship with her "took the fire off his hard-on." Production was originally to have begun on June 2, then postponed to June 9, and then to June 16. The delays were caused by a real-life event when eight Nike missiles exploded accidentally in New Jersey, killing ten people. This made McCarey reconsider the film's original ending where the trigger mechanism control button was accidentally pressed and launched a Nike anti-aircraft missile into a suburban community. He created two or three different comedy finales.

Producer Lawrence Weingarten said that the Newmans were hot properties and either of them could have their pick of roles. And in a fit of madness, she gave in to her husband's demand to do a comedy. Woodward reported that he really had to sell Fox on using her in the film since the pair had had a hit in a drama and that was the formula the studio wanted to repeat. Also, despite her Oscar, they feared the audience still didn't know the actress's name. She had reservations about the script but agreed to do it because Newman was again on loan to Fox. The actress contributed to his character's wardrobe, making a bathrobe, sweater, socks and sports shirt. But Woodward loathed herself in the film. She made some wrong choices: When she wasn't playing small, she was busy making faces. Newman commented that he liked working with her because they got along pretty well, despite the fact that they worked very differently. She was immediate and instinctive and started the character internally. He could see her knitting or sewing but her mind was snapping like a grasshopper until she finally soaked it up into her intellect. He started in the intellect, then mulled it over until he wound up internally. The couple were also different types off the screen too, but it was amazing that they could be together as much as they were. When they worked together, Newman said they couldn't get away with any old tricks, because the other one was sitting there nodding his head knowingly and saying, "Yes, I seem to remember doing this on the 28th page of *The Helen Morgan Story*."

Woodward improvised during the scene where Grace read *Cinderella* to her sons and three-year-old Barry Livingston sneezed unexpectedly. She looked at him with what was said to be motherly concern and casually interjected a "God bless you" into the take before continuing to read. McCarey wanted full credit for the sneeze since it made the take more natural and admitted he would not have dared, even if he had thought of it, to ask the boy to attempt to sneeze on cue. The scene remains in the film. However, the part of the boy, Danny, is said to have been played by Ralph Osborn III and his older brother Stanley Livingston played the older Bannerman son, Peter. A source claims that McCarey did not get along with the Newmans, despite his encouraging his actors to make suggestions and improvise. Apparently the director felt uncomfortable with them being the new generation of New York Method actors. Joan Collins commented that the fault was with McCarey, whom she considered "an old Hollywood has-been who seemed to have had a sense of humor bypass." Another source quotes Collins saying that she was unaware of any tension on the set and was in awe of the director. The actress also said that the Newmans were so down-to-earth and un-luvvie that she really didn't think people would be in awe of them.

Woodward left for Louisiana to begin Fox's *The Sound and the Fury*. It was shot from mid–August to mid–October 1958 on location near Baton Rouge and back at the Fox Hollywood studios. The screenplay was by Irving Ravetch and Harriet Frank, Jr., based on the novel by Faulkner, and the director was Martin Ritt. The novel had been previously adapted into a 60-minute episode of NBC-TV's live anthology series *Playwrights '56* (December 6, 1955).

The Compson family of Southern aristocrats in Jefferson, Mississippi, are trying to deal with the dissolution of their clan and the loss of its reputation, faith, fortunes and respect. Woodward was the narrator and also played the part of teenage Quentin Compson, a student at Miss Baines' School for Young Ladies. The actress is billed second after Yul Brynner, who plays Quentin's step-uncle and general store worker Jason, although she has more scenes than he. Her costumes are by Adele Palmer. Her hair by Helen Turpin is short and straight blonde with bangs. Woodward uses a Southern accent. She has lipstick rubbed off her mouth by Jason, is carried by Charlie (Stuart Whitman) and Jason, and choked by Benjy (Jack Warden). Her mannerism of self-conscious self-touching is a plot point since Jason tells her not do it. The actress is funny and her best scene is perhaps when Quentin reunites with her mother Caddy (Margaret Leighton) where her character changes from happiness to beseeching for help to disappointment.

The film was previewed on March 19, 1959, with a special screening at the Fox projection room in New York as a benefit for the Virginia Day Nursery. It was released on March 27, 1959, with the tagline "William Faulkner's blistering story of love that breaks

Woodward in *The Sound and the Fury* (1960).

the unwritten commandment!" It was praised by *Variety*, who wrote that Woodward gave firm conviction to her part. Bosley Crowther in *The New York Times* said Woodward was incongruous as a teenage high school girl since her mannerisms and general deportment were those of an accomplished woman of the world. The film was not a box office success. It would be remade in 2009 and 2014, with Joey King playing Miss Quentin in the latter.

It had been commissioned by Fox as a return trip to Faulkner territory after the success of *The Long, Hot Summer* and reunited that film's producer, director, screenwriters and Woodward. She became pregnant during shooting so had to be photographed carefully to conceal it. The actress wondered why she and Ritt made the film, seeing nothing socially conscious about the material, and she laughed at absurdities like Yul Brynner wearing a wig. However the character of Quentin had a redeeming value, since she was closer to her than most. Ritt helped by telling her the character had such a tremendous appetite for any experience that there was no halfway measure for her. Woodward said she did not find the character until her hair was cut and then she knew just what to do.

That summer, the Newmans spent some time with Gore Vidal at his house at Edgewater. The actress was considered for the title role in Fox's remake of their 1917 silent historical biography *Cleopatra*. Studio chief Spyros Skouras wanted her when the film was planned to be a relatively small production, with her status as a new Oscar winner helping to sell the idea. Fox's head of production Buddy Adler wanted Joan Collins, but producer Walter Wanger preferred Elizabeth Taylor and wanted the film to be a mammoth production to match its mammoth star. Writer-director Joseph L. Mankiewicz reportedly had the notion of casting both Woodward and Newman since they were a real-life couple, but this idea was dropped.

Woodward was named the Number One Star of Tomorrow in the 18th annual poll of motion picture exhibitors conducted by the *Motion Picture Herald*.

The Newmans moved into a cozy Greenwich Village duplex on East 11th Street which had a small garden, fishpond and trees. Woodward moved all her furniture from her old New York apartment there and they shipped their books, paintings, four lamps and most of their clothes by express from California. In their new home, the actress's Oscar was placed on a mantel in the den. The couple planned to name the next child Joshua if it was a boy, for Joshua Logan, or Quentin if it was a girl, after her *Sound and the Fury* character. She spent much of her time with her two Chihuahua dogs El Toro and Little Brother and perfecting her dressmaking and knitting skills. After having only been married a year, Woodward had already knitted Newman 37 sweaters which he said was more than he could use. She also sat around and read cookbooks, and waited for her husband to come home from rehearsals of the stage play he was doing, *Sweet Bird of Youth*. Woodward said she loved being totally domestic, but was surprised at her feeling, guessing that her childhood conditioning had really stuck. A baby had always been a possibility but it wasn't scheduled time-wise, yet the timing was clever, since she wanted her husband to be close when it was born. The expectant mother kept praying she would have it during the day or after midnight when Newman wouldn't be on stage. The actress also conducted correspondence courses in algebra, anthropology and the history of philosophy. She planned to enroll at Columbia when Newman's play was run, since Woodward always regretted not having a college degree. *Sweet Bird of Youth* opened on March 10 at the Martin Beck Theatre and ran until January 30, 1960.

The couple spent their free time alone together, generally reading, and frequented the bar-restaurant Jim Downey's in the theater district. They also socialized with Gore Vidal, Christopher Isherwood and Tennessee Williams. Their home became a salon for the radical chic where people from the political world mingled with people from show business and the literary world.

Although they claimed to discourage media coverage of their home life, the Newmans appeared on the December 26, 1958, episode of *Person to Person*, directed by Franklin J. Schaffner. Host Edward R. Murrow reported that the couple had moved into their duplex a week prior to their interview. On the show, a visibly pregnant Woodward wears a dark-colored elbow-sleeved knee-length maternity dress with a nautical collar and a jewel at the bust. Her hair is worn short in a sculpted style and mostly off her forehead. Our view of the apartment includes the nursery, the downstairs visitor's guest room, and a room with a Christmas tree and the actress's Oscar on a shelf. The couple say that they are only allowing the cameras to show the uncluttered part of the house. She comments that their Christmas had been hectic, although the year had been pretty hectic since in one year she had married, had her first trip to Europe, won the Academy Award, done two films, moved twice, and now was expecting a baby. Newman showed an original watercolor of George Bernard Show which they planned to hang over the crib because they believed in osmosis. In the guest room den, Woodward sat on a wooden rocking chair and then on a sofa where she knitted. Morrow reminded her of the carriage lamps the actor had given her as a Christmas gift the year before. Newman said they were now unable to find them but they had to be in the house because his wife never threw anything away. This Christmas the actress gave him a Leica camera with two lenses and all the equipment and more books than he had ever seen. He gave her a little tiny Nicholas II Russian antique sherry glass with the coat of arms laminated, which were no longer made, and a bathrobe. Woodward showed her Oscar which she described as her favorite child of the moment, and next to it was Newman's Noscar, her second favorite child. This was the award he was given by Charlie Schnee and Robert Wise the previous year for not being nominated for *Somebody Up There Likes Me*. Woodward read the inscription: "The Schnee/Wise Noscar award to Paul Newman for best portraying a terrible no-good blankety-blank. For turning him into a charming and lovable sprite and for thereby doing what Lincoln said what should never be done i.e. Fooling all of the people all of the time." Murrow reminded the actress she had wanted to marry an actor better than she, and Woodward was quite lucky because that was exactly what she did. The actress felt that Newman was not only a great actor but he could produce and direct and was a pretty good writer. All she could do was act. Woodward did not agree with her husband's views on acting or life in general. The couple had great arguments about it that would go on for hours, being great ones for sitting up all night long. Newman reported that it did rather irritate his wife when, right in the middle of a discussion, he got up to cook a large batch of popcorn and open a quart of beer and build a fire at three o'clock in the morning. He said the actress was a wonderful wife and a good shopper. She started filling a piggy bank with change early last February and when they opened it up before Christmas there was $156 in it, which they were going to save for gifts. Woodward had a huge pocketbook that she carried into some of the chic Beverly Hills shops, and she paid $22.50 in change for an item which was pretty embarrassing for the sales clerk. Woodward was amazed at the expression on the face of the clerk, who kept asking if she wouldn't prefer to charge it. Now that the couple were living in New York, they said they wouldn't miss California living.

They also appeared in the December 28 episode of the CBS comedy musical variety show *Toast of the Town* which was filmed in New York. As Joan Collins also appeared on the show, presumably the actors were there to talk about *Rally 'Round the Flag, Boys!*

The couple celebrated their first wedding anniversary on January 29, 1959, at their rented apartment on 51st Street in Manhattan with the writer A.E. Hotchner and his wife, then went across the street to Lutece, the reigning four-star French restaurant at the time.

By February Woodward was out of contention to play *Cleopatra*, considered not quite voluptuous enough to be the Queen of the Nile. Elizabeth Taylor would play the part and the film would be released in 1963.

On March 6, Woodward was cited by Harvard University's Hasting Pudding Institute of 1770 for screen achievement and accepted a "woman of the year" award from the organization at a reception held at 21 on West 52nd Street in New York.

Woodward was cast in *Orpheus Descending*, an adaptation of the Tennessee Williams play that was being headlined by Marlon Brando and Anna Magnani. The film was a United Artists release to be directed by Sidney Lumet.

She gave birth to a daughter on April 8 at Mount Sinai Hospital in New York. The girl was named Elinor Teresa Newman, after her two grandmothers, but known as Nell to her parents. She was born in time for Newman to welcome her into the world before he had to be at the theater to play the matinee. To help care for her, Tressie, a fulltime nanny, was hired. Gore Vidal was asked to be Nell's godfather. The actress even said she didn't like children. Woodward also spoke about being a stepmother. Woodward took three months to get back in shape and, being very disciplined, within five weeks she was ready to go back in front of the cameras.

Orpheus Descending was retitled *The Fugitive Kind* (1960). The play had run on Broadway from March 21 to May 18, 1957, at the Martin Beck Theatre in a production directed by Harold Clurman. The screenplay for the black and white film romance was by Williams and Meade Roberts, and it was shot on location in Milton, New York, and at the Gold Medal Studios in the Bronx from June 22 to September 4, 1959. Rehearsals took place from June 9. Brando stars as Valentine "Val" Snakeskin Xavier, a 30-year-old former New Orleans entertainer, who comes to the Mississippi town of Two River County and gets a job as a clerk at the J.M. Torrance Mercantile store. Woodward played the alcoholic, sex-crazed Carol Cutrere, which had been played by Lois Smith on stage. She is billed third after Brando and Magnani, who plays Lady Torrance. Her hair by Mary Roche appears to be peroxide-blonde worn straight and shoulder-length with a middle part, and her makeup by Robert Jiras and Philip Rhodes includes white-pancake makeup and kohl-rimmed eyes. She only has one costume by Frank Thompson, a white knee-length sleeveless dress, worn with light-colored overcoat, scarf and cap. The actress is heard before she is seen and uses a soft Southern accent. The role sees her attempt to give oral sex to Val. Woodward's performance here is less mannered and she is funny. Her best scene is perhaps when Carol explains what "juking" is at Ruby's Bar-B-Q, where the actress throws herself around to "make a crazy show of herself."

The film was released on April 14, 1960, with the taglines "Three Academy Award winners ... the Pulitzer Prize author ... and now the screen is struck by lightning!" and "Three Academy Award winners—the most explosive star combination of the year in Tennessee Williams' most shattering drama!" Bosley Crowther (*The New York Times*) wrote that Woodward was perhaps a bit too florid for full credibility with her dipsomaniacal maunderings being flush with theatricality. *Variety* said that the actress provided a distasteful and often ludicrous extra dash of degeneracy. In *The United Artists Story*, Ronald Bergan wrote that Woodward was unconvincing. It was a box office failure. The film was remade for television as *Orpheus Descending* (1990) with Anne Twomey as Carol.

According to *The Hollywood Reporter* of February 27, 1959, Carroll Baker was considered to play Carol. One of the reasons for the delay in principal photography was Woodward's pregnancy. She was borrowed from Fox for the role and was reportedly so taken with it that she told the producers she'd do anything to keep another actress from playing it.

The July 5, 1959, *New York Times* featured an article by Richard Nason written on location in Milton, New York. Nason reported that the cast stayed in a hotel in Poughkeepsie. When rain interrupted filming, Woodward withdrew into the home of Matthew (Doc) Jannelli, the Milton postmaster who had provided it for makeup and rehearsals. She tattered a scarf to suit her frantic costume. A shot was then filmed with Brando climbing into the driver's seat of a Jaguar also carrying Woodward. Three takes were made before Lumet was satisfied.

She was visited on the set by Newman and Gore Vidal. The actress didn't know whether she was any good in the film because all Woodward could see was the insecurity in her eyes. And she hated working with Brando, resenting his pauses and vagueness, and feeling he was *not* there. The actress had nothing to reach out to, and she complained to Lumet that Brando was a complete blank "regardless of how much money he was hauling in for this turkey." The actor had been paid $1 million for the film, as opposed to her $30,000. Woodward stated the only way she would work with Brando again was if he was in rear projection. A source claims that the actor mistreated her to get back at Newman who was now considered a greater exponent of the Actors Studio Method than he. To torment both Newmans, he supposedly spread the rumor that he was shacking up with Woodward during the making of the film. Though it was untrue, Newman knew that Brando had dated her briefly in 1953 and he suspected that Brando had seduced the actress. Brando also seemed to be antagonized by the fact that she was friendly with Magnani, who shared Woodward's disenchanted view of the Hollywood scene.

The actress loved Magnani. Woodward thought her beautiful, very kind and very gentle in her own strange way. Brando was mean to Magnani and Woodward hated him for that. The older actress (age 51) was very ambivalent about her looks. Woodward found it touching how Magnani would hide her neck with scarves and she was constantly pushing them closer to her chin line. She said as one got older and the wrinkles came, you realized the tragedy of the worship of the young in films.

Sidney Lumet considered Woodward smart and funny and sweet—a real divinity of a woman, as Tennessee Williams put it. She and the writer became fast friends. Williams had first seen the actress in the 1953 *Philco Television Playhouse* drama "A Young Lady of Property."

Woodward returned to domestic life. Tennessee Williams called her "just plain old Mary Cook from across the street," and Gore Vidal "that clever girl who had everything under control." The first description amused the actress but the second irritated her, amazed that the man she considered one of her four closest friends would think that. Woodward admitted to being impatient, overly emotional, and almost hysterical, having tantrums and throwing things. Her ambition was to be the best actress in the world, as well as the best wife and mother, and to do some real good in the world.

When in the summer of 1959, Newman went to see Jack Warner to prematurely end his contract with Warner Bros., the studio chief reportedly made a comment about Woodward. With three years left, Newman was unhappy with what the studio was doing for him, but Warner told him he had saved both their careers. *Confidential* was planning to report that the couple were both gay and married to serve as each other's beards. Warner paid off the magazine with $20,000. Newman said the story was a lie and he and his wife were very much in love. Warner didn't believe it but he didn't care what kind of arrangement they had. The actor negotiated his release with the help of his new agent, Lew Wasserman.

On October 17, the Newmans served as king and queen of the Mediterranean Masquerade Ball sponsored by the junior committee of the women's division of the American Friends of Hebrew University. This was held in the Starlight Room of the Waldorf-Astoria Hotel. Proceeds from the fete were to be used for the establishment of a new School of Fine Arts at the university in Jerusalem.

Woodward was set for a leading role with Newman in producer-director Otto Preminger's film version of *Exodus*. It was based on the best-selling novel by Leon Uris and would start filming in January. The part that Woodward was to have played—the American nurse Katherine "Kitty" Fremont—was taken by Eva Marie Saint.

The Newmans appeared as the mystery guests on the November 8 episode of the CBS-TV game show *What's My Line?*, shot in New York. Woodward wears a light-colored strapless knee-length dress with many necklaces and her hair tied back off her forehead in a bun. She uses her acting mannerisms and answers questions in a British accent, with the pair's identity guessed by panelist Arlene Francis. Francis had seen her in the play *The Lovers*. Panelist Dorothy Kilgallen reports that she had seen her in the beauty parlor recently and has heard wonderful things about the yet-to-be-released *The Fugitive Kind*, which the actress had also yet to see. Woodward only liked to see her films in the cinema with an audience so she could hide and watch. The actress reports that her new baby ate a cigarette the day before but she is fine.

The couple next co-starred in *From the Terrace* (1960), an adaptation of the John O'Hara novel. The Fox production was directed by Mark Robson and shot from early December 1959 to late February 1960 on New York and Pennsylvania locations with interiors at the Fox Movietone Studios in New York and in Hollywood. Woodward went to Hollywood to finish her scenes in February. The Ernest Lehman screenplay begins in 1946 in Port Johnson, Pennsylvania, where former Marine Alfred Eaton (Newman) meets Wilmington heiress Mary St. John (Woodward) and becomes a Wall Street executive. Her hair by Helen Turpin is shoulder-length silver-peroxide worn with a side part, and gowns by Travilla include a blue wedding dress and furs and a tiara. The role has Woodward ice-skate. It's fun to see her play a bad girl. The actress's best scene is perhaps when Mary tells Alfred she won't divorce him. Woodward transitions from Mary's nasty anger at Alfred having a girlfriend to an attempt at seduction, saying they could still have an enjoyable relationship as friends.

The film was released on July 15, 1960, with the tagline "It is being talked about as few motion pictures in recent years!" Neither Newman attended the New York premiere. It received a mixed reaction from Howard Thompson in *The New York Times* and Michael Kerbel in *Paul Newman*. Thompson wrote that Woodward had skillful, silken sensuality. The film was a box office success.

It was reported the Newmans were instrumental in having Patrick O'Neal cast as

Dr. Jim Roper. He was a fellow student of the Neighborhood Playhouse and the Actors Studio. O'Neal had performed a Dorothy Parker short story at the Studio, and afterwards the couple told him how much they had liked it. When casting was being done for the film, his name was mentioned to Mark Robson, who had not heard of the actor. The Newmans denied they had anything to do with Robson contacting him or his casting but O'Neal was sure they had everything to do with it. Newman joked about Woodward's love scenes with Patrick O'Neal. When she finished, Newman let her have it across the behind, just in case the actress got any romantic notions.

She defined her role as being a mean, nasty witch but a good part. The actress told reporters that she and Newman could get out all their own frustrations by screaming at each other in character on the set. Once that was done, they could go home and make like turtledoves. Woodward loved the way she looked in the film—like Lana Turner. The actress had 22 wardrobe changes and hoped Fox would give her the clothes. Woodward had only browsed through the O'Hara book but felt she had played too many Southern belles. The actress feared if she got much nicer, the public would get wise to her.

Woodward went back to studying with Sanford Meisner, saying the experience was a revelation and the whole turning point on her growth as an actress. Woodward also read the Evan S. Connell novel *Mrs. Bridge*, about an upper middle class, bourgeois Kansas City family in the period between the First and Second World Wars, told mostly from the perspective of the mother. She said the main character's sociological background was very much like her own. She envisaged playing Mrs. Bridge though Woodward at the time was too young.

In January 1960, she attended a performance of *Sweet Bird of Youth* late in the run and chastised her husband for putting in what the actress considered a half-effort. Newman said she was right because had rushed through the show but his last ten performances were just great. On January 1, the couple was photographed in Times Square for *Town and Country Magazine.*

On February 9, Woodward was said to have become the first actress to receive a star on the newly established Hollywood Walk of Fame. The legend originated because she was the first to pose with her star for photographers, but in fact there was no first recipient. The original terrazzo and brass stars were installed with no individual ceremonies.

Woodward traveled to Israel and Cyprus with Newman and their daughter Nell for the filming of the United Artists historical actioner *Exodus* (1960). This was shot from mid–March (one source claims the start date was March 27) to late June. The Newmans remained in Israel for three and a half months. He said that the couple had endured few long separations due as much to her intelligence as his insistence. His wife would have many opportunities to go abroad or on location by herself and she had turned these offers down in order to stay with him. He feared Woodward had done this much to the detriment of her career but it helped keep them together.

During production, director Otto Preminger noted that Newman was an oddity in the business because he really loved his wife. He was a sex symbol who was off limits to that special breed of Hollywood woman who circled young men like sharks ready for the kill; the actor could not be seduced. When the director had telephoned to tell him he was wanted for the film, Preminger advised not to bring his wife on location. But when he did, the director told the press that she was no doubt protecting her own interests. The Newmans spent time sightseeing, with Woodward doing so alone while her husband worked in the day. She toured historic locations and took Hebrew lessons, but soon learned that walking around became impossible. The actress said that Israelis were movie-mad and the Newmans could not walk down the street because they would be followed by 1500 people, which terrified her. Newman reported that people stood in front of the hotel all day staring in at the lobby or hollering upstairs into unknown windows. Once when the family was breakfasting in the hotel dining room, they saw more than a hundred people staring at them through a window. Another time Woodward was having breakfast on the terrace when she saw 50 people standing and staring. The actress commented that she would never be able to go to the zoo again. The day they left the country, all of the film's company went to visit Prime Minister David Ben-Gurion. Woodward reported when they all walked in, Mrs. Ben-Gurion pointed to Newman and asked if he was the handsome one they all talked about because she didn't think he was so handsome. The actress reported that Newman was unhappy with his performance in the film, and couldn't stand to talk about it or even think about it.

One source claims that the Newmans left Israel for Paris but another says that they first went home to New York for the summer and then went to Paris in the fall. They reportedly moved from Greenwich Village to an apartment in a venerable old building in the East 80s with enough space for their growing household. At Kenyon College on June 4, Newman accepted an honorary doctorate of human letters degree, and donated $10,000.

Woodward won the San Sebastian Cinema Festival's Grand Prix for the best feminine performance of the year for *The Fugitive Kind*. She was tentatively set for the second female lead in Newman's new film *Paris Blues*. This was a modern jazz comedy-drama about a pair of expatriate musicians, to be played by Newman and Sidney Poitier, and their complicated romantic relationships with two uninhibited American girls.

The Newmans helped to create the Theatre Group, where famous representatives of the theater and movies worked with the University of California to lead to the establishment of permanent professional theater companies in Los Angeles and New York. These would tour colleges throughout the country, presenting the best of classical and modern plays.

The actress was confirmed to be in the United Artists musical romance *Paris Blues* (1961) and the director was Martin Ritt. It was shot on location in Paris and at the Studios de Boulogne from October 10 to December. The screenplay was by Jack Sher, Irene Kamp and Walter Bernstein, adapted by Lulla Adler from the novel by Harold Flender. Trombonist Ram Bowen (Newman) and saxophonist Eddie Cook (Poitier), American ex-pat jazz musicians living in Paris, perform at the Club Prive. They meet and fall in love with two American tourist girls on a two-week vacation. Woodward played Lillian "Lilly" Corning, a divorced mother of two. Her hair by Carita is blonde, and worn in a short sculptured style with bangs. Her wardrobe includes a black shimmery short-sleeve knee-length dress with a wide coat, and in one scene the actress wears only a chemise. She is heard before she is seen and the role allows her to play the piano, take a photo of Newman with a camera, and speak one word of French. Woodward's best scene is the one where Lilly tells Ram she wants them to be together in America.

The film was released on September 27, 1961, with the tagline "A love so spectacular, so personally exciting, you feel it happening to you!" It was not a box office success but its music score was Oscar-nominated.

Marilyn Monroe was also considered for the part of Lilly but declined. Marlon Brando's company Pennebaker produced the film and, after he decided against playing

Ram, he reportedly cast Woodward before signing Newman. Woodward described the film as strange, interesting and ahead of its time.

Diahann Carroll, who played Connie Lampson, called Woodward a great actress. She said being on the same soundstage every day with someone as gifted as Woodward was a constant reminder of how fine film acting could be. As Carroll watched the rushes of one of Woodward's scenes, Martin Ritt marveled at the things her co-star could do in front of the camera. Carroll learned much from watching and working with her, and said the experience was tremendously important to her own development as an actress.

During filming, Woodward became pregnant again. She reported that they rented a place in Montmartre. One source claims it was a two-story house, another that it was an apartment that Picasso had once lived in. Sources do agree there was a backyard garden. In her time off, the actress visited museums and looked after Nell and the Chihuahuas. She was also visited by her mother for three weeks. The Newmans grew tired of the French food that Desiree, the studio-provided maid, prepared, so Newman set up a barbecue in their garden. After this too became a bore, the couple frequented an American Southern–style restaurant they found just below Place Pigalle. To the Parisians they did not look like movie stars, with Woodward described as looking like a Kansas housewife. The couple was seen one night dining with Louis Armstrong at Haynes, a Harlem-inspired restaurant on Rue Chauzel. (Armstrong played Wild Man Moore in *Paris Blues*.)

Hollywood gossip columnist Mike Connolly reported the Newmans had separated while making the film. Newman was so wild with anger that, with the help of his friend Joe Hyams, he wrote an article regarding the Connolly allegation. The actor stated that for the columnist's benefit, he was going to try to take some steps to split from his wife. Newman would start complaining about how she made hollandaise sauce, and that he hated the way the actress held her fork when she ate. The actor would be a prime mover in the marriage for the use of twin beds or, even better, separate bedrooms. He promised to tell Woodward daily what a lousy wife and mother she was, and how he loathed the color of her hair. The article appeared just as Newman had written it and Connolly never again printed his name.

The Newmans toyed with the idea of buying an apartment in Paris and relocating but then lost interest. They sailed back to the United States and reportedly lent their support to John F. Kennedy, the Democrat presidential hopeful. The couple also campaigned for Gore Vidal in his unsuccessful run as a Democrat for a Congressional seat in New York State. To counter the issue of Vidal's homosexuality, he reminded the press of his previous engagement to Woodward. She also spoke for Vidal at a rally which 1400 attended.

The actress was sought for a leading role in *The Rich Boy*, a film of the F. Scott Fitzgerald novel about an emotionally unfulfilled, wealthy youth during the Jazz Age. Richard Burton and Sidney Lumet were to co-produce as an independent production to be shot in the summer in June or July. Burton would act in the film, which had a screenplay by Walter Bernstein, who had written a television adaptation for *The Philco Television Playhouse* in 1952. This film was never made.

The couple took Piper Laurie to a benefit ball for the Actors Studio at Roseland with Gore Vidal as her date. She was Newman's co-star in the Fox sports drama *The Hustler* (1961), which had begun production on location in New York on March 6.

The Newmans moved to Hollywood with Nell while he made the film version of *Sweet Bird of Youth* (1962). The MGM production was shot from July 6 to early October

1961 on location in Malibu and at MGM. She said Newman thought making it would be a breeze because he had played it on the stage but the movie version was so different it was almost like another story. The couple rented a Beverly Hills house with a garden and a pool from actress Linda Christian. Woodward had a hard time with Nell, who was going through the terrible twos. The actress engaged a Southern woman as a nanny for the girl and who would also help with the baby on the way. Woodward felt that the baby would be the best thing that could happen to Nell and admitted that she and Newman were hoping for a boy this time. The actress said there was no jealousy between her daughter and Newman's children, who visited.

Woodward was to head the cast of the screen version of the Enid Bagnold play *The Chalk Garden*, to be produced by Ross Hunter. The play had run on Broadway from October 26, 1955, to March 31, 1956, with Siobhán McKenna playing the part of the governess Miss Madrigan, the part that Woodward was presumably to play. Previous actresses who had been announced for the role or were said to be interested were Audrey Hepburn, Ingrid Bergman and Vivien Leigh. The play's location of London was to be changed to San Francisco and the production was to begin in New York on January 15.

The actress gave birth to her second daughter, Melissa "Lissy" Steward, on September 27, 1961, at Cedars of Lebanon Hospital in Hollywood. The name Lissy was in honor of the Newmans' screenwriter friend Stewart Stern and also the name of the character Woodward had played in *Count Three and Pray*.

This time Woodward hadn't been signed to work right away so she let herself go, not exercising and eating too much. She had gained 35 pounds when she was pregnant and then had to lose 20, vowing never to put on that much again.

Delbert Mann was announced as the director of *The Chalk Garden*. Woodward was also to star in *Celebration*, the screen version of William Inge's play *A Loss of Roses*, for producer Jerry Wald. The Fox production was to begin the first week of December. The play had a short run on Broadway from November 28 to December 19, 1959, with Carol Haney playing the protagonist Lila Green.

In early 1962, the Newmans were given a free cruise from New York to the Mediterranean in exchange for being the featured on-ship celebrities on the ocean liner *Leonardo Da Vinci*. They had initially gone to see their friend Gore Vidal leave for Palermo to meet up with Howard Austen, and at the last minute decided to join Vidal on the cruise. The writer was apparently sitting alone at dinner in the ship's dining room when he looked up and saw them heading towards his table. At first he assumed they had failed to get off before the ship sailed. The threesome spent as much time as they could boozing and gossiping. The Newmans had to present their films as part of the agreed arrangement, so one evening's entertainment was the screening of *The Three Faces of Eve* and *Cat on a Hot Tin Roof*.

They appeared on the television special *At This Very Moment* which was broadcast on ABC on April 1, 1962. It was written by Arnold Peyser and Lois Peyser and directed by Dick Schneider. The variety show was presented under the auspices of the American Cancer Society and its affiliate, the Eleanor Roosevelt Cancer Foundation, saluting 25 years of progress in cancer control and inaugurating Cancer Control Month.

The couple also attended the Academy Awards on April 9, 1962, at the Santa Monica Civic Auditorium. The ceremonies were broadcast on ABC with the television show directed by Richard Dunlap. Piper Laurie was nominated for the Best Actress Academy Award for her performance in *The Hustler* and had asked Woodward to accept for her, partly because she knew the actress was going to the ceremony anyway. Woodward and Anthony Franciosa presented the Best Sound Recording Award to Gordon E. Sawyer and Fred Hynes for *West Side Story* (1961). Laurie lost the Best Actress Award to Sophia Loren for the war drama *Two Women* (1960). Woodward wore a light-colored beaded dress with long white gloves and a fox jacket. Newman was nominated for Best Actor for *The Hustler* but lost to Maximilian Schell for *Judgment at Nuremburg* (1961). The Newmans went backstage to congratulate Schell, but Woodward reportedly refused to speak to him. She had thrown a fit when Schell's name was announced by Joan Crawford. Woodward was ashamed to admit she was wild, furious, upset and in tears. She made a terrible spectacle of herself, being sure her husband was going to win, and knew the loss made him bitterly hurt and disappointed. Crawford launched an attack on the actress, calling her behavior tacky and so typical. She predicted that Woodward would never work in Hollywood again, which proved untrue. One source claimed that the Newmans had a very big fight over her behavior, with him feeling she had embarrassed him. But the actor said his wife helped him through the loss of the award. After the ceremony, they drove home and she acted like the perfect therapist. The actress dragged Newman by hand to the garage where they had a little hideaway. Woodward told him they were going to take a little caviar and a little champagne out there and watch a very bad show on television. Newman said they never got around to the show.

The Chalk Garden was said to be the next production for Ross Hunter with Woodward and a screenplay by John Michael Hayes. However she was replaced in the film by Deborah Kerr when it was made by Hunter and director Ronald Neame for Universal Pictures.

The Newmans moved back to California since they were both working in Hollywood. *Celebration* was now before the cameras, with the title of *A Woman in July*, but it was finally known as *The Stripper* (1963). The black-and-white romance was shot at Fox from June to August. The screenplay was by Meade Roberts and the director was Franklin Schaffner. Lila Green (Woodward) is a failed Hollywood actress and showgirl for The Great Ronaldo and Madame Olga Magic & Mirth Par Excellence vaudeville show, which comes to a small town in Kansas. Her hair by George Masters appears peroxide-blonde and is worn in a straight short bubble style with bangs. Travilla gives Lila an all-white wardrobe, which includes a midriff-baring pants and top outfit, and a jaguar fur jacket. The role sees Woodward participate in a magic act where she is supposedly beheaded and she does a stripping sex act singing "Something's Gotta Give." Director Schaffner and Travilla protect her from being physically exposed in the stripping scene, as she wears a fishnet and tassel under-costume and balloons are strategically placed over her. The actress is sometimes mannered and over-gestures and at one point she even bites her hand, but her performance is mostly controlled. Woodward is touching in the scene where Lila gently rejects Kenny (Richard Beymer) but her best scene is probably when she remembers her first day of school and tells the story of the loss of roses.

Murray Schumach reported from the set for *The New York Times* on July 2. On this day, Woodward and Claire Trevor prepared to do a scene and Woodward made wigwagging gestures with her arms and hands as a way to stimulate herself for the camera. In her dressing room she knitted a woolen sweater for the older of her two children. The actress was curious about the quantity of flowers being sent to her virtually every hour on the hour by Newman, who was making the drama *Hud* (1963) at the Paramount studio several miles away. It was no special occasion; he just knew she liked them. The film was notable as being the only one being made at Fox at the time, since the studio was in a financial slump, with Woodward being the solo remaining Fox contract player working.

Producer Jerry Wald died on July 13 and the associate producer Curtis Harrington was credited as producer in the final film. The Newmans attended Wald's funeral, which was held on July 16 at the Church of the Recessional at Forest Lawn Memorial Park in Glendale. She commented that Wald was a good friend and, as his death occurred when *The Stripper* was in mid-production, the company was devastated.

The film was released on June 19, 1963, with the tagline "The story of a girl.... And the Men who led her to become 'The Stripper.'" The advertising campaign was provocative, featuring a likeness of Woodward in her stripper outfit. The film was lambasted by Bosley Crowther in *The New York Times* and Pauline Kael in *5001 Nights at the Movies*. Tony Thomas and Aubrey Solomon in *The Films of 20th Century Fox* wrote that Woodward worked hard at the role but her obvious intelligence was greater than that of the pathetic character. Kael wrote that everything that the actress did here was worth watching, that she didn't do anything conventional and gave the Marilyn Monroe–ish role a nervousness that cut through its pathos. The film was not a box office success but Travilla was nominated for the Best Costume Design Black and White Academy Award.

The role of Lila had been originally intended for Monroe. Kim Novak had been announced to replace her before Woodward was cast. Her hairstyle recalled that done for Monroe for the unfinished Fox comedy *Something's Got to Give*, as did the use of the title song. Monroe's death on August 3, 1962, also contributed to the idea of her ghost hovering over the part. There had been a specific reference to her that was cut, when Lila was seen walking down the street. Originally an observer asked who the woman was and commented that she looked like Monroe, and a second person said that it was her. The name was changed to Jayne Mansfield and Woodward said it just wasn't right. She also said that she had a visual image of Lila as Monroe but she wasn't imitating her. Lila was.

The actress described the film as a mess and was sorry that it was so badly botched. She felt it was one of the few times that Richard Beymer was well cast and very good and Claire Trevor was also good. Woodward loved the part, loving how childlike Lila was. Screenwriter Meade Roberts invented a wonderful prop for her: the teddy bear she held onto. There was a vulnerability and resilience in the character that the actress tried to capture in her walk, a combination of a jiggle and a voluptuous swagger. She

A portrait of Woodward in *The Stripper* (1963).

felt Travilla had a great sense of character and style and they had decided wardrobe was an homage to Monroe (who was still alive in pre-production when such choices were made) and Lana Turner in *The Postman Always Rings Twice*. Lila had a suntan which was not so readable in the black and white film, and she had fake breasts made because Woodward wanted them to bob up and down when she walked. They had a wonderful time rehearsing and the script was charming but the death of Jerry Wald saw Darryl Zanuck, now back as Fox studio head, take over. He saw a rough cut and threw Schaffner off the film. Zanuck said that the actress couldn't sing or dance so he cut almost of her dancing, which had been choreographed by Alex Romero, though Lila not being able to sing or dance was the point. He also cut a scene where she tried to slit her wrists. Richard Beymer commented that Woodward was swell and a very giving person.

Doing publicity for the film, the actress said she had wanted to be a kook or something and then she realized she didn't have the personality that hit people in the eye right away. It just wasn't important for her to have an image, since what kind of image did Alec Guinness or Laurence Olivier or Geraldine Page have? If you had an identifiable personality, you ended up playing the same role all the time. Shirley MacLaine commented that Woodward didn't have an image. In her quest for this image, Woodward became a different person at every interview.

The Newmans had been apart since the actor went on location in Texas for *Hud,* which was shot from May 21 to early August 1962. In the middle of the night one night, a drunken coed from the local junior college repeatedly tried to break into his motel room. When his wife heard about this, she threatened to fly down to Texas and slap some sense into the college girls if it was necessary.

5

Connecticut

The couple impulsively went house-hunting in Connecticut. Newman had fallen in love with the New England countryside after attending Yale Drama School and when they had shot on location for *Rally 'Round the Flag, Boys!* Connecticut also made sense because it wasn't far from New York, and it had a respected regional theater, the Westport Country Playhouse. They saw four or five houses before finding one in the wooded portion of the seaside town of Westport, with a middle school right across the street, on a busy-ish road ending on a bluff over the Aspetuck River. The former coach house was now a low-ceilinged farmhouse or barn which dated from either 1736 or 1780 (sources differ). Woodward was immediately taken by the tree house on the property and after taking a quick look inside, they paid $96,000 for house and property. The 11 acres contained an apple orchard and part of the river which had trout and was deep enough for boating. The couple shared a boat they named *Ca Ca de Toro*, which meant *bullshit*, with their neighbors A.E. Hotchner and his wife Ursula. The Newmans would also join the Hotchners and anyone else who were interested in a Yuletide tradition of going from home to home in their little section of Westport, singing Christmas carols.

They remodeled the house and filled it with bedrooms and a big open area to live in and eat. There was also a pool, cabana with sauna, a guesthouse that doubled as a den with pool table and screening room, and a tombstone commemorating all the family pets who had lived and died there. A source claims the guesthouse did not come with the purchase, and shortly after moving into the main property, the actor sent out a polite inquiry through a third party to see whether its owner might want to sell. Newman was concerned that another buyer might possibly cut down some of the adjoining woods and diminish the family's privacy. The owner was an elderly lady of proper breeding who was disdainful of the Newmans being in show business and declined the offer.

Woodward said it was the most beautiful house that was ever designed for a family with five children. They named it Nook House, which came from Newman's daughter Susie, since it had a lot of nooks and crannies. In the main house, the wooden beams and stone fireplace were complemented with antiques, including the famous brass bed, lots of framed photos of family and friends, books, flowers, comfortable furniture and a couple of bits of film and stage memorabilia. These included Woodward's Oscar, tastefully off to the side on a bookcase. They had some advice from decorators like stage designer Ralph Alswang, but she mostly relied upon her own eye and sense of gesture. There was an enormous dining table which had been a 17th century Irish wake table placed around the coffin to allow the grievers to sit and weep and eat. The tree house became an adults-only space for the couple. They repaired there with newspapers and beer and sherry, or on special nights, champagne and caviar. At first it was a summertime idyll but after she had it winterized as a present for Newman, it was available to them all year round.

The actress commented that she had long adjusted to her husband's status as a superstar and sex symbol. The only place Woodward was a sex symbol was at home, she said, and she was very lucky that Newman thought her sexy. She didn't worry about women coming on strong with him because she knew what he thought of them. A long-time friend described the Newmans as the most hand-holding couple ever to be seen and it was he who reached for his wife's hand more often than the other way around. Woodward said acting was a career for him. Being Newman's wife was her career, and she never did anything which would let him think Woodward wouldn't be there when he turned to her. The actor sent flowers one day in September for her birthday. Born in February, Woodward pointed out that his *first* wife was born in September, but forgave him for the mistake.

The couple now had three homes—in New York, Hollywood and Connecticut—and the household included their children, two dogs, two cats and a nurse. Rather than taking clothes back and forth across the country, she had three wardrobes, one in each house.

The actress found a script she liked, sent to her by Mel Shavelson. It was the dirtiest one she had every read, and had a role Woodward thought Newman was perfect for. The comedy entitled *Samantha* was scheduled to be produced and directed by Shavelson for Paramount. A bonus was that location shooting would be done in Paris, which would give the family another working vacation. But he didn't like the script—her part was cute but his was a bunch of one-liners. The actor didn't think it was fun. He didn't think it was *anything*. Newman said she could do it and he would watch and clap soundlessly from the wings. Woodward got angry, reminding him she had made her career subservient to his, followed him all over the world with their family, and raised not only their children but his children from another marriage. Newman changed his mind and agreed to do it. However he told Shavelson it was against his better judgment as the couple were not Rock Hudson and Doris Day.

Filming began in October in Paris, New York and Hollywood. The mistaken-identity plot dealt with a fashion designer in Paris who becomes involved with an unsuccessful reporter. The romantic comedy was released as *A New Kind of Love* (1963) with interiors shot at Paramount in Hollywood. Woodward played the parts of 25-year-old head buyer of ladies' dresses for J. Bergner Incorporated Fifth Avenue, Samantha "Sam" Blake, and the Parisian *fil de jour* Mimi. The actress is billed second after Newman (who plays journalist Steve Sherman), although she has more scenes than he. Her hair is by George Masters, styled in a brunette short straight cut with bangs, and she also wears a peroxide-blonde shoulder length wig with bangs. Sam's mannish haircut is a plot point since when Steve first sees her he assumes she is a man. Additionally, she keeps pencils in her hair. Ironically, the blonde wig is unflattering, making her look like a drag queen. Woodward's clothes are by Edith Head, with accessories of blue sunglasses for Sam and a long cigarette holder and beauty spot for Mimi. Head also has the actress in her underwear at various times, in a sheer exercise body suit, and in a golden midriff-baring outfit of shorts and long-sleeved top when Mimi plays soccer. Woodward imitates the Hungarian accent of Eva Gabor (who plays Felicienne Courbeau) to be Mimi, plays cards, gets drunk, climbs a ladder, has a beauty treatment, rides a bike, and has her dress torn off by Steve.

Shavelson includes an extreme and unflattering closeup of the actress' face and one eye during the beauty treatment scene. She is occasionally mannered and over-gestures though the latter has context for the character of Mimi. While Woodward has some funny moments, again she is less accomplished in comedy than Newman. Her best scene is the long final one where the actress expresses Sam's mix of fear and desire at Steve's seduction, shock and anger at her pretense as Mimi exposed, an apology for the deceit and admission of being in love with him.

The film premiered in the United Kingdom on October 10 and was released in the United States on October 30 with the tagline "The picture that takes a new attitude on love!" Bosley Crowther (*The New York Times*) wrote that Woodward looked fetching even in cap, raincoat and trousers but was entirely improbable and not particularly comic as a self-made expensive demimondaine. The film was lambasted by Michael Kerbel in *Paul Newman*. It was a box office failure but was nominated for the Best Color Costume Design and Best Score Academy Awards.

Woodward called the film a fast-moving comedy and reported that the company had plenty of laughs making it. She confessed she didn't know what Newman would do next in the sequence of comic situations, which was good for her as it was a new challenge. After a screening, the actress admitted the film was not good but didn't blame herself or her husband. He told Shavelson that the only reason she wanted to do the film was to be seen on the screen in expensive French lingerie, and after making *The Stripper*, Woodward thought she was Marilyn Monroe. It was reported that the actress had to warn off Eva Gabor who made a play for her husband. Gabor commented that Woodward's blonde wig looked hideous on her.

Woodward in *A New Kind of Love* (1963).

The Newmans spent Christmas of 1962 in Hollywood and instead of spending money on presents they sent money to CARE, the major international humanitarian agency delivering emergency relief and long-term international development projects. The couple stayed in Hollywood where Newman was set for a number of films.

They said they were dead-set against becoming a permanent screen team, but announced they would do a Broadway play together the following season. She had been approached by James Costigan to appear in his comic play *Baby Want to Kiss*. Woodward wanted to do it, thinking it would be fun, and as a favor for a friend. The actress also wanted to do it with Newman, who had reservations but gave in to her request. Under the auspices of the Actors Studio Theater, the show was to be a double bill written by

Costigan, with the curtain-raiser yet to be selected, and directed by Frank Corsaro. *Baby Want to Kiss* was the story of a pair of Hollywood stars who visit a reclusive writer friend (to be played by Costigan). The opening was planned for January 1963 with the engagement limited to four or five months.

On August 28, the Newmans were part of a Hollywood contingent that joined the civil rights march on Washington. She commented that you couldn't just sit around and be hysterical. You might not be able to change anything, but at least you could try.

Her next film was the MGM black and white crime thriller *Signpost to Murder* (1965), which began shooting in November. The screenplay was by Sally Benson based on the play by Monte Doyle and the director was George Englund. Alex Forrester (Stuart Whitman), a convicted murderer and escapee from the Milhampton Asylum for the Criminally Insane, takes refuge in the country house of American Molly Thomas (Woodward), who has dark secrets of her own. Woodward is billed first, although she has fewer scenes than Whitman and plays a supporting part. Her hair by Sydney Guilaroff is blonde, straight and short with a side part, and her costumes by William Travilla include a bathing suit. The role sees Woodward have a knife to her throat. Molly also has off-screen sex with Alex and an off-screen suicide, and director Englund has a shot of her in shadow with implied nudity as she removes her bathing suit. The actress makes Molly's anger funny. Her best scene is perhaps when Molly is visited by the vicar (Alan Napier) and Mrs. Broome (the uncredited Hallene Hill). Molly's extended sobbing is used by Englund to transition to the next scene after her guests have left.

The film premiered in West Germany on December 4, 1964, but wasn't released in the United States until May 19, 1965, with the taglines "Are We All Potential Killers?" and "Don't watch this picture if you are afraid of what it may reveal about yourself!" It was lambasted by Howard Thompson in *The New York Times*. The film was remade as the Indian *Ittefaq* a.k.a. *Coincidence* (1969) and *Ittefaq* (2017).

It was a reunion for Woodward and Stuart Whitman, who had appeared together in *The Sound and the Fury*. She said Englund was an awful director and the last scene was so bad that they decided to throw it out and improvise on camera. The actress liked how she looked in her mad opening scene in bathing suit, large hat and high heels. What she remembered most was that they were shooting the day John F. Kennedy died, November 22, 1963.

The Broadway production's double bill changed as Costigan decided to drop the curtain-raiser and expand *Baby Want to Kiss* into a full-length work. After 16 previews from April 6, it opened at the Little Theater and ran from April 19 to August 22, 1964. Woodward played the part of Mavis. The show was negatively reviewed by Howard Taubman in *The New York Times*, who wrote that Woodward wore her clothes by Peter Harvey elegantly; that in sinuous movement or seductive repose the actress was the very model of a dazzling film beauty, and that she had a few amusing moments. It was a financial success but was thought to have damaged the reputation of the Actors Studio, seen as selling a cheap bill of goods on the basis of attractive star names.

During the play's run, the Newmans commuted between New York and Connecticut in his Volkswagen. Their appearance in the show's previews kept them from attending the Academy Awards, which was held on April 13, 1964. Newman was nominated for Best Actor for *Hud* but lost to Sidney Poitier for the drama *Lilies of the Field* (1963).

The settlement of a June 7 strike by Actors Equity Association against the producers of 17 Broadway shows resulted in the couple receiving a raise after they had been playing for scale ($117.50 a week). Woodward said the run was more limited than imagined but it was an interesting play. She was amused that her husband played an aging juvenile and she a fading ingénue, characters that resembled their real-life personas. Rehearsals were difficult. Woodward said the script was full of non sequiturs and the ending was a problem. Frank Corsaro said it sank like the *Titanic*. He also had a problem with Costigan, who was unwilling to change things.

Critics were harsh with Newman, with Howard Taubman writing he was like an actor who had wandered into the wrong theater. Woodward defended her husband. For her, he was marvelous on stage and she preferred him in theater rather than in film. As an actor, Newman was larger than life and on screen that quality had to be contained.

Woodward rejected the part of Mabel Cantwell, wife of a presidential candidate, in the drama *The Best Man* (1964), directed by Franklin Schaffner; Edie Adams was cast. Woodward was asked to appear in the film version of a TV episode titled "Ride with Terror." It was to be shot in the fall and the actress was reportedly intrigued by the prospect. Nicholas Baehr's script involved a group of apathetic riders of the New York City subway confronted by a trio of menacingly hopped-up kids. She would not do the film, which was eventually released as *The Incident* in 1967.

In the fall, the actress (again pregnant) traveled with Newman and their daughters to London, Paris and Nice when he made the MGM comedy *Lady L* (1965). For the second time they rented a place in Montmartre. The couple was visited by Newman's children, Gore Vidal and Woodward's mother, who was sent for after the nanny suddenly took ill. Vidal reported that Woodward was suspicious of her husband's relationship with his co-star Sophia Loren. Newman denied any interest in her. Director-screenwriter-co-star Peter Ustinov said Woodward had nothing to fear. According to one source, Loren found him vulgar and uncouth. Ustinov said the Newmans were one of the very few couples who were privileged to be in love, and because they loved and quarreled occasionally, they could afford to be quite brash about each other. One night they and Loren went out to a restaurant. She threw a sable across her shoulders and swept through like a queen, but the Newmans entered like crabs, skulking behind the head-waiter. Loren was not the least un-comfortable about the attention she received from the other diners but the Newmans were.

Portrait of the Newmans for the Broadway play *Baby Want to Kiss*, which ran from April 19 to August 22, 1964.

Newman celebrated his 40th birthday on January 26, 1965, with a party thrown by Gore Vidal. She said that after her husband got to be 29 years old, he stayed 29 years old year after year while she got older and older.

Woodward was one of the sponsors for the evening of music and drama on behalf of the scholarship fund for the Hebrew Arts School for Music and Dance on April 4. On April 20, she gave birth to another daughter at the Mt. Sinai Hospital: Claire Olivia Newman, to be known as Clea. For the occasion, Newman gave his wife a diamond tiger pin from Cartier's. She said Clea was the only child who wasn't immediately turned over to a nanny while she (Woodward) went off to make a movie. She also reported that her husband took pride in being the father of six children and never having changed a diaper.

Reflecting on this time, Woodward said she probably had a movie-star dream which faded somewhere in her mid–30s, and it was painful. The actress had curtailed her career because of her children and resented it, which was not a good way to be around them. Newman was away on location a lot and now she wouldn't accompany him because of the children. Previously, if they were left behind, Woodward became overwhelmed with guilt.

After having Clea, she was intent on regaining her figure, which the actress said was plump around the middle and affected by breast-feeding. Her six-year-old daughter Nell took ballet classes and when her teacher told Woodward there were also adult classes, she signed up. The actress found ballet like a drug and got hooked. Her lessons increased from three to five times weekly and before long became daily. Woodward wished she had found a love of dance at the age of six or seven because one could not begin at 35. She had no elevation, but could do pique-turns around the floor. She said she was the saddest, most frustrated not-quite ballerina there had been in years.

They again rented a home in Hollywood as Newman made the Warner Bros. action crime drama *Harper* (1966), which was shot from June 7 to August 20. Woodward visited the set. Newman's co-star Pamela Tiffin commented that, while Woodward didn't have a great sense of humor, she was a woman of strong character. Tiffin described Woodward as sober and said her marriage appeared to be a working one, steady, not capricious or flighty.

Woodward made the Warner Bros. romantic comedy *A Fine Madness* (1966) which was shot on location in New York and at the Warner Bros. Hollywood studios from September 20 to December. The screenplay was by Elliott Baker, based on his novel, and the director was Irvin Kershner. Sean Connery starred as Samson Shillitoe, a New York office cleaner for Athena Carpet Cleaners and a poet, and second-billed Woodward played his wife Rhoda, a waitress at Rick's Restaurant and Delicatessen. Her hair by Jean Burt Reilly is blonde and worn in a short straight thick style with bangs, and costumes are by Ann Roth. The role sees Woodward get hit and punched by Connery, run in the street, and hit a woman at the Cultural Luncheon for the Women's League of the Seven Arts with her handbag. A fall down stairs was presumably done by a stuntwoman as her face is obscured in the shot. Woodward uses a New York accent which is inconsistent, with her yelling more abrasive than funny. Her best scene is perhaps when Rhoda beseeches Dr. Oliver West (Patrick O'Neal) to help Samson.

The film was released on June 29, 1966, with the taglines "We should all be so crazy" and "Any time ... any place ... at any game ... Samson Shillitoe can out-fox them all!!" *Variety* wrote that Kershner drew an effective performance from Woodward, "almost unrecognizable in face and voice via a good characterization of the loud-mouthed, but loving, wife, done in the Judy Holliday style." The film was not a box office success.

Woodward was reunited with Patrick O'Neal, with whom she had appeared in *From the Terrace*. He recalled that the actress organized the company into a movie fan club and every night there was a screening at the Beverly Hills Hotel which she attended with Newman. Members of the cast picked their favorite film to see, Woodward choosing the romantic comedy *Mr. and Mrs. Smith* (1941). O'Neal said that working with her was a pleasure. She was not laid-back but a hard worker, willing to take chances and create.

The actress was apart from Newman as he made the Universal thriller *Torn Curtain* (1966) which was shot October 18, 1965, to February 16, 1966, on locations in Denmark and Germany, New York and Universal Studios.

The *New York Times* of January 23, 1966, included Woodward in the collection of intelligent and promising actresses that Bosley Crowther wondered what had happened to, in the article "Where Are the Women?" The Newmans were apart again when he went on locations in Arizona and Nevada for the Fox western *Hombre* (1967), shot from February 28 to June 1966.

Woodward was a guest on the March 2 episode of the CBS-TV variety series *The Danny Kaye Show*, shot in Hollywood. She appeared in three sketches: "Run for Your Life" as the wife of Kaye who plays a man with 18 months to live while Robert Goulet plays his best friend who is madly in love with her; making fun of actresses on TV commercials; and one with Kaye and Goulet about life on a Southern plantation. At the 38th Annual Academy Awards, held on April 18 at the Santa Monica Civic Auditorium and broadcast by ABC, Woodward and George Peppard presented the Best Screenplay Awards to David Lean (accepting for Robert Bolt for the MGM war romance *Doctor Zhivago*) and Connie Stevens (accepting for Frederic Raphael for the British romance *Darling*). Before presenting the awards, Woodward quipped to Peppard that she had never changed any writer's words. When he said they were pleased to present the award, the actress asked whether "privileged" would be better, but agreed with Peppard's suggestion of "honored." She wore a floor-length sleeveless green and white patterned gown by Travilla with her blonde hair in a sculptured bun and with bangs. Remembering Joan Crawford's remark about her homemade gown at a previous Oscar ceremony, the actress said she hoped this gown made Crawford happy.

The Warner Bros. Western *A Big Hand for the Little Lady* (1966) was shot on location in Arizona and at the Warners studios. The story had originated as an October 7, 1962, episode of NBC-TV's *The DuPont Show of the Week*, "Big Deal in Laredo." The teleplay was by Sidney Carroll and the director was Fielder Cook, who both also did the film version. A crew of card sharks get revenge on the rich townsmen of Laredo who play an annual poker game in the Paloma Hotel dining room. Woodward played Ruby, who pretends to be Mary, the wife of Meredith (Henry Fonda), a San Antonio farmer who joins the game. Ruby had been played by Teresa Wright in the TV version. The actress is billed second after Fonda but she has more scenes than he. Her hair by Jean Burt Reilly is blonde and tied up in a sculpted bun with a side part off her forehead. She uses a Southern accent for the part, which sees her play cards and drive a team of horses and wagon. Woodward gives a funny reading to the line "He wants me to play the hand?!" The actress' best scene is perhaps when Mary tells the players she is going to the bank to get the money needed to continue the game on Meredith's behalf and refuses to let her cards out of her sight. This moment has an added dimension since we learn that Mary is Ruby and only pretending to be an innocent Texas farmwife.

The film premiered in Houston, Texas, on May 31, 1966, and then opened in New York on June 8 with the taglines "Rule of the game: you must sit in from the beginning! And it's the wildest poker game in the west!" and "Don't tip the little lady's hand or your friends will hate you!" The film was praised by Robert Alden in *The New York Times*. It was not a box office success.

Woodward observed that Fonda liked to do needlepoint between takes, and she was a needlepoint addict since childhood. The actress reportedly suggested that Newman also take it up as a hobby, but he laughed.

The Newman family spent two months on vacation in the summer in Connecticut with the children from his first marriage. They drifted lazily on their own private stretch of the Aspetuck River in inflatable yellow boats, swam and picnicked on the grassy banks. The couple spent time alone in their barn and drove to New York for an evening of theater and dinner out, capped off by a romantic night spent in the privacy of their Manhattan *pied-à-terre*.

Woodward was under consideration for a part in a Broadway revival of *A Streetcar Named Desire*. It was to be pro-

Portrait of Woodward for *A Big Hand for the Little Lady* (1966).

duced by ABC and Talent Associates for a limited run in the spring and then be taped for TV broadcasting. It appears that neither this stage revival nor the TV version was made.

A November 6 *Times* article revealed that before the Newmans were married, they often sat in the back row at the Radio City Music Hall, chomping on popcorn he had made. They always waited for the audience's big laugh before opening the cans of beer Woodward smuggled into the theater in her oversized purse.

Newman commented on his marriage, saying it was not harmonious all the time. He was all in favor of a good screaming free-for-all every two or three months which cleared the air, got rid of old grievances, and generally made for a pleasant relationship. His wife had a habit of rationalizing, and that's when the actor turned ugly. But when Woodward told him what she instinctively felt, he played very close attention. The actress had concerns over the children, not wanting them to be photographed by the press so that their sense of importance was for and within themselves, and not because their parents were movie stars. However she also had conflicting feelings about motherhood and work, believing her career had suffered because of her children and her children had suffered because of her career. It was an unfair, frustrating predicament which had a heavy inner toll in the form of dissatisfaction and unhappiness. She wasn't alone in this predicament, for many of her friends who were working mothers had also been unable to resolve the dilemma. Her husband knew Woodward had missed out on things, Broadway plays for instance, but if she had to be at the theater every night and he was on the Coast, there would have been no marriage at all. Sometimes the actor came home and found her wandering around the house muttering, "What am I doing cooking for seven people?"

Woodward, very unhappy, felt that her career had ended. She was not a movie star anyway. The actress had never been the same person twice on screen and Hollywood never really knew what to do with her. When you were in that boat, you either became a successful established character actress or you did anything you could get. She was determined to do nothing rather than just work for the sake of having a job, and even more determined to never do anything again unless she felt strongly about it. When Woodward started, she just wanted to act. There had been some good things, like *The Three Faces of Eve*, but also some things the actress didn't care about that had taken two or three months out of a life she enjoyed. Now the older Woodward got, the more she realized life was like cotton candy. Take one bite and it's gone. She hated wasting time and refused to fiddle away her life in dribs and drabs. Something she would say to her children was, "Tell me anything, get mad, yell at me, but never say you're bored." She said her husband got all the wonderful parts and she always seemed to be the afterthought. The actress finally decided that she had to find a script herself because good things were seldom offered to her. Preferably a little film that meant something to her as she had felt uneasy in big productions.

A possibility emerged: Her old friend and agent John Forman had recommended the book *Jest of God* by Canadian writer Margaret Laurence. Foreman was also business partners with the Newmans in the newly formed Kayos Productions. Woodward liked the book's theme that things never stopped and tomorrow was another day and took an option for a film version, asking her friend Stewart Stern to write the screenplay.

Woodward and Stern went around offering themselves to everybody, aware that what was being offered was hardly like offering Elizabeth Taylor and Tennessee Williams. They couldn't get anyone interested until Newman agreed to direct. He hadn't been as impressed with the book as she, and though the actor saw that his wife was a good choice for the leading role, he didn't think it was movie material. But he trusted her impeccable taste.

The Newmans and Stern went to Palm Springs to work on the script. The writer left at one point, saying he could not deal with arguing over whether the title character would masturbate lying on her stomach or her back. The following day, Newman showed up at Stern's home dressed head to foot in a Nazi SS uniform. He banged on the door and marched in to tell the writer who was the boss. The actor did this crazy stunt to keep his friendship and collaboration with Stern alive, but from then on, Woodward was not included in the script discussions. She made some suggestions after Stern and Newman did a rough draft, which led the writer to a second and third until finally everyone was satisfied.

Daily Variety confirmed Newman's involvement as director on February 27, 1967. But he still had trouble finding a studio that would back the new project. Even though they considered Newman a star, they thought it was too big a gamble to let him direct. And they didn't consider Woodward a financeable name after the failures of *A Fine Mad-*

ness and *A Big Hand for the Little Lady.* Paramount wanted Shirley MacLaine. Columbia said that it had been so long since Woodward had a hit that she had become a footnote in Hollywood history. And as for the films the actress had made with Newman, an executive said, "I'd rather suck rotten possum eggs than sit through one of them." MGM had said the material was too downbeat and not commercial. Universal said it sounded like a dud and had as much appeal as Jerry Lewis starring in *Hamlet.*

Warner Bros. made an offer to back the film if the couple would sign for more films at less than their regular salaries (he for two films and she for one). One source claims they would not accept the deal but according to a November 8, 1967, *Daily Variety* article, the film was set to be one of four pictures Newman was contracted to direct or star in for Warner Bros.-Seven Arts, two of which (including this one) would star Woodward. The actor had inserted a clause into the contract that if the studio's creative management team changed, this would nullify the agreement, which is what happened. Warner Bros.-Seven Arts agreed to finance the film and the Newman-Foreman production company was the credited producer. The Newmans accepted deferred salaries in exchange for heavy profit participation, with one source claiming they were promised a third of the profits.

To save money, it would be shot in Connecticut, where the story was set. An old gymnasium in Danbury was converted into a workable studio and sound stage. Location footage could be easily taken in the town and local people were used as extras and to play small parts. Nell played Rachel as a young girl and two-year-old Clea Newman was the baby with Rachel on the beach at the end of the film. Woodward quipped that it was cheaper to use your own children.

If the film had been totally unsuccessful, Woodward would have been heartbroken—not for her own sake but because they filmed every bit of their insides, and it would hurt if people didn't like it. Newman said one of the reasons he did the film with his wife was because she had really given up her career for him and to make their marriage work. Stewart Stern added that the director had a real sense of adoration for what Woodward could do and was constantly trying to provide a setting where the world could see what he saw in her. She said that making this film was not at all like working in Hollywood where the grips played poker and had no idea what it was about. Everyone from the little boy who helped the grips was involved, and the Newmans were off in their little corner creating. About halfway through, they began to feel like the Moscow Art Theatre.

The romance had had the working titles of *A Jest of God* and *Now I Lay Me Down* but was finally known as *Rachel, Rachel.* It was shot in the summer from August to October 16, 1967. One source gives the start date as August 25 but a slate seen in a making-of featurette reads August 8. Woodward played the leading role, Rachel Cameron, a 35-year-old schoolteacher who lives with her mother May (Kate Harrington) as her housekeeper above the Japonica Funeral Chapel. Costumes are by Domingo Rodriguez, with hair by the uncredited Colleen Callaghan; Woodward wears it in a dirty-blonde shoulder-length straight style with bangs. The role has her collect wildflowers, get a kiss on the mouth from another woman, ride a tractor, and operate a sewing machine. She is also seen semi-naked in bed with Nick (James Olson) and in her slip. The role allows us to view the actress in a more transparent way than ever before and this is no doubt due to Newman being the director. She makes Rachel funny and touching. Woodward's best scene is perhaps when Rachel is in bed with Nick, telling him it is a new experience for her to have contact with anyone and declaring her love for him.

The film was released on August 26, 1968, with the taglines "Who cares about a 35 year old virgin?" and "If you passed her on the street you wouldn't notice her. On the screen she is unforgettable." In *The Warner Bros. Story*, Clive Hirschhorn wrote that Woodward gave a stunning performance. *The New York Times*' Renata Adler said Woodward was extraordinarily good. In *Paul Newman*, Michael Kerbel said it was her finest performance. But *Variety* said that were the actress not there, it could have been a shambles. A box office success, the film received Academy Awards nominations for Best Picture, Best Actress for Woodward, Best Supporting Actress for Estelle Parsons and Best Writing Screenplay Based on Material from Another Medium for Stewart Stern. Newman and Stewart Stern contemplated writing a sequel, to be filmed in Central Africa, but this never eventuated.

Woodward said Rachel was a character to die for, and more than anything, it was the right part for her to play at the right time. Rachel was at the exact middle of her life at the age of 35 (Woodward was 37). The filming itself was absolute heaven and everybody in it was so good. The lovemaking scene, which was discussed a lot when the film came out, was completely from Rachel's point of view. It made you understand her better and was also the turning point in the character's life. There was nothing in the film that wasn't absolutely necessary. Almost everything they shot was in the final cut. The Newmans and Stern had worked together so long on it, it was truly a magic time, and Woodward didn't think she ever had a better experience.

They hated having to release the film because it was like breaking the umbilical cord. The Newmans had actually toyed with the idea of making a 16mm print to show only at home. The fact that strangers identified with it and liked the film was a great surprise to the Newmans and Stern. Woodward observed that young people seemed to like the film enormously, which she found very strange as she wouldn't have thought they would have understood Rachel's problem yet—though in the larger sense, the problem that people should not stagnate could exist at any age. Woodward also said that what had been her "brainchild" had revived her career, since some people had thought she had gone underground.

The actress was asked if *she* now wanted to direct and said she didn't have the attributes of a director. Actors *didn't* make good directors, since they had such a strong sense of personal identity and ego that it was difficult to have the patience and kindness to allow others to do things *their* way. Woodward was impressed that Newman was able to take everything from his acting experience and use it as a director, but the difference between them was that she loved to act and he loved to rehearse. Her husband turned out to be marvelous and the best director she had ever worked with—but who could direct better than the person you lived with? He knew all there was to know about her. Woodward acknowledged that she had worked with some great directors, but just wished Newman could direct every film she would ever do again. The actress said he never lost his temper, which must have been difficult working with her and Nell. She had said all along that her daughter should have played Rachel as a child, because except for the eyes, Nell looked like her mother. To watch her husband work with their daughter was beautiful.

Newman said his wife was brilliant in the film, inhabiting the part completely, and he couldn't think of another actress that the experience could have been better with. When friends asked him about the love scenes with another man, he had a pat answer: I put her there! Woodward almost always deferred to his perception, and in the rare instance when they disagreed, Newman had her show him what she wanted to do and then let the actress do it her way. They had the same acting vocabulary and that made it easier. In directing Woodward, he used the active verb, and she sucked that sensation into her body, adding a certain physical quality. The couple had had several big squabbles during filming but it had nothing to do with work. On the set, they had never had one harsh word in that period because they trusted each other.

Reporter Gene Wilson described the couple working together as almost totally physical, their communications sometimes suggesting two deaf-mutes. Newman put the palms of his hands on her cheeks, bent forward and peered into the eyes, snarled, and then moved his hands to the back of the neck and pushed the head slowly from side to side. In reaction, she nodded in strong agreement. When Newman sat down on a box to rest before the next take, without speaking the actress began to massage his neck and shoulders, occasionally bending the head forward sharply, and then jerking it back again by the hair. Stewart Stern commented that she had the capacity to be invisible to everything but the camera and her husband's eye.

For Christmas, Newman gave his wife a complete print of the Rudolf Nureyev-Margot Fonteyn British musical romance *Romeo and Juliet* (1966). Their Connecticut master bathroom in the Newman bedroom also had a tribute to Nureyev: a huge poster pasted on the outside door. Woodward's mother asked her how she could do that, and the actress laughed, saying it was the best of both worlds. Newman would comment on his wife's love of ballet, saying there must have been something kinky about it. The actress was never going to be another Fonteyn but she still got her kicks from it.

The Newmans on location for *Rachel, Rachel* (1968).

Woodward appeared in the March 8, 1968, episode of NBC-TV's *The Bell Telephone Hour*, "Man Who Dances: Edward Villella," which was shot in New York. The show was directed by Mike Jackson. On March 10, the Newmans attended a party at the Unicorn Theatre for the opening of the French-Italian comic adventure *Weekend*.

In late March or early April, Woodward co-hosted a "Cook-in for McCarthy," an event to support the presidential campaign of Senator Eugene J. McCarthy, held at the Manhattan discotheque Arthur. She had done a television commercial for McCarthy. The actress commented that she had not seen her husband since he started campaigning for the Senator. Her appeal to vote for McCarthy came with the line, "Help bring my husband home." Woodward felt she was not a good public speaker so she just opened discotheques and hosted dinners. But Newman was not the best public speaker either, citing a speech he made for McCarthy where she nearly died because the actor talked and talked and didn't know how to get himself off the stage. The couple were also sponsors of Eugene's, the political cabaret run by McCarthy backers, which opened on April 7 with tributes to the slain civil rights leader, the Reverend Dr. Martin Luther King, Jr.

The 40th Annual Academy Awards were held on April 10, 1968, and Newman, nominated for the Best Actor award for *Cool Hand Luke*, lost to Rod Steiger for *In the Heat of the Night* (1967). Woodward said that her husband didn't mind losing to Steiger because he was a fellow Actors Studio graduate and it was like losing to a real pro. At the 22nd Annual Tony Awards, April 21 at New York's Shubert Theatre, the Newmans presented awards. The actress wore a silver floor-length short-sleeved dress. Her dirty blonde hair was shoulder-length with a part in the middle.

6

Winning and Race Car Driving

Woodward's next film was the Universal sports actioner *Winning* (1969), shot on location at the Indianapolis Speedway in Indiana, the Riverside International Raceway in California, and in Wisconsin and Indiana. Scripted by Howard Rodman and directed by James Goldstone, it starred Newman as Frank Capua, a rising star on the race circuit who dreams of winning the big one: the Indianapolis 500. Woodward played Elora, divorced mother of the teenager Charley (Richard Thomas) who works at Avis Rent-a-Car in the small town of Redburne where Frank races. Woodward's costumes by Edith Head are period-garish and include the repeated use of a colored nightgown. Hair by Larry Germain is dirty-blonde worn straight and shoulder-length with bangs and off her forehead. Elora also wears a blonde short sculpted wig in one scene. Her best scene is perhaps when Frank discovers Elora in bed with Lou Erding (Robert Wagner), where she has silent reactions of shock, shame and fear, and cries.

The film was released on May 22, 1969 with the tagline "WINNING is for men who live dangerously! WINNING is for women who love recklessly! WINNING is for young people who live for now! WINNING … is for everybody!" In *The New York Times*, Howard Thompson wrote that Woodward was splendid in a complex characterization she shaded with wise reserve. The film received a mixed reaction from Michael Kerber in *Paul Newman* but was panned by Roger Ebert, who wrote that Woodward's talent shouldn't have been wasted on it. It was a box office success.

The project was a reunion with Robert Wagner, with whom she had appeared in *A Kiss Before Dying*. Although their love scene is not explicit, Newman supposedly gave Wagner points on how to make love to a wife. Not wanting the film to become X-rated, he didn't say how to hit all of her hot spots. During filming, the Newmans arranged a screening of *Rachel, Rachel* for the company.

Woodward objected to her husband's refusal to use a double in race sequences, although he went through training to prepare, and opposed his getting involved in the dangerous sport. But racing became Newman's new passion. She blamed this on making the film and said his life was at risk ever after. The actress admitted to getting chills every time she saw him speed by her at 150 miles an hour. Woodward knew he was a natural athlete but she worried about the unpredictable—wheels falling off, things breaking down, spinouts. Wanting to share his enthusiasm for racing, the actress agreed to take a run around the track with him at the wheel. They didn't get out of second gear and she was holding onto Newman so hard that she left fingerprints. She did drive one lap around the Indianapolis but at 40 miles an hour, perhaps a record for slow speed, and her husband admired her for trying. The actress thought competitive driving was the silliest thing in the world and it was also very scary to her. Newman said he could be killed driving on any American highway, even crossing the street. She quipped it wasn't always easy living with Sam Superstar, having to dwell in his shadow. He gave off such a glow that Woodward would be blinded if she didn't have a good old shade tree somewhere.

The atmosphere of the racetrack was uncomfortable for her and Woodward would skip her husband's racing practices as often as possible. Trackside in Indy, she didn't know what was worse: the prospect of Newman killing himself in a crack-up or the clutches of screaming women holding up signs pleading "Paul, Please Slow Down" and clucking over him as he walked around the track. Woodward grumbled to a reporter, wishing she wasn't married to him, and that a mind was a terrible thing to waste on a Trans Am motor. The couple made an agreement where Newman would continue to race and also accompany her to the ballet and dance recitals. This was a concession on his behalf, as while he enjoyed all aspects of the theater, seeing *Giselle* for the 19th time was less palatable. The actress even suggested her husband should try ballet since it was the most athletic sport of all, but he declined.

Newman, interviewed in the July 1968 *Playboy*, spoke about his marriage. It was not always fine and dandy, since it involved two people with very different approaches and attitudes to things. They had gotten through periods when they considered themselves bad parents and periods where they saw each other as only reflections of themselves. But there was affection and respect and a good deal of humor. Another ingredient to their success was the avoidance of the social whirl enjoyed by most celebrities, with the party they threw for Gore Vidal on his return from Europe being the first and only one thrown by them in ten years. They didn't have time to be social while raising three children continuously and six part of the time, maintaining a couple of houses and continuing their careers. It was not a glamorous Hollywood marriage. For privacy, the couple slipped away to their New York apartment now and again, and their house in Beverly Hills with a billiard room and a swimming pool where they spent a great deal of time unwinding. Woodward still thought he was sexy, and vice versa. The actor also reported that she was rather a good cook and made the best hollandaise sauce he had even eaten.

The actress was interviewed by Rex Reed for the September 1 *New York Times* article "The Doug and Mary of the Jet Age." She was then working on *Winning* and, while Reed spoke to her, two Universal makeup artists were waiting to Max Factor her. Woodward joked they would be calling the film "Cool Hand Luke Finds Rachel in the Sack with the Saint!" She planned to take the Super Chief train back to Connecticut the following week, after which Newman was to start a new western in Mexico. This was the Fox biographical crime drama *Butch Cassidy and the Sundance Kid* (1969) which was shot on location in Mexico, Arizona, Colorado, New Mexico and Utah from September 16, 1968, to March 13, 1969. She had been instrumental in the casting of Robert Redford in the part of Sundance in the film, after Steve McQueen and Warren Beatty declined it, as Woodward knew Redford's work and thought he was the best. During the shooting, Newman had her sew and frame a sampler with the caution, "Punctuality is the courtesy of kings," which he presented to Redford, who was always late for work and dinner.

For the interview, she sat on a sofa in the library eating chocolate chip cookies and drinking iced coffee, and later was in the kitchen, with the baby in one arm and two dogs yapping at her feet. The actress had glorious white skin, twinkling naughty eyes, and her hair was long and golden and soaking wet as she had just come from ballet class. Ballet was her favorite thing in the world. Reed wrote that the actress' delicate Southern accent was more magnolia blossom than hominy grits. Woodward didn't really do interviews, and was content to take a back seat to fame and glamor, preferring to emerge in the roles she played. For Reed, she was the star without an image, the girl with many faces, none of which ever got recognized by the dime-store clerks who rioted when Newman walked in. Woodward didn't attract the oddballs who wanted her husband to take off his sunglasses so they could see the famous blue eyes. She felt it must be sad to be like Elizabeth Taylor who hadn't been to a supermarket in ten years out of fear of being descended upon by hordes of fans. Woodward did all her own shopping and had nothing to worry about whenever she went out in public alone. She wasn't grabbed at and mauled the way she had seen Marilyn Monroe at an Actors Studio premiere for *East of Eden*. The Newmans had a hand-painted sign on the lawn of their Beverly Hills house that read "PLEASE—THEY HAVE MOVED!—THE PIERSONS." This was to discourage the myriad of tourists who visited and trampled on the sculpted lawns.

Woodward dodged the Hollywood scene and spent all of her free time in her Connecticut home. She hated Hollywood's superficiality and her frankness on the subject made her unpopular and the town's joke. Maybe the actress was perverse since life was pleasant but it would never be home. Even the house where they lived at present wasn't hers since it was rented out all the time, and it had just been sold. The family, which included a sparrow named Baron, was to move into a place with a prize-winning cactus and three big palm trees in the yard that she was having cut down and replaced with magnolia trees and rose bushes. The children went to a very proper school where Debbie Reynolds was head of the Girl Scouts but Woodward couldn't wait to get them out of there. She didn't like the way Beverly Hills looked, loathing manicured lawns and palm trees. People expected the Newmans to have big houses and servants, but the actress hated houses with no personality. They had a driver who took the children to school but she had to keep thinking of things for him to do, like taking Lissy down to the store to buy her some pencils. Woodward said her life was all about her children who were all marvelous and beautiful and slightly insane. Newman got most of the fan mail and she was still waiting for one that began with "Gee baby, you were great." The only fan mail the actress received was from 12-year-old boys who loved her because she reminded them of their mothers.

The Newmans were among the group of 20 Americans prominent in the film industry who expressed concern for Czechoslovak filmmakers in a letter delivered to Anatoly F. Dobrynin, the Soviet Ambassador to the United States. Woodward made the first of three 1968 appearances on the ABC-TV talk show *The Joey Bishop Show*, shot at the Vince Street Theatre in Hollywood. She was a guest on the October 19 episode of the BBC music TV series *Dee Time*.

The actress appeared as part of a celebrity panel on the November 5 ABC television telethon to support presidential hopeful Vice-President Hubert Humphrey. She was the subject of the November 14 episode of the British documentary film television series *Cinema*, which was directed by Eric Prytherch and broadcast on Granada Television.

The Newmans were awarded the William J. German Human Relations Award of the American Jewish Committee in recognition of their good works. They appeared as themselves in the black and white biographical documentary *Ely Landau's King: A Filmed Record...Montgomery to Memphis* (1970) which followed Martin Luther King's life and decades-long civil rights activism. The project was conceived by Landau, with speech research by Mitchell Grayson, and the uncredited directors were Sidney Lumet and Joseph L. Mankiewicz. The film was shot in 1968 to 1969 on locations in Alabama and Tennessee.

It was released on March 24, 1970, with the tagline "A motion picture tribute to Martin Luther King in 1,000 theaters across America. One night only. All proceeds go to the Martin Luther King, Jr. Special Fund for the war against poverty, illiteracy and social injustice." Woodward appeared for one minute in one of the black and white cameos by celebrities inserted between the newsreel footage. She wears a light-colored suit with a flower-patterned scarf, and her hair is in a straight collar-length style with a side part. Woodward clasps her hands as she recites a poem about four little girls who were killed when a Birmingham, Alabama, church was bombed. Footage shows that King spoke at the funeral service for the victims of the bombing. The film was nominated for the Best Documentary Feature Academy Award.

The couple attended the reception held on January 26, 1969, at the Rainbow Grill in New York to receive the plaques for Best Director and Best Actress for *Rachel, Rachel* by the New York Film Critics Society. She commented on the upcoming Academy Award nominations, hoping that Newman got the Best Director Oscar. She felt he had been nominated so often as an actor that it would be a crack-up for him to win as a director.

On February 6, they attended ceremonies in a Senate hearing room that preceded the introduction of a bill in Congress to create a federal department of peace. When the Oscar nominations were announced on February 24 and Newman was snubbed, Woodward said she or Estelle Parsons couldn't have been nominated without his being the director. It negated the whole purpose of the Academy, and the actress was going to boycott the ceremony. Newman felt she was being too emotional and Woodward changed her mind. At that year's Golden Globe Awards ceremony, he won the Best Director and she won the Best Actress in a Drama awards for *Rachel, Rachel.*

Her next film was the Paramount romance *WUSA* (1970), which was shot from April 3 to late June or July 1969 on location in New Orleans and at the Paramount in Hollywood Studios under the working title *Hall of Mirrors*. The screenplay was by Robert Stone based on his novel *A Hall of Mirrors* and the director was Stuart Rosenberg. In the movie, a New Orleans radio station becomes the focal point of a right-wing conspiracy. Woodward played Geraldine, a former prostitute from West Virginia. A widow, she starts a relationship with Rheinhardt (Paul Newman) who gets a job at the station as a disc jockey. Her hair by Sydney Guilaroff is dirty blonde worn in a straight style off her forehead, and her wardrobe is by Travilla. Woodward also wears a scar on her right forehead courtesy of makeup by Lynn Reynolds and Jack Wilson. The role has her use a Southern accent, chew gum, jump in the lake and swim in her underwear (perhaps a body double was used) and commit suicide. She adds to her mannerisms by playing with her hair, though it has context since Geraldine sometimes does so to hide her facial scar. Woodward's best scene is when Geraldine is imprisoned and the actress has a silent reaction of fear, stopping herself from screaming in hysteria, and observing how she can kill herself.

The film was released on August 19, 1970, with the taglines "Newman/Woodward 1970," "Love it or leave it" and "A picture for our times." It received a mixed reaction from *Variety* and negative reviews from Roger Greenspun in *The New York Times* and Pauline Kael in *The New Yorker*. The film was not a box office success.

The August 7, 1968, *Variety* had reported that Newman and John Foreman were to produce the film. *Variety* on August 8 said the film would be a Universal production. It moved to Paramount early in 1969. The actress said the film was a fair statement about the country at that time, though later felt it didn't come off and disliked it. She only appeared in it because her husband was involved and because of the New Orleans locations. Woodward discounted the talk that they were the current screen duo and claimed the only reason the couple continued to work together was that it was convenient for their family life if they were on the same schedule. But she regarded Newman's performance as one of the best he ever gave. Newman said that her performance was very sexy and vulnerable, thinking she was spectacular.

Stuart Rosenberg found her so controlled that he virtually never needed to repeat a direction, although sometimes it was necessary to prod Woodward to try a different approach. He found both Newmans to be virtuosos and observed the different approaches they took to reach the same brilliant performance level.

Warren Cowan outlined the publicity strategy he managed for *Rachel, Rachel* in the April 13 *The New York Times*. It included having Woodward on TV talk shows. Cowan also took Woodward to London for a week of appearances. This included a speech at the Royal Academy of Dramatic Arts, where one source claims she received an award for the film. The couple was on the October 18, 1968, cover of *Life* magazine. The photo, shot by Mark Kauffman, was a closeup of them lying on a carpet in their rented Malibu beach house. The cover line was "Director and Star: The Newmans Triumph with *Rachel, Rachel.*" Cowan reported that it was not in their nature to pose all day for the shot but the film was very special to them.

They both attended the 41st Annual Academy Awards ceremony, held at the Dorothy Chandler Pavilion on April 14, 1969. In the Best Actress contest, Woodward lost to the tie of Katharine Hepburn for the historical biography *The Lion in Winter* (1968) and Barbra Streisand for the biographical comedy *Funny Girl* (1968). Woodward wore a white and red patterned high-collared dress and had her hair up, sculpted and off her forehead. The actress said she would never forgive the Academy for not giving Stewart Stern the Oscar for his *Rachel, Rachel* screenplay, instead rewarding James Goldman for *The Lion in Winter*. The couple skipped the post-awards ball and attended a private party given by friends, not feeling they were snubbing the Academy because the Newmans had never been avid partygoers. At the party were Warren Cowan and his wife, actress Barbara Rush, who noted how Newman stayed very close to Woodward, seeming to rely on her. People often commented how lucky the actor was to be married to her.

The New York Times of July 20 reported that the Newmans were visitors to the Washington office of Senator Eugene McCarthy. In the autumn, Newman commented to Robert Peer in *Photoplay Film Monthly* that he and Woodward had things pretty well worked out between them. Married eleven years, they been away from each other no more than ten or twelve weeks, and were frank with each other about everything which was important. But at this time there were rumors of trouble in the marriage and the couple briefly separated. He was said to have had an affair with journalist Nancy Bacon, who had visited the set of *Butch Cassidy and the Sundance Kid* to write about the film. Gossip columnist Joyce Haber announced that she had heard fascinating rumors, so far unchecked, that the Newmans would soon get a divorce. They responded by placing a signed half-page ad in the *Los Angeles Times* that stated three things: They recognized the power of the press, feared to embarrass a journalist, and, terrified to disappoint Miss Haber and her readers, would try to accommodate her unchecked rumors by busting up their marriage even though still liking each other. Later in the year, a gossip magazine published Bacon's tell-all about the affair, supported by a photograph of her with the actor looking chummy on the set. Bacon also devoted a chapter to Newman in her 1975 autobiography

Stars in My Eyes…Stars in My Bed. She wrote that Newman had left Woodward at a party and missed a plane he was to catch with her to be in Bacon's bed. Bacon had also encountered the actress at the Factory once, when she and Newman walked in with his children. When he went back to his wife in Connecticut, the actor reportedly told her, "I'm home. But I must warn you, the fires of autumn burn on a very low flame," a line taken from a Gore Vidal play.

The Newmans didn't take out any ads to counter Bacon's assertions. They went on vacation to London after wrapping *WUSA*. He commented that for two people who had almost nothing in common, they had an uncommonly good marriage. She admitted that he was right, but they were interested in *what* the other did. Newman explained their different personalities, saying Woodward was like nitroglycerine and he was diesel fuel. He was a morning person, and she was not. He also compared her to a light bulb and cannon, bright and explosive. But while she lost her temper easily and quickly forgave and forgot, Newman rarely became angry but tended to hold grudges.

Working with Warren Cowan, the couple decided to talk about their marriage with selected press. They targeted women's magazines and used female reporters from major news outlets, like *Good Housekeeping*, *Redbook*, *McCall's*, *Ladies Home Journal*, *Cosmopolitan*, *Playgirl* and *The New York Times Magazine*. Newman told the *Times'* Maureen Dowd that he and Woodward had had difficult confrontations but they hadn't surrendered. The actor had packed up and left a few times, and then realized he had no place to go, and was back in ten minutes. In *Good Housekeeping* Woodward said that Newman spent more time with his kids than most fathers who were home all the time. He was extremely home-oriented, which didn't really go along with his sex symbol image. The actor was not a great disciplinarian and most of the time the actress did the scolding, like throwing a pitcher of water over Lissy who was having a tantrum. Woodward also explained the couple's differences. He liked fast cars and swimming and fishing and playing pool. She loved ballet, the theater, opera and museums. The actor had boundless energy and the actress had low blood pressure and often pooped out. He was a conservative dresser and she liked him to wear shirts with ruffles that he hated but wore just to please her. She drank nothing but a little sherry and he drank nearly everything. Often the actress would hear herself say to Newman, in a voice which was a cross between a howl of fury and the whisper of a saint, that he was getting stoned and she could see it in his eyes. She felt nothing was worse than somebody doing that. Their battles mostly came from the fact that Woodward was grumpy in the morning and Newman was so damnably cheerful. Always after a fight he bought her a present, and very often he gave her something just for nothing. As a result, she had the wildest collection of nutty underclothes.

The actor demonstrated his commitment to his wife by making sure that almost everything he would produce or direct in the future would include her. Newman also encouraged her love of the ballet, giving the actress gifts of ballet-inspired artwork and helping her fund a dance company of her own.

She was named female "Star of the Year" as the leading box office attraction in the annual poll of the National Association of Theatre Owners, cited for *Rachel, Rachel* and *Winning*. Her award was to be presented at the annual association convention in November in Washington. On September 23, the Newmans attended the Los Angeles premiere of *Butch Cassidy and the Sundance Kid*.

On October 13, the Newmans attended a press conference for the London premiere of *Winning*. On October 15 in London, they joined more than 200 singing and chanting students in an antiwar demonstration in Grosvenor Square in support of Vietnam Moratorium Day. The actress was considered by screenwriter-director Frank D. Gilroy for the character of Sophie Bentwood in the Paramount drama *Desperate Characters* (1971) but Shirley MacLaine was cast instead.

In the fall, the Newmans went to San Francisco where he was feted at the San Francisco Film Festival at the Palace of Fine Arts. The press seemed to depict Woodward's more unusual public-spirited gestures as mere eccentricity. In New York she picked up trash in Central Park, assisted by her children. When onlookers did not follow her lead, the actress was disappointed. In response to the energy crisis, the Newmans ditched their unnecessary electrical goods, like the can opener, and she swapped her Mazda for a more fuel-efficient Honda. They switched to organic foods as the couple were concerned about their diets. Woodward was also involved with Planned Parenthood, peace groups and ecology groups, saying she was in despair about the country and worked very hard to do something about it.

The actress' next film was the Universal romantic comedy mystery *They Might Be Giants* (1971), shot on location in New York and New Jersey from November 22, 1969, to mid–February 1970. James Goldman adapted his own play and the director was Anthony Harvey. The play had been produced in London in 1966 at the Stratford East Theater, but not in the U.S. Classic paranoid jurist Justin Playfair (George C. Scott), convinced he is Sherlock Holmes, is treated by Dr. Mildred Watson (Woodward) of the Manhattan Strauss Clinic. Woodward's costumes are by Ann Roth, and her hair by Romaine Greene is a short, straight style with blonde tints, worn with a side part and a few strands on her forehead, and a hair clip. She gets some funny lines. Justin asks Mildred if she wants to get them killed, and the doctor replies, "No, just one of us." When he comments that her house is nice and a mess just like her, she tells him, "Somehow that just misses being a compliment." Woodward here is perhaps the funniest she has been on screen to date. Her best scene may be when Justin visits Mildred's apartment for dinner. The actress is funny, romantic and fearful when he is shot.

The film was released on June 9, 1971, with the tagline "When they reach out for each other … they touch every heart … with warmth, charm and laughter!" It was praised by Les Keyser in *Hollywood in the Seventies* but panned by *Time*'s Stefan Kanfer, who wrote that Woodward's real sweetness becomes ersatz and saccharine. The film was not a box office success.

Woodward felt that if Newman had directed the film, it might have been a great one instead of a good one. Woodward got along well with the cast and crew but did not enjoy making it. She said the experience almost drove her out of the business. Her unhappiness may have been due to the arctic winter conditions and a garage strike in New York at the time. The Newmans' company produced the film, which meant there were practical concerns to be dealt with and pressure overshadowing the creative input. She said good little films could not be made any more; either one was a huge hit or a disaster. Anthony Harvey reported that Woodward remained upbeat throughout filming, and she had no problem with her co-star Scott, who had a bad reputation. The actress described him as a gentleman and said acting opposite him was acting with an erupting volcano. She gave Scott the gift of three doves after filming was completed.

The film's publicist was astonished that Woodward did not care at all which still pictures of her the studio released, even though she had shot approval, a contractual privilege actresses generally fought for. The actress only cared about looking in character, so if the

Poster for *They Might Be Giants* (1971).

pictures showed her with crow's feet around the eyes or other imperfections, she didn't care. The wrap party was held at Mama Leone's restaurant in midtown Manhattan. There Woodward did not come on as a star but instead seemed like just another member of the company, and was mainly interested in talking with the crew members about their families and their plans for the future. The publicist didn't think her behavior was an act and got the impression she was a thoughtful and generous person. The actress admitted she was probably as self-centered as most actors, but also Southern, and that upbringing had stayed with her. Southern ladies were not rude and thoughtless. For them, life was role-playing to a great extent and that happened to be a very comfortable role to play.

Anthony Harvey commented that Woodward and Scott worked differently. Her Actors Studio background meant it was important to develop a character, whereas he had contempt for the Studio. Despite this difference, they played well together because the pair had the chemistry of two strong, interesting people. The director said she gave a moving performance.

Woodward and the girls visited Newman in Washington College, Chestertown, Maryland, where he was acting in and directing the Universal action adventure *Sometimes a Great Notion* (1971), but while he was making this movie, mostly she stayed in Los Angeles with the children. Woodward expressed her dislike of the city with the comment, "Eleven years to emphysema in Los Angeles."

Woodward helped Newman campaign for the Congressional candidates the Reverend Joe Duffy in Connecticut and Pete McCloskey in California. While Newman made personal appearances, the actress felt she lacked his political acumen and stayed at home, telephoning and writing letters to try and get out the votes. Concerned about the growing problem of drug abuse among teenagers, the actor narrated a film on drugs and attended a screening at a local high school in Connecticut. Woodward reported that parents called to tell her that was the first time they ever heard their kids say the message really got through to them.

She had thought living in Connecticut was a lot healthier for her children until a proposal came up to bus in disadvantaged kindergarten students from Bridgeport. Woodward said the attitude of many was so extraordinary, so biased that she wondered whether this was the town they all thought so lovely, with high taxes and a lily-white school system. The actress supported the proposal, believing that bringing outside children would have helped their own who were growing up in a very one-sided atmosphere. She didn't like New York any better, being concerned about the air pollution, and that people didn't seem to care about it. Becoming conscious of the environment, Woodward tried to get her grocer to stock certain products, like bio-degradable soaps and pure white paper products, rather than color-treated items. Discussing the future of the world, she said conservatively, people had at most two or three generations left, and she was raising her children not to have any of their own.

She was to star in the movie version of Iris Murdoch's *A Fairly Honorable Defeat*. Peter Ustinov was to adapt the novel and also direct, and the film was to be produced by Newman and John Foreman. The novel was about an evil genius who manipulates the lives of others, including a married couple, a female professor and a pair of homosexual lovers. Filming was to begin on location abroad later that year. The title was changed to *Mirror, Mirror* but the film would not be made.

Between L.A.'s smog and a severe February 9, 1971, earthquake, Woodward made up her mind to leave. She said it was perfectly absurd to have a beautiful home and to drive weekends to the beach so her child, who was allergic to the smog, could breathe, and then on top of it to be victimized by an earthquake. The actress herself had even been known to break out in spots from the smog. She convinced her husband they should sell their Beverly Hills home and move back to Connecticut for good, which is what they did when the school year was over.

Woodward continued her interest in ballet, taking lessons from David Leshine in Los Angeles. She also took tennis lessons, then realized she had no interest in the game and chose piano lessons instead. The actress accompanied her husband and children when they went skiing at resorts in California and Vermont. She was only there for companionship as she did not ski and was not about to break a leg trying to learn, saying she was undoubtedly the only person who rode the ski lift down. At the resorts, she read, did needlepoint, played the guitar, exercised or answered her mail. At this time she described herself as schizophrenic, manic-depressive, lazy, emotional, compulsive, theatrical and prone to playing roles.

She was a guest on the November 21, 1971, episode of the BBC talk show *Parkinson*. Woodward had gone to England in the fall, alone, for the British opening of *WUSA*. She narrated and appeared in the ABC-TV documentary *Eagle and the Hawk*, broadcast on ABC on November 26. In it, she, daughter Nell and wildlife expert Morlan W. Nelson spent several weeks observing the living habits of eagles and hawks in Idaho's rugged, picturesque Snake River County country. They also watched as Nelson prepared to set free a red tail hawk, which had been wounded and then nursed back to health. Woodward's commitment to the film came from the Newman children's love of animals which was indicated by the fact that they had menageries at the family's homes on both coasts.

The made-for-TV movie *All the Way Home* was broadcast on NBC on December 1, 1971, with the tagline "Love was their legacy." Rehearsals took place in New York and the show taped in Toronto, because of union costs. The teleplay was by Tad Mosel, based on the James Agee novel *A Death in the Family*, and the director was Fred Coe. The play had been produced as a Danish made-for-television movie (*I havn*, broadcast on May 2, 1959) and a Paramount film which was released in 1963 with Jean Simmons in the leading role. Set in Knoxville, Tennessee, "some time ago," the story centered on Mary Follet (Woodward), who has a five-year-old son, Rufus (Shane Nickerson), and is pregnant again. Her husband Jay (Richard Kiley) dies in a car accident. Her clothes by Ann Roth are pastel colors except for an ankle-length black mourning dress with hat and veil. Her hair is worn in a long, straight graying-brown style with a side part off her forehead. The actress uses a soft Southern accent and the role sees her faint. Woodward's anger is funny, especially when Mary beats Ralph (Pat Hingle) to try and get information he is concealing. She delivers a four-minute monologue about Jay's drinking, but her best scene is perhaps when Mary reacts to the description of her dead husband's body by Andrew Lynch (James Woods). While the actress does some over-gesturing in the scene, this is acceptable given the hysterics she displays. The play was later remade as made-for-TV movies with Sally Field as Mary in the 1981 version and Annabeth Gish in *A Death in the Family* (2002).

Woodward commented that she had almost forgotten how much fun there was for an actress in a television drama. Doing the show brought it all back to her, especially with the people she worked with. Coe, Kiley, Hingle and Eileen Heckart, who played Aunt Hannah Lynch, were all associated with New York television shows when Woodward was starting her career. She knew James Agee from the *Omnibus* show "Mr. Lincoln," and said he was a wonderful man and that everyone adored him. Woodward felt she really matured as an actress through her work in television shows.

In his memoir, Luke Yankee wrote about his mother, Heckart, making the show. Woodward was on a veritable campaign to get Heckart to stop smoking, something which did not amuse the older actress. She thought Heckart could quit if she had something else to do with her hands and suggested needlepoint, because it was not hard and incredibly relaxing. Heckart said she was not good at handicrafts and they didn't interest her. Woodward fished in her purse and pulled out a small, half-finished needlepoint sampler of a butterfly which her six-year-old daughter Clea had started. The actress handed it to Heckart, saying if Clea could do it, so could she. The next day, Heckart walked into Woodward's trailer and tossed the completed sampler onto her lap, saying Clea did shitty work. Woodward scored half a victory as from then on, Heckart was rarely without a needlepoint canvas in her lap when she was on a movie set or backstage in her dressing room. But the older actress had a cigarette in one hand and the embroidery needle in the other.

In 1971, the Newmans made a $500 contribution to the campaign of openly gay Frank Kameny, who was running for Congress in the District of Columbia. The check was said to have arrived too late to be used by the campaign so instead it paid for tickets for some staffers to go to New York and meet with representatives of the Gay Activists Alliance which supported Kameny.

Woodward acquired the novel *Mrs. Beneker* by Violet Weingarten as another possible vehicle for herself playing a guilt-ridden matron. The author's agent was Gil Parker, who had another client, Paul Zindel. The latter's comic play *The Effect of Gamma Rays on Man-in-the-Moon Marigolds*, about a bitter mother and her two troubled daughters, had been filmed as a 60-minute October 3, 1966, episode of the television series *New York Television Theatre* which was broadcast by National Educational Television. Later it was produced off-Broadway and had run from April 7, 1970, to May 14, 1972, with Sada Thompson in the leading role.

Parker brought Zindel together with the Newmans, suggesting the playwright do the *Mrs. Beneker* screenplay. Zindel said he didn't know very much about Woodward, other than she was a star. But he was thrilled to be working for them and the more he saw the impact and the power they had, the more impressed he was. The three hit it off so well that they also saw each other socially, including an excursion to the ballet. Zindel was invited to the Newmans' East Side apartment and she made her caviar omelet, learned from a master omelet chef in New York. After eating, the three went to the ballet via limousine. When the car was a block from Lincoln Center, Newman took out a vial and put a little Murine in his eyes, so that his famous blue eyes could be seen by the public. When the Newmans walked down the aisle of the theatre, the whole place turned around to see them. People asked for his autograph, which he did not give, but no one asked for hers. Newman said that in public he was the star and the actress supported him.

The couple was eager to see Zindel's play on stage so he got them tickets but did not go to the performance. She thought the lead character was a miserable, hateful woman and the only reason her husband related to the story was because he had a very difficult mother. Woodward didn't know what his attraction to the story meant to her as his wife and what he was telling her but the actor was determined she was going to do it. He called the playwright from the theater, wanting to buy the film rights. During negotiations, the three continued to meet socially as Zindel worked on *Mrs. Beneker*. He was invited to their Connecticut home more than once and was shocked that the couple wore caftans. The playwright observed that she was a rather secure woman, who gave a sense of the family life and what was being protected. While the Newmans were specialists in their acting talents and they could tell when something was missing in a script, the couple couldn't tell you how to solve it. They just knew it needed more energy, and discussed the things that needed punching up. On July 7, it was announced that the Newman-Foreman Company had acquired the film rights to *The Effect of Gamma Rays on Man-in-the-Moon Marigolds*.

Zindel decided he did not want to write the *Effect of Gamma Rays* screenplay but was still working on *Mrs. Beneker*. He and Woodward met to discuss the script over a Mandarin dinner of Mou Ling pork and sizzling rice soup. The playwright hired a limousine to take him from the Beverly Hills Hotel to pick her up, and he said she was very nice and as nervous as he was. As they drove to the restaurant on Sunset, the car stopped at a light and another car pulled over next to them. Although it seemed to Zindel that the passengers were simply looking over at the limousine like anybody would do in the situation, the actress yelled out to them "Yes, there's a star in here!" He said it was a nervous reaction more than anything else. At dinner when she began discussing the *Mrs. Beneker* script, the playwright was completely stunned when Woodward said that she didn't know who the character was and went down a list of five things that Stella Adler would ask. He couldn't answer her, so while the food was delicious, the meeting was clearly unsatisfactory. She was very nice about it, though, and Zindel drove her home to her mansion. The actress invited him in for a glass of water and to show him the nine small Utrillos that she had found in a junk heap and hung on her wall. When he left, the limousine broke down in the driveway and the playwright had to go back to have the chauffeur call for a replacement. As it turned out, Woodward had reservations about the *Mrs. Beneker* script, but the Newmans were still interested in having him continue, with his status enhanced after *Effect of Gamma Rays* won the Pulitzer Prize. However, Woodward rejected Zindel's first draft.

Newman and John Foreman had had trouble getting studio backing for *Effect of Gamma Rays* until Newman agreed to sign away final cut of the film. He joked that perhaps if he had played the lead female character and Woodward had directed, there would have been more interest. In the late winter and spring of 1972, the Newmans were back in Connecticut to make the Fox drama on location from April 10 to early June. The screenplay was by Alvin Sergent and Newman was the director.

After two weeks of rehearsal, filming took place in Bridgeport, with interiors shot in an abandoned parsonage of a church. The Bridgeport location being so close to the Newman home in Westport was thought to be an advantage but the situation ultimately proved otherwise. After a strenuous day on the set, Woodward was not able to go home and unwind, having to contend with a houseful of demanding kids which she found detrimental both to them and herself. She was unhappy, disliking her hair and wardrobe (the makeup made her look worse than if she had worn none), the dreary set of the house, and the hopelessness, boorishness and negativity of the character. She was used to playing character parts but considered this one to be the frumpiest woman of all. Her hair was dyed a mousy brown and she hated the gooky rinse they put on it, that got all over the pillowcase at night. The character's clothes were sloppy because they were her mother's. The woman was a pack rat, never throwing anything away, so Woodward went through her closet and dragged out a lot of old junk and dyed it an icky color and wore it. She was so depressed and suicidal during the film, she couldn't stand it. The actress claimed to be obsessed by demons and admitted to coming close to sheer insanity. There were such ugliness and putrefaction inside the character and she understood her too well. If someone was rejected and she rejected herself, then the goodness got swallowed up by the ugliness. At home, Woodward was a monster and the Newmans avoided each other as much as possible. Newman said that in all their years of working together as co-stars or as director-actor, it was the only time she let herself get overwhelmed by a role, being a "real pain in the ass." Of all the characters the actress had played, including functioning voluptuaries and very comedic ladies, it was amazing to him that she would choose to take this one home with her. Woodward became that miscreant, vulgar, punishing, impossible woman and she became so hostile every single night that it made the actor flee. One night Newman asked to occupy the spare room of A.E. Hotchner, saying if he had to spend another night with her, one of them would not be on the set the next day. The actress said the relationship with her family was strained to the limit, and they thought that if she didn't get through the film they were all going to have to move away. Her kids hated her, Newman hated her, and everybody including herself wished Woodward would leave home.

On the set, the couple fought with onlookers surprised by the intensity of their arguments. She said that her husband was the easiest person in the world but they still had big fights. This time they were not clicking on how the character should be played. The actress wanted a little humor and compassion to shine through the character's repulsiveness, but he felt there was nothing in the script that lent itself to that. Newman said the actress was uptight because she thought she wasn't funny enough or sad enough and some of the scenes eluded her. Also, Woodward got really off-balance and out of synch, to the point where it affected her physical appearance and her face just went sour all of a sudden. But he thought his wife had a lot of guts and strangely, because she was being difficult, that translated itself into her performance, which was sensational to him. The actress had kind words about Nell, who also appeared in the film, who loved the money because she had a whole menagerie to support. The girl wanted to be an ornithologist and the Newmans gave her an electric handsaw for Christmas so that she could build pigeon houses. Woodward thought her daughter only acted in the film because her father had told her he refused to pay for her pigeon food any more. Now the other children wanted to know when they would get to be actors too. Woodward believed they thought it was always fun to go to work if Daddy was directing and Mommy was starring, but if the children ever had to face the reality and toughness of the business, they would change their minds.

After filming was completed, the actress drove to her New York apartment, leaving her family behind in Connecticut. She was physically and mentally worn out and wanted a few days on her own. But the first night, Woodward woke up screaming like a mad creature, and called Newman in a panic at four in the morning. She told him she was going crazy and he raced to Manhattan to be with her. When the actor arrived, the actress burst into tears. She said the film left scars.

The story concerned middle-aged, alcoholic, eccentric widowed Beatrice Hunsdorfer *née* Betty Frank (Woodward), whose "craziness" has her labelled Betty the Loon. Her daughters attend Warren Harding High School: epileptic cheerleader Ruth (Roberta Wallach) and shy science student Matilda a.k.a. Tilly (Nell Potts). Woodward's costumes by Anna Hill Johnstone include notable red robe, red cape, and a shimmery black knee-length short-sleeved dress worn with black gloves, black wrap and a black turban. Hair by Romaine Greene is a collar-length wavy dark brown-black worn off her forehead. The role has the actress try on wigs in a thrift shop, and mistreat and off-screen kill a rabbit. She is also funny and her likability makes Beatrice's hatred of the world empathetic. Her funny lines include a comment about Mr. Goodman (David Spielberg): "He's poetic all right. I've never seen a more effeminate look on a man." To Floyd (David Venture): "You made such a lovely speech at my wedding about how we'll all stick together through thick and thin. Well, it's thin, Floyd." Woodward is touching when Beatrice drunkenly attends the school's Science Fair and tells Matilda, "My heart is full," but her best scene is perhaps her first when she silently tries on wigs. We see the actress do so much with her face in her reactions to her mirrored reflection with each wig.

The film was released on December 20, 1972, with the taglines "If you had a mother like this, who would you be today?," "Mother of the Year," "The Paul Newman Production of the 1971 Pulitzer Prize winning play," "Joanne Woodward stars in it. Paul Newman made it. The electrifying team from *Rachel, Rachel*" and "Life's been a real bitch to Beatrice Hunsdorfer. And vice versa." *Variety* said that Woodward brilliantly projected the pitiable character. Roger Ebert wrote that the actress was not like anything she had ever done before, played with great energy, and served notice that she was capable of experimenting with roles that were against type and making them work. Vincent Canby in *The New York Times* at times had the feeling that Woodward was auditioning for the role of Sadie Thompson. Pauline Kael in *The New Yorker* found the actress unconvincing, and Michael Kerbel in *Paul Newman* said she displayed remarkable range. The film was not a box office success.

Newman said Woodward was brilliant in the film and he wanted to get a bunch of film critics together and run a reel of *WUSA*, *Rachel, Rachel*, and this film back-to-back. To him she was absolutely unrecognizable from one to another, either in terms of physical mannerisms or basic quality, and there was something of witchcraft in there.

Initially Zindel was not happy with the film or Woodward's performance. He felt she had played too far away from herself, and was defeated by the challenge to play nasty and mean combined with the humor that was natural to her. Instead Zindel found Woodward to be one-note and forced. But when the playwright later saw the film on television, he liked it more. There the performance, pushed down from the large screen to the small screen, became less strenuous and less transparent.

Woodward in *The Effect of Gamma Rays on Man-in-the-Moon Marigolds* (1972).

At this time, Woodward commented on her relationship with her stepchildren. She said she had experimented on them to their detriment, and maybe to the betterment of her own children. They were all friends, though there had been rough times. Scott Newman had not spoken to her for several years, perhaps because the actress resented the fact that he wasn't standing on his own two feet and was using his father. Another problem child, teenage Susan, became very ill after losing 40 pounds on a diet, and became involved with an older man. When any of the children were near the actor in public, they were pushed aside literally by fans who wanted to get near him. It was as if they were nothing in themselves, and also it must have been disturbing for his daughters to know that their friends were madly in love with their father. Additionally, it was difficult for them to grow up in multiple homes at multiple schools on two coasts in a bohemian household with celebrity parents.

Woodward said she had her own frustrations when Newman was away working. One time he was gone all fall on location, came home for two weeks, and was off again. The actor would go drinking or fishing or racing cars, and his wife would wonder when she would get a vacation.

Martin Ritt wanted her for the part of Tillie in *Pete 'n' Tillie* (1972) but she didn't feel right for the script. Woodward also wanted to stop playing parts that started out with her sitting crying in her bathrobe. Carol Burnett was cast instead.

A likeness of the actress was used for the painting of Marguerite Wyke, who is never seen in the mystery thriller *Sleuth* (1972). The portrait was based on a photograph of her. It was said to be a private joke, since the Newmans were friends of director Joseph L. Mankiewicz. The film was remade as the 2007 crime drama mystery with the same title, and the character of Marguerite (renamed Maggie) was seen only in photographs and credited as Carmel O'Sullivan.

The Newmans made a special effort to see their friends in the theater. Once on the West Coast, Barbara Rush was starring in the romantic comedy *Forty Carats*. The couple hadn't told her they would be in the audience and even took balcony seats so as not to be spotted, acutely aware of actors' nerves before a performance. Woodward said she adored the play but Newman did not. It was pure entertainment with no underlying message, something which the actor felt was important. Woodward loved light and airy material, soap operas and comedies that had nothing important to say. Woodward wanted to do *Forty Carats* on screen and was considered by director William Wyler when he was attached to Columbia's 1973 film adaptation. But after he bowed out, Liv Ullmann was cast.

7

Summer Wishes, Winter Dreams

Woodward was next in the dramatic film known as *Death of a Snow Queen*, then *Souvenir*, and released as *Summer Wishes, Winter Dreams*. Scripted by Stewart Stern, it was shot from late October to early December on location in New York, London and Bastogne. Top-billed Woodward's Rita Walden is a middle-aged New York City homemaker who finds herself in an emotional crisis which forces her to re-examine her life. Her earth-toned costumes are by Anna Hill Johnstone and include a knee-length brown mink coat. Hair by Romaine Greene is a short sculpted dark brown style with a side part off her forehead often worn with hair clips. The role sees the actress hold a baby, attend a screening of the Swedish romance *Wild Strawberries* (1957), have her dying mother (Sylvia Sidney) propped on her knees as Rita sits on the floor, climb a ladder, and ride a London rail escalator. Director Gilbert Cates supplies an extreme closeup of her in the scene where Rita dreams of being in a falling plane. She is funny when angry, especially in Rita's reaction to Harry telling her about a beautiful woman he saw in the street which was actually her. Woodward's best scene is perhaps in the family farm hayloft when she cries over the memory of her dead farmhand Carl (Lee Jackson) and then argues with Anna (Dori Brenner) over selling the farm.

Arthur Bell in *The New York Times* of December 17 reported from the Studio Cinema in New York where a scene was to be shot with her. The actress chewed gum and read about Orson Welles as she waited. Woodward told another interviewer on the set that when not making films she went to class, raised her family, did needlework, made attempts to play the guitar, played the recorder, went to the ballet, and worked on causes. The actress also read a new biography of Isadora Duncan, Simone de Beauvior's new book that Newman had given her, and Anthony Trollope. For two years all she read was Trollope, except for an occasional lapse into Agatha Christie.

The Columbia film premiered at the San Francisco Film Festival on October 17, 1973, and then received a wide release on October 21 with the tagline "Beautiful. Frigid. She is called a Snow Queen" and "She's beautiful ... but frigid." Woodward attended the October 21 premiere at the Plaza Theater in New York. *Variety* wrote the actors were first-rate and created genuinely tender moments. Nora Sayre of *The New York Times* wrote that Woodward acted as if she had been drinking Drano; the moments of vulnerability just weren't convincing. In *The New Yorker*, Pauline Kael said Rita was the least vital of the actress's afflicted women, and asked, "Haven't we suffered enough with Joanne Woodward?" Woodward was nominated for the Best Actress Academy Award and Sidney for Best Supporting Actress.

Stern's script was about his parents and himself, and he had written it for her. The actress felt it was a beautiful script and that Rita was a wonderful character. She was a reactive woman who had things happen to her and rarely instigated anything, being at the mercy of her mother, her daughter, the son and the husband. But Rita had made the awful discovery of how brief life really was, too brief even to correct one's mistakes and, even worse, too brief really to ever change. Woodward found her breakdown in the London subway affecting. She could see why the film's bleakness made it unsuccessful. A source quotes her saying it was very depressing and the actress had just about had it with being depressed.

This time she chose to go home to her empty New York apartment at night to spare her children the suffering they had endured from her on *The Effect of Gamma Rays on Man-in-the-Moon Marigolds.* But toward the end of filming, Woodward's nerves were frayed. One source claims she and Cates had arguments over the handling of the material. Another cites a day when the actress got angry when she discovered Stern and Cates had decided to cut the dialogue of a scene Woodward had carefully planned for. She thought they could have warned her and told Cates that they had to finish the film by the end of the week because she was going to Switzerland. Cates responded that would be done as *he* was going to Florida. Regretting what she had said, Woodward would have to send him flowers, and reported she wanted to go home and get drunk but only drank sherry

Portrait of Woodward for *Summer Wishes, Winter Dreams* (1973).

which you couldn't get drunk on. The actress later said she loved doing the film because it was so inner.

Martin Balsam, who played Harry, commented that Woodward was one of the finest actresses he had the pleasure of working with. Just to watch her listening, he said, was a course in acting in itself. Sylvia Sidney, another Connecticut resident, remained friends with the Newmans.

By late 1972, the *Mrs. Beneker* project had been shelved, and the film was never made. Paul Zindel remarked that *Summer Wishes, Winter Dreams* had an identical character and story. The thrust was used to embody that script, despite Stern's claim that the material was autobiographical.

Although the Newmans no longer lived in Los Angeles, they still managed to maintain a medium-high profile in the movie community. They regularly attended parties held by super-agent Sue Mengers at her Dawn Ridge Drive home, despite the couple's normal dislike of such affairs. The parties seemed to be informal but they were actually business opportunities, a place where established and rising film people could mingle. Woodward would sit in a chair and knit but if anyone lit up a joint, the couple would leave. They were liberals in most respects but didn't want to be associated with the drug culture, disliking this aspect of the New Hollywood scene.

Meanwhile, her schedule was full with going to classes. She was tired of playing worn-out, depressing ladies in frayed bathrobes, though she admitted to having a joyous time later playing Amanda in *The Glass Menagerie* in a frayed bathrobe. The actress enrolled at Sarah Lawrence College in Yonkers, New York, which was convenient from both her Connecticut and Manhattan homes. She started out majoring in philosophy and then changed to art history and astronomy at the college's Center for Continuing Education. Woodward had never graduated from college, after dropping out of Louisiana State University, and always had a lingering drive to go back and finish. She only wanted to enrich her mind. It was an act of great indulgence, and the actress had a great time, joking that she was the oldest living undergraduate. Woodward was thrilled when one of her history professor returned a term paper with the comment, "Good thinking." That was something that no Oscar could begin to compare with.

Simultaneously she was raising her family. She described her home as a madhouse and very messy. Nell was training a hawk in her bedroom, and there were papers all over the place because they had an undetermined number of pigeons, too. The household included the actress's two younger daughters, her two stepdaughters, four cats, two dogs, two horses and a chicken named Dorothy who thought she was a dog. She also agreed to be a chairperson for a Planned Parenthood benefit scheduled for late in the year, to be held at the American Shakespeare Theatre in Stratford, Connecticut. Woodward was vocal about the cause, saying she believed every woman should have the right to say how many children she wanted. In addition, the actress wanted to write a biography of Margaret Sanger. She said the concept of going into parenthood with conscious thought was not something people of her generation did. They just had babies.

The Newmans were guests on the January 23, 1973, episode of *The Dick Cavett Show* and Woodward reportedly brought a clip from *The Effect of Gamma Rays on Man-in-the-Moon Marigolds,* playing a scene with Nell. Cavett said he thought Nell might be even more beautiful than her mother. The actress replied that it was no surprise because of who the girl's father was.

The New York Times of February 13 reported that the Newmans had contributed $5000 to the presidential campaign of Senator George McGovern. On March 16, she introduced Nancy Hanks, chairman of the National Endowment for the Arts, who spoke at a midnight supper in the Atlanta Civic Center auditorium.

On April 25, she was one of the participants in a noon protest in New York's Duffy Square against the plight of Soviet Jews, calling on Americans to support the right of Jews and other Soviet minorities to emigrate and to live in freedom. The rally was sponsored by Writers and Artists for Peace in the Middle East and the National Conference on Soviet Jewry.

In 1973, the Newmans made their first-ever appearance at the Cannes Film Festival to promote *Effect of Gamma Rays*. On May 25, she won the Best Actress Award at the Festival but had her husband accept for her.

In the July 5 *Rolling Stone*, interviewee Newman talked about his wife. He stated that he would never enter politics because it would blow his marriage, because she would never throw one of those fancy Washington bashes. He also spoke about the actress making of *Effect of Gamma Rays* and how she got him to do *A New Kind of Love*.

On September 13, the Newmans attended the opening night party of *Waltz of the Toreador* at Pub Theatrical in New York. On September 17, they attended the "We Believe" United Nations Dinner at the Waldorf Astoria Hotel in New York. She was to read a preamble to the United Nations Charter on September 18 for the annual dinner of the liaison organization between industry, business, labor and the United Nations. The event was to take place in the Grand Ballroom of the Waldorf Astoria.

To publicize *Summer Wishes, Winter Dreams*, Woodward agreed to give interviews, something she disliked doing and felt she was not good at. When questioned about her sex life, the actress laughed wildly and admitted the rumors of a marriage of convenience were all true. They were sex maniacs and everything in between, and she thought that made it so much more interesting. Her daughters were also all nymphomaniacs, as were the chicken and the skunk. Another reporter asked Woodward why she didn't stop Newman from racing, particularly as he had been involved in an accident. She reportedly bristled at the question and stated that she couldn't stop him because he was an adult man with a mind and a will of his own.

On October 28, Woodward, co-chairman of Connecticut's Planned Parenthood League, celebrated its 50th anniversary with a benefit gala called Stars Over Connecticut at the American Shakespeare Theater in Stratford. The Newmans were at the Actors Studio 25th Anniversary Honoring Elia Kazan at the Actors Studio in New York. One source gives the date of the event as December 6 but another as January 20. She was the narrator of "The Fragile Mind," an ABC-TV special on mental health broadcast on January 9, 1974. The show profiled a representative group of Americans who had suffered some of the more common varieties of mental and emotional distress and detailed how they had been helped through appropriate treatment.

Woodward won the Best Actress Award for *Summer Wishes, Winter Dreams* in the 39th annual poll of the New York Film Critics Circle. The award was presented on January 27 at Sardi's Restaurant with the Newmans in attendance. The couple also attended a party that Ray Stark and his wife, Fran, threw for her in honor of her Film Critics Award. The Starks were famous for their lavish and elegant soirees and it was commented that the actress was beautiful to look at and beautifully mannered, and had a commodity that Hollywood couldn't fake: class.

She and Robert Shaw were to make their Lincoln Center debuts in August Strindberg's *Dance of Death* for the New York Shakespeare Festival's subscription season at the Vivian Beaumont Theater. The play, directed by A.J. Antoon, was to open April 4 after a series of previews starting March 21 and to run to May 5. Before its local presentation, it would be done for two weeks at the Annenberg Center in Philadelphia beginning in March. But Woodward withdrew from the production. In a statement released by the Festival, the actress was quoted as saying that after a week and a half of rehearsal, she did not feel she could do justice to the role of Alice, the embittered wife. Both Antoon and festival director Joseph Papp had encouraged her to remain and work her way through but Woodward knew she would not perform it properly. One source reported that Shaw and Woodward fell out during the first week of rehearsal. Shaw said that she was nervous about returning to the stage after such a long time. The actress also objected to his heavy drinking, especially during rehearsals as she had little time for actors who did so when working. Zoe Caldwell replaced her.

Woodward won the Best Actress Award for *Summer Wishes, Winter Dreams* from the Young New York Film Critics Association. It appears that the Newmans attended the 31st Golden Globe Awards that was held on January 26. She was nominated for Best Actress in a Drama for *Summer Wishes, Winter Dreams* but lost to Marsha Mason for the romance *Cinderella Liberty* (1973).

Woodward was nominated for the Best Actress Academy Award for *Summer Wishes, Winter Dreams*. Vincent Canby of *The New York Times* predicted that, despite her film not being a box office success, she would win, having already won the New York Film Critics prize. (Canby added that he would rather predict the outcome of a turtle derby than any Oscar contest.)

For her 44th birthday, Newman reportedly gave his wife a motorcycle. The couple attended the 46th Annual Academy Awards on April 2 at the Dorothy Chandler Pavilion. She was nominated for the Best Actress Award presented by Charlton Heston and Susan Hayward, and shown when her name was announced. The actress wore a black spaghetti-strapped dress which had a matching black cape and white collar. Her hair was worn shoulder-length blonde with a side part off her forehead. Woodward lost to Glenda Jackson for the romantic comedy *A Touch of Class* (1973) and was seen to gasp and raise her eyebrows in reaction to the news. She claimed that the Oscar was only significant as a political or a business gesture.

The Newmans agreed to appear at a film symposium conducted by critic Judith Crist in Tarrytown, New York. It was reported that they were refreshingly candid and honest at the question-and-answer session.

A lot of mornings the actress said she could hardly get out from under the covers to be herself, feeling unfulfilled and incomplete. Woodward figured the best thing her husband could do was to take her out back and shoot her like a crippled horse. But Stewart Stern reported that Newman had no such conflict because she was a source of reassurance and nourishment for him. Her love for Newman was as total as his for her, and Stern said they found constant comfort in one another. She admitted it wasn't easy living with him, and Woodward was a complainer rather than a grin-and-bear-it person. The difficulty came with relating to Newman as a superstar, which had nothing to do with the man. Friends thought she tended to downplay her contribution to the couple's successful relationship and their family life. Gore Vidal found this quality of modesty refreshing in a world where most people went in the opposite direction. The actress has misgivings about her performance as a mother, rating herself 6.5 on a scale of 10 though believing her daughters would rate her even lower. She said all of the Newman children were different and as much of a mystery to her as they had been when they were younger. But, although communication with them was sometimes difficult, Woodward talked to the children a lot more than her parents ever talked to her. She didn't think her daughters had too much to rebel about, all things considered, because they led a very atypical and interesting existence. No child had parents who were home all the time and who were all-knowing and secure and capable of solving any problem. There were certain things kids needed to work out for themselves, and the actress wanted to be sure to give them the leeway and support to do this. If outside help was needed, she would see they got it.

On April 21, Woodward attended the Tony Awards after party, held at Sardi's in New York. On April 24, the Newmans went to the opening of Bloomingdale's model rooms exhibit at night after the store closed, but the actress was disappointed that she could not shop. Woodward used to drop in there on Saturdays when she lived in a coldwater flat and couldn't afford to buy anything, and just look at the rooms. Now the actress didn't show up so much because it was so crowded. On April 29, they were at a benefit gala at the Circle in the Square-Joseph E. Levine Theater. The couple were among many actors and actresses and singers and dancers, many of them alumni of the Circle, who entertained with dramatic scenes and readings.

A May 5 *New York Times* article about the Chateau Marmont in West Hollywood included the claim that Woodward and Newman had met for the first time in a Marmont elevator. On May 20, the *Times* reported that Woodward was one of 21 women who had sent a telegram to Senator Bayh, chairman of the Senate Judiciary Subcommittee on Constitutional Amendments. This was concerning the three "right to life" amendments that had been introduced in Congress, which would ban abortions. The women stated they deplored that so few females had been allowed to testify at hearings in March this year, since they were the ones who would suffer from government attempts to control their reproductive lives.

She was one of the signers of a May 21 letter to the editor of the *Times*, as part of Writers and Artists for Peace in the Middle East. The letter was provoked by the May 15 attack by the Popular Democratic Front for the Liberation of Palestine in Maalot. It protested the use of children and civilians as political pawns and called upon the civilized world to join in demanding the United Nations condemn acts of terrorism and devise suitable measures against those countries which harbored terrorists.

Her next film was the Warner Bros. action crime mystery *The Drowning Pool* (1975), originally titled *Ryan's the Name*. It was shot from mid–October to December 24, 1974, on location in Louisiana and at Universal and Warner Bros. This sequel to *Harper* (1966) had a screenplay by Tracy Keenan Wynn, Lorenzo Semple, Jr., Walter Hill and an uncredited Eric Roth, based on the Ross MacDonald novel. The director was Stuart Rosenberg. Lew Harper (Newman), a Los Angeles private detective, travels to New Orleans to help Iris Devereaux (Woodward), an old girlfriend who is worried that her wealthy playwright husband (Richard Derr) will learn that she is cheating on him. She is billed 13th after the film's title with a "with" credit. Wardrobe by Donald Brooks includes an ugly ruffled long-sleeved blouse. Hair by Carrie White is worn in a gray-blonde shoulder-length straight style with a side part and bangs. The actress uses a Southern accent and the role calls for her to also be seen as a corpse. Woodward's best scene is perhaps when she talks on the phone with Lew when Iris is drunk and cries before committing suicide off-screen.

Preview clips of the film were shown May 5, 1975, during the fourth annual gala of the Film Society of Lincoln Center in New York City where the Newmans were honored. The film premiered on June 18, as a benefit for the Policemen's Association of New Orleans, held at the Saenger-Orleans Theater. It was released on June 25, with the taglines "Harper days are here again…" "Your favorite private eye is back in *The Drowning Pool*" and "Just a guy trying to keep his head above water." The film was not a box office success.

Newman reported that it was her idea to relocate the novel's location from Los Angeles to New Orleans. She reportedly told Melanie Griffith, who played Schuyler, that her three goals in life had been to marry a movie star, have beautiful babies and win an Oscar, ambitions that Griffith tried to copy. Anthony Franciosa, who plays Broussard, has one scene with the actress, though she is dead in it, which is a reunion for them after *The*

Long, Hot Summer. Woodward was also seen in the Ronald Saland–directed featurette *Harper Days Are Here Again*. After completing *The Drowning Pool*, Woodward said that it would be very difficult for her to do another film, particularly one with Newman. She had to do something that was hers, not as an appendage.

The Newmans co-starred in *The Wild Places*, a conservation-themed NBC special made in conjunction with the Sierra Club and broadcast on December 2, 1974. Directed by Lee Mendelson, the show was divided into four basic areas of wilderness: mountains, swamps, rivers and deserts. It told the story of the people in these areas. One of the locales was the White Mountain National Forest in New Hampshire where the couple marched with daughters Lissy and Clea.

Woodward said she was aware of the difference in status between herself and her husband in the industry. He was the big movie star and she was a character actress, and things would probably be more difficult if it were the other way round. Woodward told of the time when the couple were walking down the street and they passed two girls who gave the usual response to him, and then one asked, "Is that *her*?" The actress had passed through the identity crisis of being Mrs. Paul Newman, though admitted that she often felt like running through the halls shouting, "I'm me, me. I don't know what my name is, but I'm me." Woodward said the couple were definitely not content, and they could get a divorce next year but they were still married. Having known each other a long time, the Newmans felt very comfortable together. They liked each other and had great respect for one another, but didn't believe in being together all the time. About half the year was spent apart and she felt the separations helped rather than harmed their marriage. John Foreman reported that the actress had creative people stashed on both coasts and in Europe and neither rain, sleet, nor snow kept her from her appointed rounds of all that was beautiful and artistic.

The Newmans bought another house in Beverly Hills but still they preferred Connecticut. He said they were very whimsical about things like where to live and, being "seasons people," loved the weather change. For the actor's 50th birthday on January 26, 1975, he assembled his family, except for son Scott, in Westport to observe his morning swim in the Aspetuck River. A luncheon followed. At night, a coterie of friends were among the 50 guests who joined the family at La Cave Henri IV in Manhattan for an evening of dining, laughs and music. After this, the Newmans sent their children home and spent the night at a Park Avenue hotel. She commented on her husband still being a sex symbol, saying he received passionate love letters from teenagers, some as young as 13. These did not concern her, and the actress never had occasion to worry about older women having a serious crush on Newman because she was always watching.

Woodward was one of the honorees at the 1975 Annual Entertainment Hall of Fame Awards, held on February 22 at the Hollywood Palladium and televised by NBC. The Newmans were to be honored for their movie achievements at the annual benefit gala of the Film Society of Lincoln Center on May 5 in Avery Fisher Hall. The event was sponsored by the society in cooperation with the Museum of Modern Art, Lincoln Center for the Performing Arts and the City Center of Music and Drama. Proceeds would go to offset deficits in the society's programs as well as those incurred by the participating organizations. A film program exploring the careers of both performers would include excerpts from films in which they appeared individually as well as a clip from the as yet unreleased *The Drowning Pool*. A party and dance at the New York State Theater would follow.

They had been invited by Robert Redford to attend the opening of *The Great Waldo Pepper* (1975) at the Rivoli Theatre and a "country-style" picnic at the Rainbow Room afterward. The guests would arrive in the new, experimental double decker buses that would be used in New York in the summer. There were to be no klieg lights or limousines and people would wear jeans instead of "penguin suits" and jewels, since the event was designed as a benefit for a "Sun Fund" in awareness of solar energy. The actress wore her blonde hair cropped short and a trendy suede outfit with calf-high matching boots. At an auction, she made a winning bid on something that Newman reportedly did not like and he got angry. The couple had words and the tension between them lasted the rest of the evening.

Their publicists made them available for interviews. Woodward commented that it was very difficult to live with somebody for a long time and like him all the time. Newman said that in their relationship they had some pretty bad hassles but it would be pretty dull if their life together had been hassle-free. He realized it had been difficult for her having his older children to contend with. Most relationships fell apart because one partner usually grew emotionally or often professionally faster than the other, but Newman claimed the process for them was more or less equal. Her talents had not been buried in the kitchen while he went from triumph to triumph in a galaxy of beautiful people. They had grown together.

Woodward was to be involved in the opening weekend of America's Bicentennial. On April 20, the Bicentennial Committee to Westport's History on Wheels inaugurated a historic minibus tour of the town's historic sites was to open to the public in the summer. A 30-page text written by Mrs. Robert Potts was to be narrated on tape by the actress.

The Newmans commented about their forthcoming May 5 honor by the Film Society of Lincoln Center in an April 28 *Times* interview. Newman agreed to meet for lunch to talk about his individual and their intertwined careers, but she at first declined, having nothing to say about movies or about acting. But on the appointed day, they both appeared at one of their favorite restaurants. Newman merrily described his wife's unexpected presence as one of those tiny little bonuses in life, and they ordered half-caviar and half-chicken omelets. The couple felt abashed to be following such grand old masters as Charles Chaplin, Fred Astaire and Alfred Hitchcock, who were totally creative, as if they were being enshrined before their time. Woodward commented on the industry, saying it had to do with economics, being almost impossible to get a film on unless it was presold with her husband, Steve McQueen or Barbra Streisand. Another problem was bad scripts which were written viscerally and inarticulately. There was a kind of innocence when they started out but now she felt a little desperate, with the only meaningful thing in the last five years being a poetry jazz concert the actress had done recently. She only liked three of the 12 movies she had made—*Count Three and Pray*, *The Three Faces of Eve* and *Rachel, Rachel*—and had a lingering fondness for *From the Terrace*. The only one Woodward disliked from the beginning was *A Kiss Before Dying*. She didn't like to talk about acting, feeling it was very private, like not talking about one's sex life. An actor was like a magician. You didn't give away secrets.

At the gala benefit retrospective, the Newmans were seated with New York Mayor Abe Beame and his wife. Martin Balsam, the actress's *Summer Wishes, Winter Dreams* co-star, introduced ten Woodward film clips. When she spoke to the audience, she actress apologized for a show that ran longer than *Gone with the Wind*. The evening went on for several more hours, with a reception for the donors in the New York State Theater.

On June 10, 1976, Woodward, chairman of the Paul Taylor Dance Foundation, was to attend the dance company performance at the Lyceum Theater, to be followed by a champagne reception in the garden of New York's Federal house. On July 28, the Newmans attended the Gala Performance of American Ballet Theatre at New York's State Theater.

The actress narrated a segment of the "Bicentennial Minutes" televised on CBS. She told of a how Nathan Hale, a 21-year-old Connecticut schoolteacher, became a lieutenant in Washington's Continental Army and spy, and was executed by the British.

Woodward attended EST sessions for self-awareness training, reportedly an attempt to stop choosing to be in her husband's shadow and to stop feeling guilty and inadequate about being what she called a creative dilettante. The actress got so much out of it that she encouraged her children to do the same. Woodward never got Newman involved, even though he complained of feeling left out of what he saw as an exclusive little clique within the family. She also continued her dancing, wanting to keep in shape, especially when she saw the youthful bodies of her daughters and their friends who were constantly about the house. Newman joked that he kept in shape because she put him on a rope at the end of the car. His insurance value appealed to her because Woodward would undoubtedly outlive him and would like to collect as soon as possible. Newman said that Woodward also made sure that after jogging, he jumped into the ice-cold river to start his heart or stop it, one way or the other. He described his wife as awfully self-effacing. She denigrated her own talent, apparently feeling that when something came easily to her, it meant the result was no good. But ballet dancing didn't come easily to her.

The Newmans' patronage of dance was reported in the *Times* of August 18, after they gave $50,000 to the Los Angeles ballet which allowed for the opening of a new school. Woodward had been an avid attendee of Lincoln Center's ballet performances, as well as a donor and patroness. Newman often accompanied her to recitals, galas and benefits in support of dancers, dance education, and new dance companies. The couple traveled the United States to see performances, and especially attended ones in New York. They gave grant money and donated to the Royal Winnipeg Ballet, the Paul Taylor company for which the actress was on the board of directors, and many small dance troupes. She gave $120,000 in seed money, which a source claims came from the No Sutch Foundation that the Newmans had set up to help various charities and causes. Woodward also became a founding board member of Dancers. The new company wanted to challenge the assumption that the performing arts must be a money-losing proposition and was designed to provide an alternative for leading dance artists not satisfied with the traditional large ballet company. Dancers was to have a roster of 14 performers. The *Times* reported on August 31 that the company had made its debut in July at the Jacob's Pillow Dance Festival, with the performances financed by a $7600 gift from the actress. She was said to be a close friend of Dennis Wayne, the choreographer and creative director of the company, and a ballet enthusiast of long standing. Woodward had also given Wayne $20,000 for his company's week in New York.

Her involvement in Dancers supposedly led to trouble in the marriage when it was reported that she was spending more time than necessary with the handsome and heterosexual Wayne. He was unpopular because of the mixed grades he had received on his work but the actress was determined to keep him on. Some described him as a man who could play women like a flute and his relationship with her as typical of the networking that went on in the artistic world between creative types and ladies with money. But an observer noted that the way she looked at Wayne was like he was a bowl of cream and she the cat. She was said to have been attracted to him because he personified all of the things the actress missed in her husband: romance, tenderness, and a true love and understanding of art and culture.

The Newmans reportedly had a nasty public quarrel at Sardi's where they used salty language. For damage control, their publicist let the press know the couple was loving and only too happy to be interviewed provided it featured the both of them. In these interviews, the Newmans stated that a marriage that had lasted as long as theirs had also had some difficult moments. On November 1, they returned to Kenyon College where he screened *Rachel, Rachel* at night in the big campus assembly hall, and produced her from the audience to join him in the Q&A.

On January 29, 1976, in Washington's New Senate Office Building, Newman announced that the couple had agreed to raise $600,000 for a newly established Energy Action Committee. The liberal Democratic Committee which called itself a new national citizens' lobby had two major initial purposes: to prevent deregulation of natural gas prices and to propel through Congress legislation to break up the big oil companies into separate producing, refining and marketing entities.

Woodward was a guest on the February 14 episode of CBS-TV's *The Carol Burnett Show*, filmed in Hollywood. The show was written by Gary Belkin, Roger Beatty, Bill Richmond, Gene Perret, Rudy De Luca, Barry Levinson, Bo Kaprall, Pat Proft, Dick Clair and Jenna McMahon, and directed by Dave Powers. Costumes were by Bob Mackie and wigs by Roselle Friedland. Burnett commented at the start of the show that Woodward was an even nicer lady than she was a great actress. She appears in two sketches and the musical finale, as well as under the show's end credits, kissed by Burnett and Harvey Korman. In the sketch "The Family," Woodward plays Midge Gibson, an old school chum of Eunice's. She wears what appears to be a brunette wig with a side part and bleached bangs, and a low-cut purple-flowered knee-length black dress. The actress uses a Southern accent, sings, dances the can-can, laughs and plays drunk. She also stammers when Midge tells off Ed (Korman) and Mama Harper (Vicki Lawrence), which may have the context of her being drunk. In the second sketch, Woodward is Clarice Trickleson, a wallflower at a dance. The actress wears a brunette short curled wig with bangs and a blue-patterned short-sleeved floor-length round–collared dress. At one point she is approached by Korman playing a married man who misinterprets Clarice saying her feet are tired from dancing. Together the women duet to "Why Can't I?" and "Let's Be Buddies," revealing that Woodward can carry a tune even if she has not got much of a voice. The actress gets a funny line when Clarice says she wants to see the film *The Hindenburg*, thinking it might be nice to see somebody else have a disaster. In the musical finale, Woodward, Burnett and Vicki Lawrence sing and dance to "Everything Old Is New Again," wearing turn-of-the-century knee-length layered pastel-colored dresses and sun hats. Woodward's dress is purple, and under the hat her hair appears to be worn short and straight with bangs. She also dances with one of the chorus boys in choreography by Ernest Flatt.

The Yale Studio had a film documentary in development on Woodward, but this film was not made. The actress headed a drive to raise $5 million for Dancers and a Greenwich Village dance center. The center would have a 500-seat theater and a school, and would also be available for lease to other companies. She had always wanted to be part of the ballet world, but unfortunately couldn't dance, so the only other thing to do was to help others to dance. Woodward said her involvement with dance was a my-activity-my-time-my-money thing, and not her husband's, since he was involved with environmental concerns. She started her day like a serious ballerina, being at the barre at 9 a.m. five days week to keep in shape. At age 46, dance was marvelous therapy for the head as well as the body.

Stewart Stern brought her onto a new project that he had scripted, the adaptation of Flora Rheta Schreiber's novel *Sybil*. This was a medical case about Sybil Dorsett, a 29-year-old substitute art teacher in New York whose harrowing childhood in Willow Corners, Wisconsin, resulted in her developing 16 different personalities. Stern had read the actress parts of the script that she found very interesting. When he heard that the project was off, Stern went to the Newman house to have a hamburger and Woodward asked what had happened. Audrey Hepburn had been offered the title role but declined. The production company, Lorimar, wanted a star because they knew it was going to be a hard sell. Woodward felt she was no longer a star in films but could be a star on television, and Stern asked her to play Dr. Cornelia Wilbur, the psychiatrist who treats Sybil, to help get the project made. Woodward had decided that television, a return to her roots, was the logical step for her career. It was also where the kind of roles she longed for were only been done now. In addition, the actress had to act, otherwise she was going to a displaced person and impossible and her family would suffer as much as Woodward. Acting was for her an innate behavior, and like being born with a deformity: You not only learned to live with it, you wouldn't know how to live without it. She was also motivated by her need to make money, particularly for Dancers, which reportedly had taken all her earnings from 1975 on.

The actress thought she could play Cornelia, but not as the doctor really was. The real doctor had flaming red hair on top of a craggy, lived–in, masculine face, and she liked to wear theatrical makeup of blue eye shadow and enormous false eyelashes, always with one that was off and sticking up. Stern brought the doctor to dinner at the Newman house on the same night that Fred Astaire attended. Cornelia arrived first and when Astaire appeared she almost fainted, and the actress thought that was wonderful. It made her love her immediately and Woodward found Cornelia to be a marvelous woman. She agreed to play the part, also because the actress would do anything for Stern, and called Lee Rich, Lorimar's founder and the supervisor of the production. Her casting therefore allowed them to look for a Sybil who wasn't a star. One star was interested, Natalie Wood, but Stern thought she was wrong for it. He wanted an unknown.

An actress was hired for the day of auditions, to read as Cornelia with people. But Woodward wanted to read Cornelia since she would be working with the chosen actress on the show. She came in from 9 a.m. to 6 p.m., allowing all the hopefuls to sit on her lap for the scene that was taken from the screenplay. The actress joked that sometimes she was squashed but Stern said Woodward showed respect and reverence and gave them everything in her readings, time after time. It got to be lunchtime after seeing six girls and Sally Field was announced as the next to be read. Stern suggested they do her fast because then they could go to eat, thinking she was going to be nothing. Woodward was also skeptical as she only knew Field from the television comedy series *The Flying Nun* (1967–70). In her memoir *In Pieces*, Field recalled she read with Stern as Cornelia, then returned to read again through April and the beginning of May and did a screen test with the older actress. But Woodward said she initially read with Field, who astonished her. They *played* the scene that the young actress had memorized, she crawling on the floor and weeping and Woodward crawling after her. Field then kneeled and laid her head on Woodward's lap and sobbing, wiped her nose on the older actress' sweater. Although they had never met before, Field instantly fell in love with Woodward because she opened her heart and her arms. The older actress believed Field had totally absorbed the character and everyone watching was crying. Field said some didn't feel she was proper casting but the older actress wouldn't do the show without her. The two did a filmed test and Field was hired.

There were problems with director Anthony Page. After a week of rehearsal, he asked for a full run-through of the four-hour piece at performance level. Field resisted, wanting to save it for the camera, but the director saw this as her being unable to play the role. She said Woodward agreed that the run-through was irrational, unreasonable and potentially destructive, but they would do it. Huddled together on the rehearsal sofa, the older actress took her hand and told Field to do the best she could. Presumably this satisfied Page, for the time being, as the next day the actors flew to New York and began shooting. But he continued to disagree with Field's interpretation, and after the third day she was taken to Woodward's dressing room and told that Page was to be fired. Another source claims that Woodward was shocked when she heard about the director's firing, though could still have known of it before Field, as the younger actress claims. The Lorimar executives justified the action, saying their vision wasn't the same as his and he had gotten in the way of Field's performance. The company was shut down for one day, then they shot on a Friday with the assistant director filling in. On Sunday, the cast were informed that director Daniel Petrie had been hired. He told them he wanted more time to rehearse and they had as long as they needed before shooting would resume. Woodward didn't know how the extra rehearsal time was possible with the budget and the schedule, but Petrie managed it. She never felt discomfort, nor did Field. Between scenes, they never left the set, with Woodward sitting in a chair doing her needlepoint. They all felt the need to protect Field and gave her the space to work. After the 16-page scene was done, where she had to portray five different personalities in rapid succession, the older actress turned to her and said that next to that, *The Three Faces of Eve* was a piece of cake.

NBC broadcast the four-hour miniseries over two nights, November 14 and 15, 1976. It was shot on location

Woodward (back to tree) and Sally Field in the television miniseries *Sybil* (1976).

in New York and at Warner Bros. in Burbank. Woodward is billed first, although she plays a supporting role to Field, and also narrates. Her hair by Janis Clark is a red straight short-wedge style with bangs, and clothes by Patricia Norris include repeated outfits which have context for the 11 years Cornelia treated Sybil. The role sees her conduct a neurological examination and hypnosis, and speak French. The actress makes Cornelia funny. Director Petrie gives her two closeups where she looks beautiful as the doctor listens to Sybil, and her best scene is perhaps when she talks to Sybil's father, Willard Dorsett (William Prince), about his daughter's childhood injuries and her now deceased mother.

John J. O'Connor in *The New York Times* wrote that Woodward remained convincing and sympathetic as the psychiatrist despite the character's tendency to call people "sweetie." Both Field and Woodward were nominated for the Outstanding Lead Actress in a Drama or Comedy Special, and Field won. *Sybil* was remade as a 2007 made-for-TV movie with Jessica Lange as Cornelia.

Woodward's praise for Field to the press was thought to be unheard of, for an actress to laud another's work in such an unselfish manner. The younger actress wrote that Woodward did not attend the industry screening for the show on November 6 because she could not stand looking at herself on-screen, and also refused to attend the Emmy Awards show.

As a board member for the Paul Taylor Dance Company, Woodward was to attend a gala benefit on November 1 at Washington's Lisner Auditorium. It was to aid the company which had announced two weeks prior its indefinite disbandment due to financial difficulties.

On September 29, the Newmans' Connecticut home was burglarized, and among the stolen items was Woodward's Oscar. Police recovered it and detectives in Westport were awarded makeshift Oscars by Police Chief William Stefan for having broken up a burglary ring preying on local stores and the homes of the wealthy. Woodward was said to have had her award returned to her in a mock ceremony.

She attended the SCCA National Championships at Road Atlanta on October 31 where Newman raced. The actress was photographed in the passenger seat of his car after his victory. She spoke on the WNYC-FM talk-radio show *Speaking of Dance* on November 13.

Woodward was a guest on the November 17 episode of ABC-TV's *The John Denver Special*. It was written by Marty Farrell and the director was Bill Davis. She and Denver did a skit in the pond at Universal where the shark from *Jaws* lived, parodying *Gone with the Wind*. The actress wore a Southern-belle organza gown and a straw picture hat, sitting in a rowboat munching on an apple and clutching a parasol. The singer was her beau, working the oars. The music from *Jaws* was heard and the shark rose up from the water and devoured them and half the boat. The pair sang "Getting to Know You" in another segment.

In the fall, she attended the wrap party for Newman's film *Buffalo Bill and the Indians, or Sitting Bull's History Lesson*, a comedy western shot in Alberta, Canada. Woodward flew in to join her husband, who had organized a prairie clambake.

At this time the family had trouble with their daughter Nell, who had gotten into drugs. The teenager dropped out of high school and had several car accidents learning to drive, and by the age of 21 she was way behind her peers. The Newmans also attempted to help Scott with his drug problem by paying for a clinical psychologist, Mark Weinstein.

The boy supposedly blamed his father for ruining his life and Woodward "for trying to send me off to another world."

Woodward was the narrator and played Marmee March in NBC-TV's ballet version of *Little Women* on December 14. The show was written by June Reig based on the novel by Louisa May Alcott and directed by Sid Smith. It centered on four sisters and their romances and tragedies while growing into womanhood in Concord, Massachusetts, during the latter part of the 19th century. The actress provided introductions to a number of danced scenes taking the form of solos, duets or ensembles.

Woodward's father Wade, 75, died on December 16 in his home in Decatur, Georgia.

On January 19, 1977, the Newmans participated in the 1977 Inaugural Committee Gala, a televised pre-inaugural concert at the John F. Kennedy Center for the Performing Arts which was broadcast on CBS. The show was subsequently titled *Inaugural Eve Gala Performance* and *The 1977 New Spirit Inaugural Concert*. On the night, she suggested that they were gathered together "to celebrate a country, its spirit and its art." A source claims the couple spoke at the gala held in Washington on January 20, the night Jimmy Carter was inaugurated as president of the United States.

The April 3 *New York Times* had an article about Dancers which mentioned the balletomane actress. Woodward said she had been involved in other ballet companies but generally speaking they had been eclectic in their intentions, not really having a dream or a total plan for what they wanted to do. Dennis Wayne did. He was the perfect kind of person to be artistic director, as he had energy and rare enthusiasm and was also a hell of a good fundraiser. The company was reported to be $54,000 in the red but the actress was to co-sign a $400,000 cash credit line.

She found a new cause, the National Society for Autistic Children. The actress had hesitated when they asked her for help, having long decided to never be an honorary anything or lend her name to a letterhead unless she was willing to get involved in the work. But Woodward couldn't turn them down and became the Society's honorary national chairperson, and got involved. She admired the devotion of those parents who could have put their children in an institution but didn't. Their special kind of love didn't stop and that's what brought her to the Society.

The Newmans also worked for the Native Americans on the Bellington Reservation and the Washington Energy Action Committee, whose purpose was to pressure the government into a saner energy policy.

An acting opportunity surfaced which Woodward very much wanted to do. This was the Arthur Laurents script for the film *The Turning Point*, about the world of ballet. She was attracted to the story of two women, an aging prima ballerina and her former best friend, who had been a dancer but gave up her career to marry and have children. A source claims that Woodward brought the property to Fox's head of production, Alan Ladd, Jr. He loved the script but not her and told the actress so. Another source claimed this was unlikely given that Newman later worked for Ladd and Fox on the science fiction mystery film *Quintet* (1979). The film romance was made with Shirley MacLaine in the part Woodward presumably sought and Anne Bancroft as the ballerina. Both received Oscar nominations.

Woodward was to appear in *The End*, a film comedy to star and be directed by Burt Reynolds. But since it was not to go into production until the late summer, the actress had time to do another role. In the spring of 1977, the Newmans went to London as she was to do a new television show. The press speculated that they had decided to live apart when Woodward took an apartment by herself. Newman returned to the States to babysit since now she was the one working on location and her husband the one to look after their family at home.

Susan Newman proved to be a point of contention between her mother and the Newmans, since Jackie could not compete in any financial way with them in providing luxuries. There were reportedly tears and recriminations when the couple gave the girl a fur coat. Scott was another continuing problem. They got him into the care of a highly regarded addiction counselor, whom he saw along with his psychologist and a nutritionist.

Woodward appeared in the December 31 episode of the British Granada television series *Laurence Olivier Presents* entitled "Best Play of the Year 1950—*Come Back Little Sheba* by William Inge," broadcast on NBC. The play was originally produced on Broadway in 1950 (February 15 to July 29 at the Booth Theatre) with Shirley Booth as the Midwestern housewife Lola Delaney. Her performance won her the Tony Award for Best Actress. She repeated it in the 1952 Paramount film version, and won the Best Actress Academy Award. The new version, directed by Silvio Narizzano, was set in a small uni-

versity town in the Midwest in the 1940s and centered on Doc Delaney (Olivier), a chiropractor and recovering alcoholic, and Lola (Woodward), his dowdy, unambitious wife. She is top-billed before the title and plays the leading role. Costumes are by Frances Tempest. Woodward wears her hair in a blonde short straight style with end curls and a side part. The actress uses an indeterminate accent and seems too physically thin for the "sloppy" character, despite apparently wearing padding on her middle. The role sees her get chased by Doc with a hatchet. She uses bad pantomime when Lola panics over the bottle of whisky that Doc has taken, and the climactic chase reads as unintentionally funny. Woodward is better in Lola's silent reactions to the drunken Doc being handled by Ed (Bruce Boa) and Elmo (Ed Devereaux). Her best scene is perhaps when Lola telephones her mother to ask to come home, where she cries and then transitions to acceptance of the rejection of her request. John J. O'Connor in *The New York Times*

Woodward with Laurence Olivier in the made-for-television *Come Back Little Sheba* (1977).

wrote that she was simply miscast, saying her confidence and intelligence were qualities that worked against the portrayal.

The actress told Olivier how she had jumped into his limousine at the Atlanta premiere of *Gone with the Wind*, and he claimed to remember the incident vividly. Woodward said she found it difficult working with him. She adored Olivier and thought he was brilliant as Doc, but there was no way the two could communicate. She wondered if perhaps the actor had chosen not to communicate, because at the time he was very fragile and fairly much to himself. Woodward returned to the States and stayed in a bungalow in the Beverly Hills Hotel.

Scripted by Jerry Belson, United Artists' *The End* was shot from July 11 to October on locations in California and at Goldwyn in Hollywood. Burt Reynolds starred as television real estate salesman Wendell Sonny Lawson, who learns he is dying of a toxic blood disease, and Woodward played Jessie, his English teacher ex-wife. The actress is billed fifth after the film's title, with an "and" credit. Her hair is by Dorothy Byrne and is worn in a blonde short straight full style with a side part. Woodward is heard before she is seen and the role has her cook and in another scene she kicks Sonny. The actress is funny in her anger. Her best scene is perhaps when Jessie is alone with Sonny in a room at the La Playa Psychiatric Hospital; Woodward is broad but still funny and sincere. Sally Field is also in the film but she has no scenes with Woodward.

The film was released on May 10, 1978, with the taglines "Are there laughs before death?" and "Think of death as a pie in the face from God." *Variety* wrote that Woodward was poorly utilized though adroitly cast. The film was a box office success.

Woodward now did what she liked to do, which was to act. If she did so in a film, it was mostly for the money because it was very expensive supporting a ballet company.

Burt Reynolds was glad to cast her, in gratitude for the actress's encouragement when he was a fresh-from-Florida apprentice actor. In his memoir *But Enough About Me*, Reynolds wrote that he first met her in the mid–1950s when they appeared in the Hyde Park Playhouse in a New York summer stock production of *Tea and Sympathy*. He says Woodward played a teacher and he played Al, though another source claims she was not in the play but only visiting to see the show. The actress said she never actually saw him perform. Woodward knew him as this cute, shy, attractive boy who had the kind of lovely personality that made you want to do something for him. Reynolds said she introduced him to her agent, who signed him. The actor thought Woodward had a crush on him though when they had a drink after one performance, she told him about her boyfriend, Paul Newman. The next weekend, Newman came up to see her and the actress introduced them. A couple of months later, she invited the actor to a party in Manhattan at Gore Vidal's. Vidal was hostile towards Reynolds because of the obvious way he was chasing her, and provoked him to behave like an idiot in front of Woodward. She drove him home and when he started to apologize, the actress said Vidal was a brilliant man but he was very drunk and testing him. Reynolds thought he had flunked but she felt Reynolds had passed but just in a different way.

At this time Woodward commented that what she had gone through was a natural phenomenon for a woman of her age. She had been raised to stay home with her children but then to get out and free herself. She hoped they would understand that although the children were adored, Woodward would not have them if she had to do it all over again, or get married either. She thought actors didn't make very good parents, because they were frustrated when not working. She believed getting married and having children should not be the sole aims of life. You had to grow up to become a human being too.

She was one of 12 women in television and film to be chosen by the American Film Institute Center for Advanced Studies to take part in the institute's 1977-78 Directing Workshop for Women. The workshop began in late August in Beverly Hills, and Woodward wrote, directed and edited a short film called *Lover*.

8

See How She Runs

Woodward returned to television for *See How She Runs* (1978), which was shot on location in Boston in the fall of September 1977. It had a teleplay by Marvin A. Gluck and was directed by Richard T. Heffron. Top-billed Woodward played Betty Quinn, a 40-year-old divorced teacher at Abraham Lincoln Junior High School. Her life is changed by her decision to enter the Boston Marathon. Her costumes by Mary Ellen Winston include a repeated yellow scarf and brown overcoat and blue t-shirt and shorts for the race. Hair by Colleen Callaghan is worn in two red-colored styles, one short and the other shorter with bangs and a side part. The role is perhaps the most physical for Woodward to date, since she plays a jogger, and we also see her punch the Handsome Man (Jim Houghton) who attacks her, and fall. Director Heffron devotes 17 minutes to the climactic race, though he includes cutaways and slow motion and deprives Beth of her victory over the finish line with a freeze frame just before she reaches it. She is funny, especially when angry, and her best scene is perhaps after Betty is attacked and she sobs to her daughters Janey (Lissy Newman) and Kathy (Mary-Beth Manning). The scene allows her to mix crying and hysterical laughter at the idea that she might have broken the Man's nose.

Broadcast by CBS on February 1, 1978, the show prompted John J. O'Connor of *The New York Times* to write that Woodward gave one of the best performances of her career, being thoroughly and affectingly convincing. The show won Emmys for her as Outstanding Lead Actress in a Drama or Comedy Special and for Jimmy Haskell for Outstanding Achievement in Music Composition for a Special (Dramatic Underscore).

The actress' habit of jogging three miles a day had gradually increased to running, and she said it was great fun and good for the behind. During filming, Woodward ran four to six miles a day before collapsing at the Somerville Holiday Inn outside Boston where the Newmans were staying.

Dennis Wayne, interviewed in the November 18 *Times*, said he met Woodward when he had an acting part in *Summer Wishes, Winter Dreams*, playing Bobby's friend. The dancer was then in the Joffrey Ballet. She had admired him as a dancer, and he spoke to her about a company. Wayne said Woodward was one of *the* most selfless people.

The Newmans appeared in the *All Star Tribute to Elizabeth Taylor* broadcast on CBS on December 1. The show was written by Paul W. Keyes, Marc London and Bo Howard and directed by Dick McDonough. The event was held by Variety Clubs International at the Warner Bros. Burbank Studios to benefit underprivileged and handicapped children. The actress, seated at a table between Newman and Henry Fonda, wore her hair in a short straight red style with a side part. She did not make a speech but her husband did.

Taylor commented in her thank you speech that she was doubly blessed that both Newmans attended.

The *Times* of December 9 reported that Woodward was on the board of the Children's Storefront, a free nursery school for children with special problems in New York. On December 13, it was reported that the Newmans had donated a personalized Christmas stocking, filled with goodies, for a charity party for Trinity Missions. The stockings were to be auctioned at the Christmas party to be held the night of December 15 at the Starlight Roof of the Waldorf Astoria Hotel. The couple wrapped their gifts in red- and white-striped paper, and she put hers in a calico stocking intersected with calico hearts.

She appeared on the television documentary special *The American Film Institute Salute to Henry Fonda a.k.a. AFI Life Achievement Award: A Tribute to Henry Fonda*, which was shot at the Beverly Hilton Hotel a few weeks prior and broadcast on CBS on March 15. The show, written by Hal Kanter and directed by Marty Pasetta, was nominated for the Emmy Award for Outstanding Program Achievement in a Special. The Newmans were part of the television musical special *The Stars Salute Israel at 30* which was broadcast on ABC on May 7.

Woodward did summer stock in Massachusetts, celebrating the 50th anniversary of the Berkshire Theater Festival in Stockbridge by appearing in Lillian Hellman's *The Children's Hour*, which opened July 26. The director was Arthur Sherman, and she played schoolteacher Martha Dobie. Richard Eder of *The New York Times* wrote that Woodward managed to suggest conflagration hidden behind a warm exterior.

Woodward in the made-for-television movie *See How She Runs* (1978).

At this time, Woodward's mother was exhibiting serious mental health issues. She had been deteriorating for years, and at first her daughter had attributed the symptoms to her being erratic and temperamental. When Woodward's Aunt Dae-Dae brought her mother to see her perform in stock, Woodward saw evidence that something had to be done. Her mother was diagnosed with Alzheimer's disease, a condition about which little was known at the time.

Sources differ as to when Newman began working on Kenyon College's production of *C.C. Pyle and the Bunion Derby*, a Michael Cristofer play about con men in the 1920s. Some say it was the summer of 1978 and others the fall. Some sources claim Woodward was with him, being a friend of the writer, and others say she was not. One source claims that the actress came out to see the play because she was already on the school's board of directors. In the play was Tait Ruppert, whom Woodward would say was the perfect Marchbanks in George Bernard Shaw's *Candida*, a project she had wanted to do on stage.

She joined Newman in his car for the victory lap at the Lime Rock Park race on September 5. Twelve days later, she attended the 30th Annual Primetime Emmy Awards which was held at the Pasadena Civic Auditorium and broadcast by CBS. The show was written by Hildy Parks and directed by Clark Jones. She was a presenter and she accepted the Outstanding Lead Actress in a Drama or Comedy Special award for *See How She Runs*.

The Newmans co-hosted the television documentary *A Salute to American Imagination* which was held at the Ambassador College auditorium in Pasadena and broadcast on CBS on October 5. The show, written by Rod Warren and directed by Don Mischer, celebrated the Ford Motor Company's 75th anniversary.

On November 19, 1978, Newman's 28-year-old son Scott was living in the Ramada Inn in West Los Angeles. Around 11:30 p.m., paramedics came to his room, found him not breathing, and took him to the emergency room of Los Angeles New Hospital. At 1:07 the next morning, Scott died from an accidental overdose of drugs and alcohol, though there was also a rumor that the overdose was a suicide. His father or the couple drove to Cleveland the next day. Then there was a flight to Los Angeles for the funeral, a small private affair for family members. Jackie and Woodward both attended. Scott's body was cremated on November 27 and the ashes interred at the Westwood Village Mortuary. While Newman did not speak publicly about the death of his son, Woodward did. She said that he was a bright kid, and maybe if Scott had known early on about the dangers of drugs, he wouldn't have started. The actress believed you had to do a positive thing for kids since negative things like throwing them in jail or sending them somewhere to be dried wouldn't work. What finally happened to Scott could have happened a lot of other times much earlier. The family knew it and they had to live with that. She also commented that maybe it would have been a good idea if they had been able to announce to the public what was happening in their household. Woodward praised Carol Burnett for doing so about her daughter's drug problem, and also discussed Nell's own short-lived one.

Woodward joined the board of directors of the Scott Newman Foundation, which Newman formed with several friends. It was dedicated to the cause of promoting anti-drug education by awarding grants to writers, producers and directors for prime-time TV programs, films and lecture tours. Because the Newmans were involved, the foundation drew Hollywood stars to the casts of its informative programs. The actress said that they didn't want Scott to have lived in vain. Within a few years, the couple doubled down in their war on drugs by donating $1.2 million to the University of Southern California to create the Scott Newman Chair in Pharmacy and the Scott Newman Center for Drug Abuse Prevention and Health Communications.

On December 3, Woodward attended a gala held to celebrate the 50th anniversary of the Neighborhood Playhouse School of the Theater, and the formation of the playhouse's new repertory company. The evening began earlier at the Shubert Theater, where Woodward and other Playhouse graduates gathered to pay tribute to the school and its renowned acting teacher, Sanford Meisner.

She made a cameo appearance for friend and director George Englund (producer of *See How She Runs* and director of *Signpost to Murder*) in his made-for-TV movie *A Christmas to Remember*, broadcast on CBS on December 20, 1978. The show was filmed in Rush City, Minnesota, and had a teleplay by Stewart Stern and the uncredited Miles

Hood Swarthout, based on the novel *The Melodeon* by Glendon Swarthout. George Parry starred as "Rusty" McCloud, a Philadelphia city-bred teenager who during the Great Depression is sent by his mother Mildred (Woodward) to live with his grandparents on their Hadleyville, Minnesota, farm at Christmas. Woodward is fourth-billed with a "Guest appearance by." She is in two scenes, with costume by Susan Hum and hair worn in a period red-colored short sculpted style with a side part. John J. O'Connor of *The New York Times* wrote that Woodward was effective.

In December, the Newmans did promotional spots that ran on ABC television for "Who Are the DeBolts—and Where Did They Get 19 Kids?," an edited-down version of the John Korty–directed biographical documentary which was broadcast on December 17. The theatrical version had been released on December 5, 1977, and had won the Best Documentary Feature Academy Award. The film told the story of Dorothy and Bob DeBolt's tale of the struggles and joys involved in their 19 adopted children, many of them physically disabled war orphans. The show also won the Outstanding Individual Achievement–Informational Program Emmy Award.

In 1978, the Newmans donated $25,000 to stage a one-day Nuclear War Conference in Washington.

Woodward visited Kalaleu, Hawaii, when Newman shot the Warner Bros. action adventure *When Time Ran Out ...* (1980). Sources differ as to when filming began on location, with one saying it was February 8 or 9, and another April 24. Either date would have been late if the visit was made to celebrate the couple's wedding anniversary on January 29. Newman presented his wife with a new evening gown in a box, an item he had picked out personally. After the actress changed into it, they flew out to a deserted golf course on the coast. There, an elegant and intimate dinner for two was served at a shady spot beside the ocean, accompanied by a string quartet. But as the couple ate, Kalaleu was hit by an earthquake. She commented that her husband picked the nicest places.

On March 30, they attended the Los Angeles World Premiere of the romantic comedy adventure *A Little Romance* (1979) honoring Laurence Olivier in Century City. On April 16, Woodward was honored as a founder and patron of dance companies at a supper-dance by the American Jewish Congress at the Promenade of the New York State Theater. The dance took place after the American Ballet Theater's opening night at the Metropolitan Opera House, where she received a lithograph of a dancer by Aaron Schickler.

The New York Times of June 28 reported that she was one of the celebrities narrating 30 and 60-second announcements by Action for Children's Television, a national citizens' group based in Newtonville, Massachusetts. Their radio announcements were about the influence of television on children, made to some 200 radio stations across the U.S.

On June 9 and 10, 1979, Newman participated in the Le Mans 24-hour race held two hours south of Paris. Woodward reportedly tried to dissuade him from the notoriously grueling event, but to no avail. After he and his team finished second, he put through a trans–Atlantic call home but she was out—watching their daughter Clea in a horse show.

The actress did not attend the Lime Rock Park race on July 1 in Lakeville, Connecticut, where her husband drove, because she was in California making a film. This was presumably the made-for-television drama *The Streets of L.A.* which was broadcast on CBS on November 13, 1979, with the tagline "A woman is tormented by Barrio hoodlums and sets out to bring them to justice. A real life drama from the General Electric Theater." The teleplay was by Marvin A. Gluck and the director was Jerrold Freeman. The true story centered on 43-year-old Carol Schramm (Woodward), a real estate agent for PWC realtors whose car tires are slashed by three Mexican youths led by the 17-year-old Ramon "Gallo" Zamora (Fernando Allende), busboy at the Fiore D'Italia Restaurant and an illegal immigrant. She is billed before the show's title and plays the leading role. Her hair by Ellen Powell is worn in a blonde short sculpted style with bangs. Wardrobe, furnished by Lillie Rubin and South/Southwest, includes one repeated blue suit representing the attire of a woman on a budget. The role sees Woodward get hosed by Gallo, attack him in the restaurant kitchen, and be attacked by and fight two warehouse winos. She makes Carol's anger funny. Director Freeman provides a full length camera-tilt up her body for the scene where she sees her tires slashed. Woodward's best scene is perhaps when she explains to her brother Walter Kiner (Michael C. Gwynne) about the bad year she's had. John J. O'Connor in *The New York Times* wrote that she was feisty and spunky, but had to work hard to avoid making Carol seem a meanie in her quest for money.

The actress commented that what happened to Carol pushed her over the edge and she simply had to confront the wrongdoers. Angry because everything was so messed up in her life, the woman found that the young Chicano men who slashed her tires were angry too, for many of the same reasons. And so the experience was traumatic—a total culture shock—for them all.

The actress donated a jewel-trimmed black chiffon dress for the annual "POSH sale," which benefited the New York Association for the Blind and ran from October 30 to November 2 at New York's Lighthouse. The couple narrated *Angel Death*, a television documentary made by David Begelman about the dangers of the highly toxic drug phencyclidine hydrochloride, commonly known as PCP and angel dust. The show was broadcast on October 29 on New York's WNEW-TV. Using documentary footage of people under the influence, it focused on a number of individuals who had become habitual users, some of them teenagers.

In an interview, the actress said she had never been bothered much by the public. She said she was not easily recognized, having no image to fasten on and tending to look different in every film. Her husband was the one who suffered from constantly being chased by fans because he was as recognizable as Mount Rushmore. That could be bothersome, but as the couple had gotten older, people treated them in that way. Rather than grabbing at them, they wanted instead to talk about things they had done—in a good way. The actress denied that she hated Newman being a race car driver. She screamed and yelled and cursed like any other spectator and rode on every victory lap. About her marriage, the actress believed in the advice her grandmother once gave her: When you pick a husband, remember that you had to be able to talk to him across the breakfast table for 50 years.

She reported Dancers was having its up and downs and Woodward didn't know whether it would survive. The possibility of survival of any art form in the U.S.—but especially ballet and opera—was very low because there was little or no government involvement. The closest she ever got to politics was serving on the dance panel of the National Endowment of the Arts for three years, and it came as a real shock to realize that the Pentagon spent more in one day than the government gave to the arts in a year. Britain and Russia fully supported the arts and the actress wondered why America had to be different when the country had more money than anybody.

She directed "Thanksgiving," the November 20 episode of the ABC-TV family drama *Family*, shot at the Fox Studios in Hollywood. The show guest-starred Henry Fonda, her *Big Hand for the Little Lady* co-star.

Her next acting project was again for television. Susan Newman and documentary filmmaker Jill Marti acquired the rights to *The Shadow Box*, another play by Michael Cristofer, that dealt with the lives of patients in a cancer hospice. It had been produced on Broadway, running at the Morosco Theatre from March 31 to October 29, 1977, and the Lunt-Fontanne Theatre from October 31 to December 31, 1977. The play won the 1977 Pulitzer Prize for drama. The women wanted to produce it as a TV movie and brought in Woodward to play the flamboyant ex-wife of one of the patients. She was said to have suggested Susan become involved in the first place and in turn suggested they ask Paul Newman to direct. He was attracted to the project, having previously directed a Cristofer play, but also because it gave his wife an opportunity to essay a voluptuous kinky character like her real self. Television networks were wary of the grim material but the producers produced reviews which said how funny the play was, as well as having the Newmans attached to the project. ABC agreed to finance and granted the production the right to a two-week rehearsal period.

The actress first had to complete another made-for-television film, *Crisis at Central High,* which was shot on location in Dallas and Arkansas and broadcast on CBS on February 4, 1981. The teleplay was by Richard Levinson and William Link based on the book by Elizabeth P. Huckaby and the director was Lamont Johnson. This was the true story of the federally ordered integration of nine black children into the white Central High School in Little Rock, Arkansas, in 1957. Woodward played the leading role, "Liz" Huckaby, the school's girl's vice principal and English teacher, and was also the show's narrator. Her hair by Monique De Sart is worn in a gray sculpted short style with a center part, and the costume designer has Liz wear a bedtime hairnet, and repeats some outfits as befits a high school teacher. The actress uses a Southern accent and the role sees her use a typewriter and be mildly attacked by Mrs. Kirby (Suzie Humphreys). Liz gets a funny line after her husband Glenn (Henderson Forsythe) tells her she looks fine in what she is wearing, saying, "Why do men think fine is a compliment?" Woodward is funny. In her best scene, Liz observes Donna Kirby (Shannon John) fail to provoke Ernest Green (Calvin Levels) in the school cafeteria. The actress' expression changes from laughing at something someone off-camera has said, concern when she sees Donna and an awareness of what she is attempting, to smiling and laughing when she sees that Ernest ignores Donna. *The New York Times*' John J. O'Connor wrote that Woodward's character was superbly realized and yet another tribute to her remarkable versatility. She was nominated for the Outstanding Lead Actress in a Limited Series or Special Emmy Award.

Woodward commented that Sandy Meisner used to say it took 20 years to make an actor. You couldn't just learn the craft; it became an innate thing, like playing the violin. She didn't prepare consciously—asking who the character was, what she was doing, why she was going into a scene, and what her action was. There was a time when the actress had done those things but now her subconscious took on technique, and she automatically came in with something. Woodward compared the process to Yehudi Menuhin not needing to ask where he put his fingers to get that note. It was said that she initially wanted to play one of the drabber parts in *The Shadow Box*, like the woman with a son whose husband is dying or the self-sacrificing daughter of an elderly dying lady. But Newman was fed up seeing her play frumps, so Valerie Harper and Melinda Dillon, respectively, took those parts. Woodward said one night as they sat in the Jacuzzi drinking wine that she finally saw that her husband was right about her playing the part. He was cueing her and the whole bizarre atmosphere lent itself to the craziness of the role. In rehearsal, the actress had tremendous difficulty, supposedly troubled by the character's husband being bisexual and how it reminded her of the rumors about Newman over the years. But he said she finally got it when she glued on the red fingernails the character wore.

It was supposedly Woodward who suggested casting Sylvia Sidney as the elderly dying lady. The part had been rewritten as a man and been offered to Laurence Olivier, who declined. The Newmans visited Sidney at her Connecticut home to offer her the part.

They rented a house in Malibu and the production was set up at a Salvation Army camp in Calabasas, California. Interiors were reportedly shot in Hollywood. Sources differ as to when production took place—one claims it was in the winter of 1979 and another the summer of 1980. Christopher Plummer was cast as Brian, and he said it was always slightly uncomfortable for the other performers when a husband directed his wife. But Plummer had the distinct impression that when they went home, the couple didn't talk about the project at all.

Woodward commented about working again with Newman, saying when they did so, that became their primary relationship. He was one of the best directors the actress had ever worked with, and his one special strength was to keep her from crying. Other directors seemed to be unable to restrain her tendency, since Woodward said she cried when happy and sad and no matter what.

The Shadow Box (the title was in lower case on screen) had a teleplay by Michael Cristofer based on his play. Three terminally ill cancer patients dwell in separate cottages on a hospital's grounds in California, where they are attended and visited by both family and close friends. Top-billed Woodward played Beverly, ex-wife of Brian (the part Patricia Elliot had played on Broadway). Her hair by Jerry Turnage is worn in a brunette straight style with a side part and bangs, and the costume designer gives her only one costume— cream-colored patterned pajamas with the top worn without a bra with a green waist sash and a yellow overcoat. The role has Woodward hum, use a Russian accent, and be slapped by and heartily slap Mark (Ben Masters). Her best scene is perhaps when Beverly drunkenly shows Brian and Mark her jewelry as mementos of her sexual partners with Woodward using physicality for sexual positions and the location of the jewels on her body.

The Shadow Box aired on December 28, 1980. *The New York Times*' John J. O'Connor wrote that Woodward revealed still new layers of expertise.

The Newmans acquired A.E. Hotchner's quasi-autobiographical novel *King of the Hill*, about an adolescent growing up in St. Louis in the 1930s, for filming by their production company, with Newman to direct. Instead it would be made by director Steven Soderbergh and released in 1993.

Woodward was quoted in a January 24, 1980, article in the *Times* by AlJean Harmetz. A report by the Screen Actors Guild claimed that when women reached the age of 40, they became almost invisible in movies and on television. The actress said her husband got prettier but she got older.

Woodward was the narrator of the music biographical documentary *Fred Astaire: Puttin' On His Top Hat* (1980), a.k.a. *Fred Astaire: Change Partners and Dance*, broadcast on PBS on March 10, 1980. The show was written by John L. Miller and directed by David Heeley. It was nominated for the Outstanding Program Achievement–Special Class Emmy Award.

Woodward visited family friend Jim Padula, who was dying in Norfolk Hospital, while Newman was making the crime drama *Fort Apache the Bronx* (1981) on location in New York. For 20 years Padula had been a jack-of-all-trades on their Westport house. One day when he was working there, the actress brought him a tray of baked Toll House cookies and she asked him to teach her how to lay bricks. The couple had also sent him Christmas presents that ranged from a pool table to a Boston Whaler. Padula became afflicted with stomach cancer and on many afternoons Woodward went to the hospital to chat and do her knitting.

In a March 30 *Times* article by Marcia Cohen about how prominent parents govern their children's television habits, the Newmans reported they required their children to be engaged in some other activity while the set was on. Lissy was 14 when she had the urge to watch late-night television, and Woodward laid down the law, allowing one-half hour per week, except for weekends. After endless battles, the actress prevailed. For Lissy, the "something else" was drawing or painting and for Clea it was needlepoint. The Newmans didn't have the same battle with Nell since she preferred to read.

Woodward was the narrator of the documentary short *The Power to Change*, which screened at the San Francisco International Film Festival in the spring of 1980 with the tagline "A timely and important film about ENERGY conservation." It was written by Melvin Farman and Jamil Simon, and directed by Simon. The short featured eight projects that were developed by people across the U.S. as ways to conserve energy, following the oil crisis of the 1970s. These included solar-heated barns and greenhouses, urban composting to reclaim vacant city lots, recycled wine bottles and a wind-driven automobile.

For Nell's 21st birthday on April 8, the couple sent her to the Road Atlanta Race School. Woodward said she went to the school to get over her fear of driving fast. On July 5 the actress attended the Lime Rock Auto Race in Lime Rock, Connecticut, where Newman raced.

In 1979, Woodward she had planned on saving a certain house in Westport to create an arts center but while the actress was away in California, it was torn down. She supposedly blamed herself for not getting a campaign going in time. The next time, things were different. A nine-room Wheeler property was described by her as looking like a bastard Victorian home in riverboat style with a fake widow's walk and wonderful wrought-iron fences. As it stood in the center of the shopping district, there were concerns that the house would be bulldozed for commercial development. This was a very important cause for the actress because she was an old-fashioned house buff and a firm believer in restoration rather than tearing down. Raised in an old house in the South where there was always a great feeling for heritage, she had bought and lived in old houses ever since. She had lived in a New England house in Beverly Hills, and had owned three other houses at one time or another in California that were all recreations of something the actress knew and loved from New England or the old South. She agreed to help the Westport Historical Society raise the needed $300,000 to purchase and restore the Wheeler property. Of that amount, $175,000 had to be found by November before the six-month option the Society had on the house ran out. They hoped to turn it into a museum with gift shop, their headquarters and a research center. One room was to be restored as a typical Victorian parlor, another as a working Victorian kitchen, and a stone carriage barn would be a museum of regional farm tools.

Part of the fundraising was to be a benefactors' cocktail party on August 15 at the house, a source claiming this was the annual summer patrons' party, which the Newmans hosted. They lent their names to a mailing list to individuals, foundations and businesses in Fairfield County who might be persuaded to help. The couple also offered the services of their gardener so the grounds would have manicured lawns, a gazebo at the back and a rose garden. Part of the somewhat dilapidated wrought-iron fencing would also be restored. Woodward was said to be so much of an enthusiast of antique fencing that the Newmans were seeking a similar framing for their Coley house. She planned to become personally involved in the restoration of the Wheeler property, after restoring her own two Coley houses and the barn on the Newman home. For the last few years, the family had only used the Westport house in summertime and Christmas holidays, living the rest of the year on the West Coast where their three children were at school. Now they planned to make Westport their year-round residence from the next spring, and she was eager to help keep the town the way it was 20 years ago. The actress had grown up in a small town and liked the feeling of having neighbors and knowing the faces. She also wanted to try and save the tumbledown Victorian gingerbread boarding house at the rear of the Westport Country Playhouse that was to be demolished to make way for condominiums. Her actor friends had always lived there whenever they came to work at the Playhouse, and Woodward thought it would make a perfect inn.

On October 4, 1980, *The New York Times* reported that Woodward was one of the winners of a raffle sponsored by the New York City Opera Guild for a pair of $1000 tickets in the center of the orchestra. The actress sent well-wishes to Sanford Meisner which were read out at the birthday party held for him at a Manhattan art gallery in the week of October 9.

Come Along with Me, shot on location in Illinois, was a PBS movie of Shirley Jackson's unfinished story made as an episode of the TV anthology series *American Playhouse* and broadcast on February 16, 1982. The teleplay was by June Finfer, Morton Neal Miller and Woodward, and directed by Woodward. Elderly widow Mabel Lederer (Estelle Parsons) begins a new career as a spiritualist when her late husband Hughie contacts her from the beyond. The director cast Parsons, Woodward's *Rachel, Rachel* co-star, and Sylvia Sidney, her *Summer Wishes, Winter Dreams* co-star. Also cast was Barbara Baxley as Mrs. Faun and Mrs. Faun's Sister in a narrative that features older women characters in main roles, with Newman (billed as P.L. Neuman) voicing Hughie. Woodward uses slow motion, sepia flashbacks, freeze frames and some slapstick in the staging though the pacing is otherwise slow and the material ultimately unrewarding.

Woodward said that acting in films was not very interesting after a certain point, and it was limiting if you had done it as many years as she had. Film was really a director's medium and it was the director who had the overall viewpoint. When she acted, Woodward sat down with needlepoint, but with directing, she never sat down. The actress reported that Newman had been helpful on the new project, suggesting camera angles, certain shots and lenses.

On February 4, 1981, she attended the Scott Newman Drug Abuse Prevention Awards at the Writers Guild Theater in Los Angeles. Ten days later, she was named honorary chairman of the committee Planned Parenthood's Women Against Discrimination in Abortion, which announced a fundraising drive to help poor women terminate pregnancies. On April 27, the Newmans attended a celebrity-studded awards dinner at the Plaza held by Consumer Action Now to celebrate and raise more money. They were also on the committee for a black-tie gala at Macy's Cellar on April 29 to introduce "Mirror." This was James Lipton's novel dealing with the trials and tribulations of a young Broadway dancer. The gala benefited the Library of the Performing Arts at Lincoln Center Research Center.

ABC-TV announced that among its scheduled projects was "The Walter Lippman Story," based on the Ronald Steel biography *Walter Lippman and the American Century*, about the life of the columnist, which would feature the Newmans. The show, later known as *The Scandal,* appears never to have been made.

Woodward was considered for a role in Tom Dulack's play *Solomon's Child* which, it was hoped, would open on Broadway by Thanksgiving. It was about the deprogramming of a young man who has been abducted from a religious cult, and was to be directed by John Tillinger. He had directed it at Long Wharf in New Haven the last winter, with the show starring Joyce Ebert as Liz, the young man's aunt and high school teacher. This was the part Woodward was presumably up for. The show ran at the Little Theatre on Broadway from April 8 to 10, 1982, with Joanna Merlin as Liz.

When Woodward's youngest child left for boarding school, it was the first time in more than 20 years she had no kids at home, and her plans included going back to acting class. The actress spoke of the importance of regional theater, and criticized President Ronald Reagan for drastically cutting the federal government's support—"and to think he was an ex-actor!" She said it was enjoyable growing older, realizing that life was finite and you had to get on with doing the things you cared about. And what she cared about now was going back on the stage.

Woodward decided to star in *Candida*. The production was done at Kenyon College's Bolton Theatre from June 5 to 21, and directed by Michael Cristofer. She was on the board of Circle in the Square and had some of her friends from the theater fly to Ohio to see the show; they decided to bring it to New York in the fall. Using an Off Broadway theater meant it wasn't so much of a gamble, since the actress didn't want to tackle Broadway or do a long run. It was her husband who got the project moving, telling her she had to do it in New York because it was the best Shavian production he had ever seen. Woodward responded to this remark by asking how many Shavian productions he had seen.

Candida was the wife of the Reverend James Mavor Morell—the 19-year-old poet Marchbanks fell in love with her. She was an extremely modern woman with Shaw being ahead of his time, thinking women were at least equal to if not superior to men. Candida was very aware of her own strengths and did not feel subservient to her husband. Although she may have behaved that way sometimes, she did it purposefully. Woodward loved how the character went through a great change in the course of one day, getting a whole new insight into her life and what she wanted out of it. Also being married to a very popular, successful and attractive man and the woman-behind-the-man was something Woodward could relate to. Despite her Oscar and some highly acclaimed subsequent work in films and television, she had worked less frequently than her husband and never achieved his level of celebrity.

Woodward said Michael Cristofer was the most patient director in the world—very caring, warm and supportive. He was the best director she had ever worked for, except for her husband. The Ohio production had been presented on a thrust stage, but the Circle in the Square space was in the round, which made her feel like a whirling dervish, trying to get to all sides of the audience. You had to keep moving, not the best strategy for a Shaw play which was full of ideas.

The New York show had 23 previews from September 18 and the season was planned to run for a limited engagement from October 15 to November 22, 1981. Woodward was interviewed for *The New York Times* of September 17 when she was in rehearsals. Dressed simply in a sweater, long denim skirt and sandals, she wore no makeup, and her hair, tinted a soft shade of red, was short and boyish. The only sign of a moneyed lifestyle was the imposing diamond-studded wedding band. The actress was leaving little to chance, working hard on her voice as the theater was big, and taking singing lessons. Cristofer had recommended Andy Anselmo, the singing teacher who worked with Mary Tyler Moore when she did *Whose Life Is It Anyway?* in 1980.

Woodward said she hated opening nights, and what made this one worse was that her husband was unable to be there, occupied at a Las Vegas auto race. But he made sure a bottle of Dry Sack sherry, her favorite, was on their bed that night with a note that read, "Just in case." Newman would subsequently surprise her with backstage visits, and also sent dirty limericks and flowers. Frank Rich of *The New York Times* wrote that Woodward, while crisp-spoken, handsome, and doing her intelligent best, lacked the requisite magnetic force of the character.

The season was such a success that its run was extended to January 3, 1982. The show was also filmed by director Alex Barker for Showtime as "Broadway on Showtime: *Candida*" and broadcast on January 2, 1983.

Woodward took part in the program held by the Theater Committee for Eugene O'Neill observing the playwright's birthday on October 19 at the Circle in the Square Theater. The actress read the charming last will and testament that O'Neill wrote for his dog. On November 8, she attended a gala evening to aid the New York Theater Studio which also saw the premiere of two one-act plays given at the Actors and Directors Theater. Theatre buffs had the opportunity to sip wines, nibble on crudités and visit with Woodward.

The actress was interviewed by Lloyd Moss on the WNYC radio show "This Is My Music" on November 14. She knitted a sweater for one of her daughters for Christmas while speaking, and talked about her acting career, the marriage to Newman, her involvement in the world of dance, and some of the music used in *Candida*. Woodward was interviewed for an article in *People* magazine dated November 30. She was then happily decorating a new Manhattan apartment, which had a spectacular view of Central Park. The actress hoped to do a repertory series on Broadway with the help of Michael Cristofer. She also wanted to ride horses, speak French fluently, and get some chickens, as Woodward used to have them and missed their cuddliness. She would have loved to run for office but that required much knowledge and the actress didn't know how to acquire it. But like her childhood heroine, Scarlett O'Hara, she believed that tomorrow was another day. At this time in her life, Woodward was a risk-taker and liked to test herself. She had finally acquired confidence in herself—and her marriage. Her former neuroses had stopped seeming important now she was in her early 50s, and she had developed a sense of humor which helped when women flocked around her husband.

The Newmans had attended the finals of the National Horse Show at Madison Square Garden where the 16-year-old Clea was competing. The girl had been halfway through the course when her chestnut 1000-pound Thoroughbred gelding What's Up Doc? stumbled over a three-and-a-half-foot fence. It fell heavily and rolled over on Clea and Woodward thought her daughter was dead. The parents frantically ran toward the ring. The girl had suffered only a bruised hip and shoulder. Woodward was scheduled to give a matinee performance of *Candida* that afternoon and as she rested in her dressing room, the accident kept replaying in her head. The cast urged Woodward to let her understudy go on, but she wasn't about to miss a performance (she said she had never missed one).

Woodward was a new but enthusiastic convert to horses, having started riding in earnest only the previous year, with an earlier attempt an embarrassing failure. When she and Newman were courting in the 1950s, they hired horses at a Hollywood livery stable. Out on the trail, her mount stopped, laid down and rolled her off. She just laughed but she had never felt such a sense of rejection, and was then scared of horses. It took a bet from Clea to get her riding again, with the actress putting herself in the hands of a California trainer, Jean Torrey. She then bought a huge 17-hand Thoroughbred hunter called Mama's Boy, and progressed to jumping, and won six ribbons in a Santa Barbara horse show. Six months later, Woodward was the owner of the ramshackle Far West Farms in North Salem, New York, about 20 miles from her Connecticut home. She had it refurbished to accommodate the 52-acre indoor show rings and stalls for 56 horses where the actress also took in boarders. This showplace wasn't for competition only, but somewhere where people could simply ride. She hosted two shows and her 20-year-old daughter Melissa also worked there.

During the Christmas season, the Newmans filled old wine bottles with Paul's salad dressing and handed it out to friends and neighbors on their carol-singing jaunts. When people came back for more, he started thinking about marketing his product.

In 1981, Woodward was awarded an honorary doctorate of fine arts by Kenyon College. The Newmans attended the closing night performance of *The Life and Adventures of Nicholas Nickleby* at the Plymouth Theatre on January 3, 1982. This was the same closing date for *Candida*.

On February 14, they participated in the benefit for the Actors Fund of America, celebrating its 100th anniversary, at Radio City Music Hall. The event was known as *Night of 100 Stars* and *Night of 100 Stars and Then Some*. The show was broadcast on ABC on March 8. It was written by Hildy Parks and directed by Clark Jones. Woodward was among the ten who lit a birthday candle on stage, as part of the description of the fund's role during its 100 years. The $1000 tickets for the event included supper with the stars at the New York Hilton. She was one of the judges of the $2000 1981 Susan Smith Blackburn Prize for the female writer of a work of outstanding quality for the English-speaking theater.

On March 8, the actress spoke (with an injured foot propped on a table in front of her) at the United Nations Church Center for International Women's Day, for a year-long American protest begun by the Women's International League for Peace and Freedom to limit nuclear arms proliferation.

A source claims that Newmans attended the 54th Annual Academy Awards which were held on March 29 at the Dorothy Chandler Pavilion. Newman was nominated for the Best Actor Award for the romantic thriller *Absence of Malice* (1981) but when the nominations were announced by Sissy Spacek, the camera did not show the couple in the audience. He lost to Henry Fonda for the drama *On Golden Pond* (1981).

On April 6, a lunch with her in New York was one of the items on the block at the Fantasy Auction at the Educational Testing Service in Princeton, New Jersey, sponsored by the Association for the Advancement of the Mentally Retarded. The Association was a private non-profit organization that provided job-training opportunities for mentally handicapped adults. In an April 25 *New York Times* article, Woodward was mentioned as once being attached to a project by Joan Didion and John Gregory Dunne called "January and February." They flew to Tucson to discuss it and rewrote the screenplay for her. The story about a social worker in Detroit and Cleveland evolved into one about a college professor's wife in Pomona whose life comes to a crisis point at the Ojai Music Festival. The writers quit the picture, which appears never to have been made.

The Newmans donated a pair of love seats for the auction held in the Old Norwalk High School in Connecticut on May 19 to 20. They also sent telegrams to support the bottle bill that New York Governor Carey signed on June 15 requiring a five-cent deposit on soda and beer containers in New York State. The couple were reported to be members of the newly formed Festival Club at the American Shakespeare Theater in Stratford, Connecticut.

They took a trip to Europe and visited Paris, Nice and Florence. Upon their return, Woodward played Judith Bliss in Noël Coward's *Hay Fever* at Kenyon College in their summer theatre festival. Newman said of her performance that he didn't know that woman and she must be a real scorcher.

In the summer, the Newmans moved across the river to a small 1736 farmhouse. The original property had been gradually improved over the decades with outbuildings but the couple still felt hemmed in. They were now able to buy the much larger parcel that the owner had previously refused to sell and the couple had up to 15 acres, plus the two main houses and the outbuildings on both properties. They built a footbridge across the river—after hassling with the town over where the hundred-year-old high-water mark should be set—and gradually turned the newly acquired house into their main residence, giving the original to their daughters as a home for holidays or whenever they happened by. In time, the Newmans would convert several of the buildings on the new property. She had a dance studio and he installed fitness equipment, and there was a barn that they turned into a screening room, recreation room and guesthouse.

On September 14, Newman was interviewed for *The New York Times* about his home-made salad dressing business. Woodward recalled her husband's earlier obsession with salad dressing. In the early years of their marriage, they had gone to the Los Angeles restaurant Chasen's for one of their first stylish meals out. There Newman washed an already oiled salad in the men's room so he could do things right with oil cut by a dash of water. Another Newman product was Newman's Own Old Fashioned Roadside Virgin Lemonade—which was Woodward's idea, based on a recipe handed down in her family.

They did a promotional launch for a national media audience, singing a salad dressing love song set to Richard Rodgers's music for "Where or When" at Hanratty's, a Manhattan bar and grill. With each new product line, the couple engaged in another corny launch at an unlikely location—Central Park, Keen's Chophouse in Manhattan where they sang to the tune of George Gershwin's "I Got Rhythm," and Ronald Buck's Los Angeles burger joint. Newman praised his wife's hollandaise sauce as the best in the world, never topped by any restaurant. She vetoed his idea of a Newman's Own beer that would have been brewed in Norwalk.

On November 11, the actress participated in a birthday tribute to Eugene O'Neill in a program entitled "Strindberg and O'Neill: A Shared Legacy" held at the Circle in the Square. It was first reported that she would narrate links for the performances of O'Neill's works directed by Jose Quintero, and written by Harry G. Carlson and Barbara Gelb. But on the night, these duties were performed by Frances Sternhagen, and Woodward simply attended.

She contributed a recipe in a new cookbook published by the Connecticut division of the American Cancer Society. Called "Connecticut Cooks, Favorite Recipes from the Nutmeg State," it contained the actress's chicken, spinach and noodle dish created in her

Westport kitchen. Proceeds from the sale of the cookbook were to be used by the American Cancer Society for research, education, service and rehabilitation.

In an article in the December 9 issue of *Time* magazine, Woodward said unworriedly that she was in a period of artistic hibernation until she began work on the Newmans' next film, tentatively titled *Harry and Son*. She had joined her husband for the Sports Car Club of America national championships in Road Atlanta. At a catfish restaurant near the track the couple argued amiably about tenors. She liked Placido Domingo and he liked Luciano Pavarotti. The article said they had their house in Westport, another in Beverly Hills, and an apartment in an East Side Manhattan hotel. On the wall in their kitchen was a sampler, which he had made to commemorate a remark made by her: "I will regulate my life. JWN." The sampler showed a lit light bulb and an exploding cannon, which was his view of the actress' character. Her past conflicts over having children and career had now been replaced by the feeling that being a full-time parent would be okay with Woodward. With what she had learned, it would be more enjoyable.

On December 13 at the Circle in the Square Theater, the actress participated in "Also Known as Eve," a celebrity review that had her sing as a fundraiser for the National Abortions Rights Action League. *The New York Times* of December 19 reported that she had made a needlepoint of the Wheeler house in Westport early in the year, donating it to the Westport Historical Society to commemorate its efforts in purchasing and restoring the historic house. In the January 20, 1983, issue of *Rolling Stone*, Newman reported that the makers of the short *The Last Epidemic* had asked the couple to introduce it. Unfortunately no other information is available about this film. Woodward had recently been hospitalized for a foot operation but, despite doctor's orders to take it easy, her husband said it would take a hand grenade to get her to lie down and be quiet. Another source claimed that his new nickname for his wife was Birdie, just liking the way it sounded when he thought about her.

On January 29, the couple celebrated their 25th wedding anniversary by renewing their vows in a private ceremony in Westport. She wore a Victorian ankle-length white lace gown. The couple managed to keep the whole thing secret as their public relations firms sent out no media releases. Close friends and relatives were in attendance. Newman stated that his wife had always given him unconditional support in all his choices and especially with his racing, even though she had never stopped disapproving. To the actor, that was love.

On February 14, she joined Joshua Logan as the emcees of an evening of entertainment for the reception held in the Rainbow Room as a gala "Celebration of Playwrighting." This was the first Kenyon Festival Theater award, a check for $25,000, and presented to a promising young playwright selected by a jury of distinguished theater professionals.

9

Harry & Son

The Newmans went to Florida to begin production on *Harry & Son*, which would be shot on location in Broward County and in Malibu from February 15 to early May 1983. The drama had a screenplay by Ronald L. Buck and Newman, suggested by the novel *A Lost King* by Raymond DeCapite, and Newman was the director. He also starred as Harry Keach, a widower who works in Florida as a crane operator on a demolition crew. Woodward has a supporting role as Lilly, proprietor of the Fin and Feather Bird and Supplies store, and the best friend of Harry's deceased wife. Woodward is billed tenth with an "and" credit. Her hair by Diane Johnson sees the actress wear a gray waist-length braid with bangs. Woodward feeds a parrot and does a phrenological reading of Harry's head. Her best scene is perhaps when Lilly does the phrenological reading and Harry does it back to her; her reaction to Harry is romantically understated.

The film was released on March 2, 1984, with the taglines "Two men with nothing in common … except the blood in their veins" and "Only a hard-nose writes off his kid—Only a hero has the courage to change." Vincent Canby (*The New York Times*) wrote that Woodward made an impression as a good-hearted woman unafraid to buck conventions as the need arose. But *Variety* and Roger Ebert had less favorable reactions. The film was not a box office success.

The film was originally known as *Harry's Boy*. Sources differ as to which Newman was the project's instigator, one saying Paul developed the screenplay with Buck. Another claims the writer brought the book to Joanne and she showed it to Paul, especially as she wanted to play the part that became Lilly. It is claimed that she also wanted to direct, and after Newman agreed to do so, Woodward was the uncredited co-director. The actor had reportedly asked her to keep an eye on him, as Newman did not like having to act in the films he directed. She was supposed to work on the more difficult scenes focusing on Harry, leaving him free to concentrate on his performance. The actress said the idea of two directors turned out to be a joke since they worked very differently. He loved to rehearse and she hated it, preferring to sit around and talk about a scene for a while, and then shoot it. When it came time for Woodward to direct, Newman said things didn't quite work out. She felt uneasy about asserting herself, and he believed his performance suffered. One scene the actress directed was Harry's death scene, after feeling she couldn't direct her husband. Woodward was said to have been moved to tears after the first take, putting his arms around her and saying she was so glad he didn't die. Newman cried after each take and with the final one, he hugged her and gave his wife a passionate kiss.

Newman justified Woodward's casting by having her character (originally an extremely minor one) expanded into a small supporting role. A source claims she was determined to be in the film so as to be with her husband on location, but she also wanted to do something a little more creative than just being her husband's second set of eyes. Woodward wanted to look different and have an unusual wardrobe. She decided to make Lilly a tribute to her daughter Nell, who dressed exotically in layers. Despite her Neighborhood Playhouse training to work internally first, Woodward started externally, and remembered a woman she had met some years ago in Maine. She lived in a messy house and was a real earth mother, with dirty feet, sandals and long gray hair and a long pigtail. The actress decided on the pigtail for Lilly, and Newman wanted it to be gray, feeling it went with her eyes.

Woodward said Newman would be a fool not to play Harry, but he felt he was not right for it. Newman had not wanted to also act in the film but he had trouble getting studio backing without playing the starring role. The actress saw how her husband worked liked a fiend and understood his desire to never act and direct in the same film again.

The Newmans took time off from making *Harry & Son* to attend the 55th Annual Academy Awards, held on April 11 at the Dorothy Chandler Pavilion and televised by ABC. The show was written by Hal Kanter, Jack Rose, Leonard Spigelgass and Rod Warren, and directed by Marty Pasetta. Newman was nominated for the Best Actor Academy Award for his performance in the drama *The Verdict* (1982) but lost to Ben Kingsley for the historical biography *Gandhi* (1982). Woodward was seen in the audience sitting next to her husband when his nomination was announced by John Travolta.

It was reported that their New York penthouse apartment had a wraparound terrace so the couple's one-year-old terrier Harry would have a private place to poop. Woodward said she was fond of New York because of her participation in actor's workshop groups, and the couple planned to spend three or four days a week in the city.

Woodward was the host of the television documentary *Hunger in the Promised Land*, broadcast on Golden West Television on June 5. The show was written and directed by Ben Moses. On July 4, the Newmans attended the Kendall Cup Nationals at Little Rock Park in Connecticut. On the evening of August 3, they hosted the Westport Historical Society's annual fundraiser and summer party in a tent on the lawns behind the Wheeler House where the couple met 800 of their neighbors and friends. The event was the third time the Newmans had been the hosts of the gathering, designed to raise money for the restoration of the Wheeler House as the society's headquarters and museum. The evening was billed as a Victorian lawn party and the invited guests were asked to dress in suitable costumes. Woodward wore the white lace gown she had chosen for her wedding anniversary in January, along with a sterling silver lorgnette. (The matching petticoat had fallen off just as she was leaving the house.) The couple was presented with a citation from the leaders of the General Assembly, praising them for promoting the preservation of historic structures.

The actress accepted a role in another television movie and the Newmans rented a house in Malibu so she could make *Passions* in the winter. The show was broadcast on CBS on October 1, 1984. The teleplay was by Janet Greek, Robin Maxwell and Sandor Stern, based on a story by Greek and Maxwell, and the director was Stern. Richard Crenna starred as 48-year-old California businessman Richard Kennerly, who has a wife of 25 years, Catherine (Woodward), and a 20-year-old daughter in Pasadena but also a six-year-old son with another woman, sculptress Nina Simon (Lindsay Wagner), in Malibu. Woodward is top-billed before the title and plays the leading role. Her hair by Virginia Hadfield is worn in a short sculpted graying brown style with a side part. The role sees the actress smash two sculpture pieces. Her performance sometimes adds over-gesturing to her mannerisms, but Woodward is funny and understated expressing Catherine's simmering anger. John J. O'Connor (*The New York Times*) wrote that Woodward's older woman was a wrenching mixture of dignity and resentment.

On October 24, the Newmans attended the Musicians Against Nuclear Arms Concert at Avery Fisher Hall at New York's Lincoln Center. On December 3, at a benefit gala at the Brooke Alexander Gallery, Woodward was among the cast members who read the winning bids submitted in the course of the tour of "Art for a Nuclear Weapons Freeze," a traveling exhibition-auction to raise money for the National Nuclear Weapons Freeze Campaign.

The January 15, 1984, *Times* reported that the couple had sold the Old Salem

Woodward in the telemovie *Passions* (1984).

Farm riding school and horse farm. The Newmans attended the 41st Annual Golden Globe Awards, held on January 28 at the Beverly Hilton Hotel. Woodward was in the audience when her husband accepted the Cecil B. DeMille Award, wearing the same hairstyle she wore in *Passions*. He thanked her in his acceptance speech.

They were among 100 entertainment figures who signed and paid for a half-page advertisement in the March 18 *Times* on behalf of Save the Theaters Inc., asking the public to write to the Landmarks Commission and the Board of Estimate in support of landmark designations. She reportedly went to England without her husband for the British release of *Harry & Son*. He was busy in the United States campaigning for Democratic presidential candidate Walter Mondale.

The *Times* of April 18 reported the Newmans were among the notable contributors to the Senate campaign of Governor James B. Hunt Jr. of North Carolina. On April 22, Woodward appeared at the Theater of the Riverside Church as one of the actors who studied under Louis Horst, the late composer and dance teacher, in honor of his memory. The couple were guests on the May 28 episode of the West German music-biographical-documentary television series *Bitte umblättern*. On June 28 the actress and the political scientist Anne Cahn teamed up to discuss the women's peace movement at a National Press Club luncheon.

On August 6, she was among the cast who read the book *Hiroshima*, John Hersey's 1946 account of the bombing, for WNYC-AM to commemorate the 39th anniversary. It was read in three one-hour installments, at 10 a.m., 3 p.m. and 10 p.m. Also in August was the premiere of the documentary *Strategic Trust: The Making of a Nuclear Free Palau* at the Chicago International Film Festival. Woodward was the narrator of the film, which was written by James Heddle and Tony Szulc and directed by Heddle.

Her singing voice was heard on the Ben Bagley album *Jerome Kern Revisited, Vol. 2*, released by the Painted Smiles label. She sang "Drift with Me" and dueted with Andy Anselmo on "Bullfrog Patrol." Paul Kresh in *The New York Times* wrote that the actress was appealing enough if a little soggy and off-key.

On September 12 in the Washington Cannon Caucus Room of the House of Representatives, she was the chairman of the first National Women's Conference to Prevent Nuclear War. Woodward was interviewed about it for the *Times* in the office she shared with Newman at the Columbia Pictures building in New York. She spoke while eating a piece of honeydew melon, sitting behind a desk in a brown leather swivel chair, above which dangled a hangman's noose. The noose was her husband's sense of humor. The actress' comments were punctuated with sweeping arm gestures and a number of dramatic desk thumps, especially when she was asked why entertainers should speak out on issues. The answer was because they were citizens and they were in a position where people would at least listen. The Newmans had long been identified with liberal causes. She had first become involved with the peace movement in the early 1960s and joined the group Another Mother for Peace during the Vietnam War, and later was involved in Women for a Meaningful Summit. Woodward was not afraid of losing roles because of her activism. There were not many roles for women her age anyway. What Woodward liked to do now was teach and direct.

The one-day event was the first time that a group of prominent American women joined together to discuss ways of averting nuclear war. She compared the nuclear problem to having your leg cut off: After a while, as awful as it was, you became used to it. Men were not allowed to participate in the conference. The group was not anti-men but pro-survival. Financed with donations from individuals and foundations, it was under the auspices of the Center for Defense Information, a private watchdog group (the actress was a board member). She had been asked to be chairman because the conference was somewhat her idea, along with Admiral Gene R. La Rocque, director of the Center for Defense Information. One of Woodward's early ideas was to copy *Lysistrata*, the Greek comedy in which women withhold sex from their husbands to get them to stop fighting a war. She said it was a matter of record that women felt more strongly about nuclear war, being the nurturers and bearers of children.

On the day, her opening remark was that women were much more inclined than men to put a priority on peace and social stability. The actress proposed a unified national campaign to register more women voters for the November 6 elections, to inform voters about nuclear war issues, and to focus attention on the nuclear policy views of candidates. Ballot boxes could be used to reverse national nuclear weapons policy. The women hoped to influence public opinion so that a halt of nuclear test explosions could be made politically possible by August 6, 1985, the 40th anniversary of the bombing of Hiroshima. A third proposal was for an international women's conference on the subject to be held in Europe in November 1985.

On October 14, the Newmans acted in a staged reading of William Gibson's play

Handy Dandy for an invited audience in Westport. The plot involved a 72-year-old activist nun and a judge who sentences her to prison for anti-nuclear activities. The event was to support the Nuclear Weapons Freeze Campaign and proceeds from the performance went to promote voter registration, the Women's Peace Initiative and the Performing Artists Nuclear Disarmament Committee. The couple were also featured in six minute-long radio commercials urging women to defeat President Reagan. The commercials were part of a national campaign, the Gender Gap Project, to capitalize on the showing in many polls that Reagan's support among women was weaker than it was among men. They attacked Reagan's approach to women's issues and the arms race, using the final line, "If anybody can upset him, women can." The spots were broadcast in the last week of the election campaign, and financed by the pro-feminist political action committee Woman's Trust Fund.

The Newmans were on the committee for the benefit performance of *Torch Song Trilogy* held at the Palace Theater in New Haven on January 15, 1985. The honorary committee was a diverse group of people from theater, politics, education and business who worked to benefit AIDS sufferers. Their object was to demonstrate that the epidemic was a crisis that affected everyone from every walk of life, not just the at-risk population.

Woodward was the host of the March 27 episode of the music television series *Live from the Metropolitan Opera* "Tosca," which was designed and directed by Franco Zeffirelli. The PBS show was directed by Kirk Browning and simulcast in stereo over WQXR-FM. It won the Outstanding Classical Program in the Performing Arts Emmy Award.

On April 14, the actress participated in the Williamstown Theater Festival's fourth annual cabaret fundraiser at New York's Studio 54. She was the host of the April 15 episode of CBS's historical documentary series *An American Portrait*, "Jane Adams." Also in April, the biographical documentary in which Woodward appeared, *Sanford Meisner: The American Theatre's Best Kept Secret*, directed by Nick Doob, was presented at the Public Theater as part of Joseph Papp's "Film at the Public" series.

In the spring she returned to TV for the family romance *Do You Remember Love*, broadcast on CBS on May 21. The teleplay was by Vickie Patik and the director was Jeff Bleckner. Woodward plays the leading role, English professor and poet Barbara Wyatt Hollis, who loses her memory and mental abilities due to Alzheimer's disease. Her red-brown hair is worn in a long wavy style with bangs, and costumes include a beautiful crème-colored layered floor-length short-sleeved dress with matching shawl. The role sees Woodward have a CT scan, lie on her desk as she teaches, and walk into a pond fully clothed. She presents Barbara's childish petulance and vulnerability but fails to make the character as funny as she is said to be. Director Bleckner gives Woodward one unflattering closeup to show Barbara's confusion. Her best scene is perhaps when she laughs with George about "the one who can't remember where anything is and the one who got to his age and never knew."

The New York Times' John J. O'Connor wrote that the actress took the character through an incredible range of emotional colors, from bratty girl to fearful woman, while never losing contact with her fierce intelligence. She was nominated for a Best Performance by an Actress in a Miniseries or Motion Picture Made for Television Golden Globe (she lost to Liza Minnelli, nominated for the drama *A Time to Live*), and won the Outstanding Lead Actress in a Limited Series or a Special Emmy Award.

Woodward disclosed that her mother was a victim of Alzheimer's and that the performance was an homage to her. She wanted to call attention to the disease and its symptoms. A source claimed her mother was diagnosed in 1978 but the actress said they didn't make any real attempt to diagnose her. She was 82 and the doctors said that all the symptoms suggested the disease. For years she had been in a retirement home for sufferers of Alzheimer's and Woodward visited her frequently. As the years progressed, her condition worsened, and by the time the actress made the show, her mother was so severely disoriented that Woodward could only sit her on her lap and rock her like a baby.

She reported that an early draft of the script was sent to her, and though the subject was important, it wasn't very good. But Bleckner kept asking her to do it. And they had Richard Kiley attached; Woodward loved working with him on *All the Way Home*, so she said yes. They worked on the script right up to the last minute. Bleckner thought Woodward was often quite depressed while doing the film. On their last day, they shot in a real convalescent home with many Alzheimer's victims, and she got very quiet. He could tell that it upset her but she was a consummate professional, and her work was never affected. She commented after the show aired that it was probably the last movie she would ever do. She was going into a new, quieter phase of her life.

Patrick O'Neal reported that he saw her in New York around this time, at a party. The actress talked about her plans to do summer stock and teach, and he was envious of her ability to stay alive and active in positive ways. She attributed it to a good Southern upbringing. It provided one with a sense of responsibility, a spiritual sense of giving it back. Also, he felt she loved to act, which not every actor did.

Portrait of Woodward for the made-for-television *Do You Remember Love* (1985).

Woodward appeared in a production of Anton Chekhov's *The Sea Gull* as Arkadina for the River Arts Repertory at Byrdcliffe Theater in Woodstock. It ran from June 25 to July 21. The actress described director Lawrence Sacharow as a dreamy director, whom she initially thought wasn't going to be helpful at all because the play was hard and he didn't say much. But what Sacharow did was just allow the actors to do it, which was the best possible thing.

In the summer, she played Amanda Wingfield in *The Glass Menagerie* at the Williamstown Theater Festival. Directed by Nikos Psacharopoulos, the production ran from August 20 to 25. The actress said she had once shared with Tennessee Williams remembrances of her mother, who was a little Southern belle. She had no education and *was* Amanda Wingfield. Williams replied, perhaps sarcastically, that he thought in writing Amanda he was writing about his mother, but it seemed like he was writing about hers. Another source claims that the playwright's remark was genuine and made after he met Woodward's mother.

The actress had first played Amanda in a Greenville, South Carolina, production, directed by Robert McLane. She got a blonde wig that looked a little like Laurette Taylor's and wanted to play it in the '30s wardrobe, wearing clothes that Amanda would have worn 10 to 15 years before because she couldn't afford new ones. Because of complicated schedules, Woodward had to learn the part alone, with only one week's rehearsal with the rest of the cast who had already been in rehearsal for weeks with someone else playing Amanda. McLane had picked out a horrible Victorian wig and Victorian wardrobe which she objected to. She felt it must have been one of the worst Amandas ever created. For the Williamstown production, the director asked her to play the part with a lot of intensity and anger, not soft and easy.

In October, the Newmans jointly received the Screen Actors Guild Annual Achievement Award. This was for fostering the finest ideals of the acting profession as well as for their charitable works, political activities and antidrug work via the Scott Newman Center. There had supposedly been a lot of discussion among the Guild about whether to give the award to her as the better actor or him as the bigger star, and the organization wondered if one would refuse if the other wasn't included. Also in October, Newman won the 1985 SCCA Runoffs in Road Atlanta, which she reportedly attended. In 1985, the Newmans were vocal supporters of Save the Children, adopted seven children through the program and appeared in print advertisements for the charity.

On January 6, 1986, Woodward was among the presenters of the seven Mayor's Awards of Honor for Arts and Culture. The awards were personalized notes of recognition on a framed scroll presented by the honorees' friends and colleagues, at a Gracie Mansion ceremony. Woodward presented one of the awards to Sanford Meisner. On January 29, the Newmans reportedly celebrated their 28th anniversary, with their homes in Westport and Manhattan filled with friends.

The Glass Menagerie was revived for a production at the Long Wharf Theatre in New Haven. Rehearsals began on February 3, with the season running from February 28 to April 13. Mel Gussow in *The New York Times* wrote that Woodward created a luminous portrait, a delicately shaded, grandly Southern characterization with humor, gaiety and, finally, a tragic dimension. After the March 29 Long Wharf show, Newman surprised her upon his temporary return from Chicago where he was starring in *The Color of Money*. He waited at midnight naked in their Jacuzzi as she came home to the Connecticut home via the garden. The actress initially thought him to be a burglar and nearly took an axe to him.

She appeared in the play for eight performances a week, and between scenes sat in the wings knitting sweaters of hand-spun wool for anybody who needed one. Woodward also plotted the design of a staircase runner which she planned to needlepoint with the help of friends, with portraits of all the pets that had ever lived in the house. The actress was also encouraging her daughters in their pursuits as an artist, an ecologist and an equestrian.

At the time she was also conducting acting classes, and directing the one-woman anti-nuclear, anti-war play *The Depot* by Eve Ensler. Ensler's stepson Dylan McDermott was one of Woodward's students at the Neighborhood Playhouse; he became her protégé after she discovered him doing workshops. Her favoring him over better actors was reportedly due to his hunky dark sex appeal which may have reminded her of Newman in his younger days. An associate said that it was pretty clear that the actress had a puppy dog crush on him but tried to cover it up with a layer of maternal concern that didn't fool anybody except McDermott. The actor used his connection to promote Ensler, showing Woodward her play *Coming from Nothing*, about a girl trying to remember her childhood. The actress loved it and directed a reading with her students. Then Ensler told her she really wanted to write her a show, which became *The Depot*. Woodward had been an incredible role model because they had both been very active in the nuclear disarmament movement. The actress was tired of going to conferences and making speeches and wished there were theatrical monologues she could do instead. Ensler's piece was a viable alternative: a consciousness-raising piece of agitprop theater that was engrossing and funny. Ensler said Woodward and actress Shirley Knight, who would star in the play, were her mentors and the writer's life forever changed as a result of doing the play. Woodward credited Ensler with helping her become a director.

On top of all that, the actress was filming interviews for a documentary on the Group Theatre she was producing, *Broadway's Dreamers: The Legacy of the Group Theatre*. She would take five years to speak to the surviving original members, with the passage of time apparent in the film from her changing hair colors and styles. Her interview with Sylvia Sidney again recalls their prior appearance together in *Summer Wishes, Winter Dreams*. The film was written by Steve Lawson and directed by David Heeley, with Woodward hosting and reading from Harold Clurman's book *The Fervent Years: The Group Theatre and the Thirties*. The actress also read from a May 18, 1941, article Clurman wrote for *The New York Times*. She was the host of the 1987 Williamstown Theatre Festival celebration of the Group Theatre; in a 1985 Master Class held by Robert Lewis in New York; at rehearsals as the director of the Williamstown production of *Golden Boy*; and in the end credits which told of the Group's legacy, telling told how she had studied with Meisner. The film has a 1988 Education Broadcasting credit but would be broadcast on PBS on the television series *American Masters* on June 26, 1989. It was praised by John J. O'Connor in the *Times*.

Woodward said the impetus for making the film was her realization that soon there might not be anybody left that knew about the Group Theatre. It took her five years because she had to keep raising money to keep going with it. Co-producer Joan Kramer and David Heeley were friends of hers and great documentary filmmakers, and the actress found the film great fun to do.

The couple did not attend the 58th Annual Academy Awards, where Newman was to be given an honorary Oscar. He initially commented that he was relieved to finally even the score with his wife, but wanted to refuse the honor. She prevailed upon him to be gracious and then he agreed. His *Absence of Malice* co-star Sally Field accepted for him on the night, with Newman seen via satellite in Chicago on the *Color of Money* set to offer his thanks.

In March, Woodward appeared in the PBS documentary *The Spencer Tracy Legacy: A Tribute by Katharine Hepburn*. The show was written by John Miller and directed by David Heeley. She spoke about Tracy's performances in the Fox drama *The Power and the Glory* (1933) and the MGM biographical comedy *The Actress* (1953).

Around this time Woodward directed an Off Off Broadway production of James McLure's comedy *Lone Star*; research did not reveal the dates or the name of the space. In June, workman built a bridge in the woods near Nook House, so that the big barn where they entertained and showed movies could be linked to the Westport house.

Woodward hosted "Katherine Anne Porter: The Eye of Memory," the July 7 episode of the PBS biographical documentary TV series *American Masters*. The show was written by Ken Harrison and Jordan Pecile based on stories by Porter, and directed by Harrison. She then hosted the *American Masters* episode "Eugene O'Neill—A Glory of Ghosts," The *Times*' John J. O'Connor said that she did a bit of overselling when declaring that O'Neill was "our Strindberg, our Ibsen, yes maybe even our Shakespeare." On September 24, the actress was one of the hosts of a cocktail party held on behalf of Project Vote, a non-partisan, not-for-profit group founded four years prior to enroll voters at New York's Harkness House.

Newman was interviewed for the *Times* on the same date and commented on his wife. Writer Maureen Dowd reported that Woodward was not available for consultation and preferred not to discuss her husband for articles focusing on him. He said, apologetically, that maybe familiarity breeds contempt. They were equals, but sometimes he forgot how incredible she was and then the actor saw something that reminded him. They had a room in the Westport home with an elegant array of antiques, chintz couches with embroidered pillows, and a baby grand piano. Newman said if anyone had ever told him 20 years ago he would be sitting in a room with peach walls, they would have been told to take a nap in a urinal. Dowd wrote that the Newmans seemed like any upper middle class couple enjoying their "empty nest syndrome." As he went out one morning, she was coming back from a ballet class. They kissed and the actor asked her to put gas in his car as Woodward went to clean the barn. When he returned, she was leaving to do grocery shopping. The actress told him that their daughter Clea had won a prize in a horse show and that she had forgotten to put gas in his car. Newman said the couple lived between two worlds and were accepted by neither. It was just like Thomas Mann's story "Tonio Kroger": The bourgeois thought they were revolutionaries and the bohemians saw that they had a lot of Jell-O and didn't wear neckerchiefs and thought they were bourgeois.

On October 8, 1986, the Newmans attended the Palladium for the New York premiere of *The Color of Money*, which was also a benefit for the Actor's Studio. On October 19, he had an accident at the national title run of the Sports Car Club of America season held at Braselton, Georgia. Woodward was in attendance to see his car hit another and force them both off the track, with the front of Newman's car smashed in. Woodward arrived at the pit shortly after his car drove in, and they reportedly had an intense exchange. It was said that the actor told her that he would now quit the sport and she jumped for joy. But when Newman returned to the racing circuit, his wife told him to do what he wanted as she had finished her obligations. The actor called this a comfortable compromise, and said she had a theory about his racing: He started because had gotten really bored as an actor and then some of the passion for that bled back into acting. Newman didn't know if this was true but it was an interesting theory.

Woodward was the honorary chairman of the daylong workshop held on October 24 at Sarah Lawrence College in Yonkers on threats to "reproductive rights" and strategies for action. Known as the Reproductive Freedoms Workshop, it examined women's birth-control rights, abortion services, medical technologies and recent legal and legislative developments. The event was co-sponsored by the college's graduate programs in health advocacy, human genetics and women's history.

Also in October, *The Depot* was first seen on its feet at Westport's Theater Artists Workshop for two performances. Woodward directed the play and her voice was heard on a tape recording describing the potential ravages of a nuclear attack. She had asked

Shirley Knight, another outspoken, cause-oriented woman, to star. The play's setting was inspired by Greenham Common, a women's peace camp built in 1981 near an air base outside London. The narrative has a nurse waking up after having a nightmare about a nuclear attack. She flees from her home in the middle of the night to take refuge in a women's peace camp near a missile site. The hour-long monologue is delivered through barbed wire to a silent soldier guarding the site. The work was later performed at college campuses and at the Kennedy Center in Washington, D.C., for three performances, under the sponsorship of the Center for Defense Information, a research organization financed and directed by retired U.S. military officers. It also toured for two years and was performed at a nuclear test site in Nevada.

The Newmans had succeeded in setting up a film of *The Glass Menagerie* with Woodward to repeat her role as Amanda. Newman was to direct and said the idea came from her; she wanted a record of the stage production and her performance. Newman said she now developed a wonderful sense of weight and command on stage that in *The Sea Gull*, *Hay Fever* and this play were dazzling to watch. She said that the film got made because her husband wanted to direct it, but it was a wonderful idea because he knew the play so well, having once played the part of the Gentleman Caller. Amanda was much closer to her now than when the actress had played her at Williamstown. In a way, she *was* her. They were both from the South and Woodward understood her. Amanda was a real survivor in a matriarchal society.

Woodward in *The Glass Menagerie* (1987).

The film was shot from October 27 to early December 1986 in the Kaufman Astoria Studios and on location. The screenplay, based on Williams' play, focused on warehouse worker and poet Tom Wingfield (John Malkovich), who longs to escape from his stifling home, where his genteel mother Amanda (Woodward) worries about the future prospects of his lame, shy sister Laura (Karen Allen). The play was originally staged on Broadway with Laurette Taylor as the Mother in a season that ran from March 31, 1945, to August 3, 1946. It was adapted into a 1950 Warner Bros. film with Gertrude Law-rence as Amanda, and remade as a 1958 West German made-for-TV movie, a 1964 episode of the British television series *ITV Play of the Week*, a 1966 episode of TV's *CBS Playhouse* with Shirley Booth, a 1967 Swedish made-for-TV movie, 1969 Norwegian and West German made-for-TV movies, 1973 Finnish and American made-for-TV movies (the latter starring Katharine Hepburn) and a 1977 Turkish-Canadian-French-British made-for-TV movie.

The new film has Woodward top-billed and playing the leading role, her first in a film since *Summer Wishes, Winter Dreams*. Her hair is by Joseph Coscia and worn in a short gray-white wavy style with bangs. Costumes by Tony Walton include a black ankle-length long-sleeved coat with brown fur trim, a white headscarf and a white layered high-necked short-sleeved floor-length dress with a purple-blue waist sash. The actress uses a Southern accent but speaks in an understated manner which becomes monotonous, though her over-gesturing perhaps has context for the theatrical character. She makes Amanda's anger funny, and is also funny when charming Jim with her "gay" Southern behavior. Woodward's best scene is when Amanda recalls her gentleman callers, where director Newman photographs her in closeup.

The film was first screened on September 19, 1987, at the Toronto Film Festival and given an American release on October 23. Janet Maslin in *The New York Times* wrote that the actress was a fluttery, garrulous Amanda who seemed too sane and sturdy for the material, but approached her role with great conviction. The film was not a box office success.

Woodward felt Malkovich was very interesting and wonderfully irritating but his performance didn't allow her the desperation of trying to get through to someone as she'd had with John Sayles in Williamstown.

Malkovich reported that Newman told him he was too rough and even cruel with his wife, but the actor saw that as how Tom communicated. He said the director tended to protect Woodward and that was perfectly understandable. Malkovich had been late for the first day of shooting because he had overslept after a trip to London. When he arrived on set, Woodward assured him that his tardiness was nothing to worry about and helped get as much as possible done in the time that remained. On November 18, the Newmans hosted a banquet for cast and friends at their New York apartment.

The actress appeared in the documentary short *Women—for America, for the World* (1986) directed by Vivienne Verdon-Roe. It featured 22 prominent American women discussing their activism for nuclear disarmament.

She met with director James Ivory and producer Ismail Merchant after seeing the romance *A Room with a View* (1985) to explore the possibility of working together. Woodward had now optioned the Evan S. Connell novel *Mrs. Bridge* and the companion *Mr. Bridge*, and had envisioned making two television movies and starring as Mrs. Bridge. At a dinner with the Newmans, Ivory and Merchant suggested combining the novels into one big-screen movie, which was fortuitous as she was having trouble interesting TV executives. Ivory learned the material was similar to the couple's own childhood and adolescence, and Newman said he would play Mr. Bridge if he liked the script.

In January 1987, Woodward was involved with the National Abortion Rights Action League, sending out a letter asking for money to underwrite the retention of legalized abortion, and to train abortion activists, build coalitions and launch an aggressive media strategy. The League's director Kate Michelman considered ultra-conservative Judge Robert Bork to be the most serious threat to abortion rights in 14 years, and the League mobilized a campaign to stop his nomination to the Supreme Court. He failed to win the nomination. The actress was criticized in right wing circles and by avid anti-abortion columnist Ray Kerrison.

She was interviewed for *The New York Times* of March 15 about *The Depot*, which was being performed at the Interart Theater in Manhattan through March 27. On March 28 it was to be at the Ethel Walker School in Simsbury, and on April 12 at the Westport

Country Playhouse to benefit the National Organization for Women. Performances at educational institutions on the East Coast were also being arranged. After each showing, a discussion took place, with Shirley Knight and, at times, the playwright and the director participating. Woodward said directing was more fun than acting, and she had been doing so for three or four years because it gave her greater creative control. She continued to connect to pacifist organizations because *not* doing so was unthinkable. She would work to put together a television adaptation of the play but this never eventuated.

The Newmans did not attend the 59th Annual Academy Awards, held on March 30, 1987. Newman was nominated for the Best Actor Oscar for *The Color of Money* but was reportedly in New York editing *The Glass Menagerie*. He won the award and Robert Wise accepted on his behalf from presenter Bette Davis. The Newmans reportedly stayed home and watched the event on TV. Another source claims they celebrated the honor with a dinner at the New York restaurant Wilkinson's Seafood Café.

On March 31, Woodward was at the private Plaza Club of Madison Square Garden to benefit Madre, a project of the Women's Peace Network that supported humanitarian services and supplies to women and children in Central America. The May 3 *Times* reported that the actress was on the board of advisers for the Sanctuary for Animals, a non-profit home for abandoned and abused animals that would otherwise have to be destroyed.

In May, the Newmans attended the Cannes Film Festival, where *The Glass Menagerie* was screened. They were put up at a palatial hotel suite in Beaulieu by the film's distributors. In the street, Woodward was mugged by thieves who took her money, identification and passport. She was physically unharmed though shaken. The May 15 *Times* reported that the actress was among the candidates for the job of president of the newly merged Committee for a Sane Nuclear Policy and the Nuclear Weapons Freeze Campaign.

She returned to the Williamstown Theatre Festival to direct a production of Clifford Odets' *Golden Boy* with Dylan McDermott as Joe Bonaparte. The *Broadway's Dreamers* documentary showed a scene of the play in rehearsal with Woodward watching and then giving notes, and then the same scene in performance. In the summer, she hosted a celebration of the Group Theatre at Williamstown, which included music, film, voices from the past, great lines from some of the Group's productions, and appearances by some of the original members.

The actress voiced the role of Elizabeth Cady Stanton for a radio series called *Voices of Freedom*, produced by Public Interest Radio in honor of the Bicentennial of the Constitution. It was sponsored by People for the American Way and the Deer Creek Foundation and broadcast on more than 2000 stations. In August, the Newmans were on their way to their Manhattan apartment after seeing the Broadway show *Fences* when they were set upon by paparazzi, who followed them into the building. Woodward was said to have swung her purse, hitting two of the males. The couple also lashed out with verbal abuse, and Woodward had to pull her husband off a female photographer. The two women nearly got into a slap-and-scratch catfight after the photographer told the actor he was getting fat and his wife was going bald. The incident was reported in a lot of columns.

On October 9, the actress attended a dinner for Martha Graham at the New York Hotel Pierre. On October 15, she was at a dinner party held for the Women's Campaign Fund, a bipartisan political committee that provided money and services to women running for local, state and national office. On October 26, Woodward performed in "An Evening of Entertainment," a benefit held at the Circle in the Square Theatre. This was to honor Martha Schlamme, a singer known for her interpretations of Kurt Weill and

Yiddish and international folk songs, who died in 1985. The proceeds were to benefit the newly established Martha Schlamme Scholarship Fund at the Circle in the Square Theater School.

To help publicize *The Glass Menagerie*, Woodward did TV commercials for Audi, which extolled her as wife, mother, philanthropist and actress and showed her driving the car. This garnered a lot of criticism because the previous year, the Audi 5000 received negative publicity alleging the car was unsafe and caused accidents. Woodward was said to have been approached because the company wanted a new image and her maturity, refinement and class appealed to the kind of audience they wanted.

In October, she was in Washington when her husband was presented with a check for $5 million by the king of Saudi Arabia for his Hole in the Wall camp in Connecticut, which benefited children with leukemia and other blood diseases.

The actress read from Washington Irving at a benefit for Sleepy Hollow Restorations, renamed Historic Hudson Valley, at New York's Plaza Hotel on November 2. On November 6, she attended a tribute to Myrna Loy at the American Place Theater. Woodward was chairwoman for a November 8 Carnegie Hall concert called "Music for Life," raising money for the Gay Men's Health Crisis and its programs of care and comfort for AIDS patients.

Woodward returned to the stage to Tennessee Williams' *Sweet Bird of Youth* as Alexandra Del Lago, a.k.a. the Princess Kosmonopolis. The production was at the Royal Alexander Theatre in Toronto, directed by Nikos Psacharpoulos, and ran from April 22 to May 26, 1988. Rehearsals took place in New York. The actress commented that she didn't really want to play the princess, thinking nobody would cast her in the part, then changed her mind. It was not the kind of character she was known for, since in the business, whatever you made your initial impact in stayed with you for a very long time. She was happy to do anything by Tennessee Williams.

Her pre-rehearsal work usually involved working out a history of the character but she found this very difficult because it was hard to dissociate herself from having seen Geraldine Page play it so many times in 1959. The actress believed she never escaped Page's shadow, though there were some places where she was fine. To create an image of the character, she thought of glasses. In life, Woodward wore glasses and was always losing them. The princess was blind as a bat and she had to have her glasses attached. The actress thought of her a movie star from the '40s—in particular Rita Hayworth—and wanted a red wig to recall Hayworth's long flowing hair in the Columbia musical romance *Cover Girl* (1944). The Hayworth connection also related to the princess as a fragile creature, beautiful and insecure, who had the heart of a little lamb, beating furiously. She was terrified of life and of getting old. Costume designer Jess Goldstein dressed her in a stunning blue-sequined gown, after Woodward and he talked about having something like what Hayworth would have worn—a Hollywood dress that had a life of its own and perfectly matched the red hair.

Dissatisfied with her performance, she believed the director was no help. The second act of the play drove her crazy. Unable to find the right intentions, the actress had to arbitrarily get herself into it.

Woodward stated that she loved working in the theater and didn't enjoy making movies, which was strange because for a long time they had been the best thing for her. She was not very theatrical and it was marvelous to have a camera up close. But she had started acting on stage and still loved working in front of an audience. What Woodward regretted more than anything was that Newman had given up the theater because he was a wonderful actor on stage. She felt it was a big mistake because film was film but there was never the same satisfaction as from a play.

In June 1988, Woodward was a witness for her husband in a trial in New York's Superior Court where he and his salad dressing company, Salad King, were accused of breach of contract. The suit was brought by a Westport delicatessen owner, 63-year-old Julius Gold, who said that Newman reneged on a promise to give him a one-twelfth share and a spinoff company that produced spaghetti sauce, popcorn and lemonade. The actor's attorney, W. Patrick Ryan, said that Gold's contribution had been minimal and that no promise of compensation had been made.

On July 20, the Newmans attended the Grand Prix Ball Benefiting Ronald McDonald's Charities at New York's Waldorf Hotel. On September 25, the couple announced the engagement of their daughter Clea to Marshall Field VI, with the couple planning to marry in June 1989.

At the Shubert Theater on November 14, Woodward paid tribute to Joshua Logan, who had died July 12. The gathering, entitled "Celebrating Josh: A Tribute by His Friends (Mostly in His Own Words)," had her read from Logan's descriptions of his studies in Moscow with Konstantin Stanislavsky. She recalled how Logan had hired her as an understudy on Broadway in *Picnic*. Woodward also reported she had once said her son would be named Josh, but she had three daughters.

Newman was unable to be with his wife for New Year's Eve since he was filming the historical biography *Fat Man and Little Boy* (1989) on location in Mexico. The actor said it was the first time apart from her on New Year's since they were married, and he cried over the loss. In 1988, Newman sent money to fund a Joanne Woodward Award for the best female student performance at the Co-ordinate College, a school affiliated with Kenyon College.

On February 7, 1989, she attended a benefit sponsored by several groups for Nicaraguan flood relief at the Beacon Theater on Broadway. The actress also attended an evening of dinner and speeches at the Plaza Hotel on April 12 to honor Robin Chandler Duke, the president emeritus of the National Abortion Rights Action. She was a guest on the April 24 episode of the Spanish television series *De pelicula*.

The couple were again apart when Newman went to Louisiana in April 1989 to make his next film, the biography *Blaze* (1989). She had returned to Sarah Lawrence College in the spring hoping to finish her degree. She received a phone call where Newman pleaded with her to join him, and she said there was no academic degree in the world that could compare in importance to the fact that the person you had loved for 31 years was missing you. So Woodward put her educational plans on hold and joined her husband on location.

10

Mr. & Mrs. Bridge

The drama *Mr. & Mrs. Bridge* (1990) was shot from August 25 to November 16, 1989, on location in Kansas City and in Canada and France. Scripted by Ruth Prawer Jhabvala, it was set in the 1930s and centered on a Kansas City upper-class family falling apart due to the conservative nature of the patriarch solicitor Walter Bridge (Newman) and the progressive values of his children. Second-billed Woodward played India Bridge, Walter's wife of 20 years. Her costumes by Carol Ramsey include nightgowns that reveal the actress's heavier physique. Her hair by Vera Mitchell is a blonde short period-sculpted style with a side part. The actress makes India funny. Her best scene is perhaps when India cries telling Walter her horoscope, saying she feels unappreciated. Woodward underplays and provides emotion.

Interviewed on location for *The New York Times*, she reported that the film was very tough, as they were shooting the schedule and the budget. It was said that the couple did not take their usual salaries to save costs. Woodward had never had many manicures in her life, but here in the jumble of years and seasons, she needed two a day. Woodward admired Mrs. Bridge's emphasis on manners, since politeness was the bedrock of her own Southern personality. But she stayed home when Ismail Merchant gave a party for the company in the last week of shooting. After having been on the set 14 hours, cried many buckets of tears and been photographed with 200 extras, Woodward preferred to get into the tub with a glass of sherry and two Advils.

The film had a Los Angeles screening on November 12, 1990, which she attended. It was released in the U.S. on November 23 with the tagline "Divided by time and tradition. United by love and hope. The story of an unforgettable family." *Variety* said the actress strongly conveyed India's gradual realization that her life had been crushed in her husband's shadow; Vincent Canby in the *Times* said the Newmans gave the most adventurous, most stringent performances of their careers. Peter Travers in *Rolling Stone* wrote that the couple's lovingly detailed and bruisingly true performances not only commanded attention but richly rewarded it. The film was not a box office success but Woodward was nominated for the Best Actress Academy Award.

Home movies show Melissa Newman as Young India with her young children. The actress reported the decision not to use her as Young India was made because she didn't look young enough to have the children. Playing the part was a joy, after wanting to get the project done for nearly 20 years. Woodward understood and identified with India, saying it was very hard to break out of your framework, especially if you had no help, and she never had any help, just as her mother had no help. You framed your home life around your boyfriend or your father or a husband, as the actress had done first with

1990

U.S.A.

COMÉDIE DRAMATIQUE

MR. AND MRS. BRIDGE
MR. AND MRS. BRIDGE

RÉALISATEUR
James Ivory

French movie card for *Mr. & Mrs. Bridge* (1990).

her father and then Newman, and it took an awfully long time to take charge and not live in their shadow.

She said her husband was wonderful as Walter, a part that was the nearest role he ever played to his own true self. Working with him bred good working conditions. She knew there were married acting couples who didn't or couldn't work together, but felt there must have been something wrong with their marriage. If it was good, you had the inner rapport that made the right things happen.

The actress reported that rehearsing with James Ivory was ideal because he liked to hire actors whom he knew could do their jobs, letting them find what they needed for themselves. She said the other actors they had, especially in the family, were wonderful and they developed a real relationship as a family. Woodward loved the scene where Blythe Danner as Grace Barron was worried about her mind, and India didn't understand. The women never talked over the scene before they shot it, and it was marvelous to work with someone like her. There was a similar experience with Robert Leonard, who played India's son Douglas. He was a much more concise actor in terms of technique but they had a great instinctive rapport. Their relationship was best expressed in the Boy Scout scene where Douglas struggled about whether to kiss India the way the other boys did. Woodward also connected with Austin Pendleton, who played Mr. Gadbury.

Newman commented that it was only poetic justice that he and his wife should be brought together on screen again. They spent a lot of time doing social things, political things, family things, so to work together professionally was somehow comforting. The couple was competitive about who made the tea at night, but not about acting. He was vulnerable to her—she would do things that just shattered and triggered him, and the actor never asked Woodward about his flaws. James Ivory claimed that in a sense the Newmans directed themselves, summoning up people that Ivory had never met who were their models.

On December, 4 Woodward attended a luncheon in honor of Vanessa Redgrave at New York's Bukhara Restaurant. On December 10, she appeared in a benefit for the Memorial Society for the Victims of Stalin's Repressions in the U.S.S.R. at the Marquis Theater. On January 31, 1990, they attended a screening of the prize-winning Italian-French drama *Cinema Paradiso* (1988) for the benefit of the American Film Institute's National Center for Film and Video Preservation at New York's Alice Tully Hall.

On April 22 a.k.a. Earth Day, Woodward, as chairwoman of Earth Day 20, presided over a musical evening in the Palace Theater in New Haven. On May 9, she was honored at the annual black-tie awards dinner of the Creative Arts Rehabilitation Center at New York's Plaza Hotel. On May 16, a raffle of movie memorabilia donated by the Newmans was held by the Red Earth Ensemble at New York's Westbeth Theater. She attended the event. On May 25, the actress and daughter Clea received Bachelor of Arts degrees from Sarah Lawrence College. Newman delivered the commencement address, saying he had dreamed the night before of being scolded by a woman for hanging onto the coattails of the accomplishments of his wife. She had been a student at the college off and on for ten years, and was a college trustee since 1986, nudging the small liberal arts institution to be more active on issues concerning the environment, human rights and poverty.

Woodward appeared in "Sanford Meisner: American Theater's Best Kept Secret," the August 27 episode of PBS's *American Masters*. Directed by Nick Doob, it was a biographical documentary of her acting teacher. On September 3, she sang a selection from *The Sound of Music* at a benefit at the Meeting Place, the Hole in the Wall Camp's new performing arts center. On September 26, the Newmans had dinner with the Prime Minister of Norway and Elie Wiesel at New York's Cafe Des Artistes.

The actress contributed to the video *The Wonderful World of Westport*, conceived and underwritten by James McManus. She was one of the local celebrities who donated their talents, expressing her thoughts about the town. The October 14 *New York Times* reported that Woodward got her opera attire at the Lee Anderson boutique on New York's Madison Avenue. This season, Anderson made her a two-ply hip-length jacket in emerald green, with floral-motif trapunto stitching to wear over matching trousers.

On November 9, the Newmans attended the 10th Annual Scott Newman Gala. The *Times* of November 18 reported they spent time in early November at a rented Malibu beach house with their daughters and other guests. On November 24, the Newmans attended a premiere screening of *Mrs. & Mrs. Bridge* and cocktail buffet to benefit the Preservation League of New York State. The Newmans were the honorary chairmen of the League.

On December 18, 1990, Woodward was voted the Best Actress for *Mr. & Mrs. Bridge* by the New York Film Critics Circle. She attended the award ceremony, but not the 48th Golden Globe Awards, held on January 19, 1991, at the Beverly Hilton Hotel where she was nominated for Best Actress—Drama for *Mr. & Mrs. Bridge*. She lost to Kathy Bates for the thriller *Misery* (1990). On February 11, the Newmans attended the NYC 20th Annual Theater Hall of Fame at the Gershwin Theater in New York.

The actress was among those that signed a letter written to the *Times*, defending the Broadway production of David Hirson's play *La Bete* which opened at the Eugene O'Neill Theater on February 10. They beseeched theatergoers to experience what they called "an amazing evening in the theatre," and to ignore *Times* critics Frank Rich and David Richards, who had found the play wanting. The letter was not published because it arrived too late; *La Bete* on closed on March 2.

On March 24, the *Times* predicted that Woodward would not win the Best Actress Oscar. She was a sentimental favorite, but their pick was Kathy Bates for *Misery*, who did win. On March 27, Woodward attended a party to benefit the American Foundation for AIDS Research at New York's Ann Taylor shop. On April 8, she was the co-host for an evening of cabaret entertainment at the Promenade Theater on Broadway to benefit the Williamstown Theater Festival.

One of Woodward's paintings was auctioned on May 17 at the Hamilton Farm Mansion in Gladstone, New Jersey. She was honorary chairman of the auction with proceeds to benefit the Matheny School and Hospital, for the severely disabled, in Peapack and the Essex Young Riders Program.

Woodward appeared in "Miracle on 44th Street: A Portrait of the Actors Studio," the July 8 episode of *American Masters*. The *Times* review reported that she provided appreciative anecdotes. The actress returned to the stage in Henrik Ibsen's *Ghosts* at the Woodstock River Arts in upstate New York from August 8 to 25.

On October 11, the Newmans were given the Freedom from Want Award, one of the 40th annual Franklin D. Roosevelt Four Freedoms Medals, in a ceremony held in Hyde Park, New York. They had been active in many human rights movements and the award cited their charitable endeavors. The October 13 *Times* reported that Woodward was one of the donors to the P.T.A. campaign of the Institute for the Protection of Lesbian and Gay Youth. On October 25, the Newmans attended the reception for a special performance of the Big Apple Circus in Damrosch Park at Lincoln Center to benefit the Scott

Newman Foundation. She went to New York's Tavern on the Green on October 30 for a Black and White Ball to benefit the Alzheimer's Association. In November, the couple attended a preview of Roger Rosenblatt's Off Broadway one-man show *Free Speech in America* at the American Place Theater in New York.

Martin Scorsese used Woodward's voice and her likeness in a painted portrait for his romance *The Age of Innocence* (1993). The film had a screenplay by Jay Cocks and Scorsese based on the Edith Wharton novel. Set in New York in the 1870s, it centered on Newland Archer (Daniel Day-Lewis), a young lawyer who falls in love with Ellen Olenska (Michelle Pfeiffer), a woman separated from her husband, while he is engaged to the woman's cousin (Winona Ryder). Woodward's name appears in the film's end credits as "the narrator." Scorsese reported he found her voice soothing. The painted portrait was at the house of Julius Beaufort (Stuart Wilson), seen at the annual opera ball. The Newmans attended the film's New York premiere at the Ziegfeld Theater on September 13.

On April 5, 1991, Woodward was at the March for Women's Lives in Washington as a delegate of the Hollywood Women's Political Campaign. On April 12, the Newmans attended the opening night of *A Streetcar Named Desire* at the Barrymore Theatre in New York. On May 4 they were at the Benefit for Friends in Need AIDS at New York's Brooks Atkinson Theater.

Woodward's mother Elinor died on September 8 at the age of 89 in Georgia. She was buried as Elinor Gasque Trimmier Carter, having married Robert L. Carter.

The actress returned to films in a supporting role in the drama *Philadelphia* (1993), which was shot on locations in Pennsylvania from October 20, 1992, to February 4, 1993. The screenplay was by Ron Nyswaner and the director was Jonathan Demme. Andy Beckett (Tom Hanks), a man with AIDS, is fired by his law firm and hires Joe Miller (Denzel Washington) to handle a wrongful dismissal suit. Woodward played Andy's mother Sarah and received special "and" billing. Her costumes are by Colleen Atwood, and hair is by Alan D'Angerio worn in a short wavy graying-blonde style with bangs. Sarah adds nothing substantial to the narrative, apart from being a supportive mother. Mercifully, she is spared director Demme's self-conscious direct-to-camera and extreme closeup camerawork.

The film was released on December 14, 1993, with the tagline "No one would take on his case ... until one man was willing to take on the system." Janet Maslin in *The New York Times* wrote that Woodward was especially memorable in her brief but luminous appearance. The film was a box office success and earned Academy Award nominations for Hanks as Best Actor, Nyswaner for Best Writing Screenplay Written Directly for the Screen, Best Makeup, etc.

The Newmans were the recipients of the 15th annual Kennedy Center Honors for lifetime achievement in the performing arts held at the John F. Kennedy Center for the Performing Arts in Washington on December 7, 1992. The awards were given for "contributions to the cultural life of the nation," with the couple cited for making some of America's most powerful films. CBS televised the event as *The Kennedy Center Honors*, a.k.a. *The Kennedy Center Honors: A Celebration of the Performing Arts* on December 30. The show was written by Bob Shrum and George Stevens, Jr., and directed by William N. Cosel. At a brunch earlier in the day the Newmans appeared a little perplexed but pleased at their selection. She said that it was so heady, and asked herself what she had done to deserve being up there with people who were her gods and goddesses. But of course Woodward was delighted. At the ceremony she wore a black sparkly long-sleeved knee-length dress with a black jacket, and her hair in a short sculpted blonde style with bangs. The couple were lauded from the stage by Sally Field, Robert Redford and a group of children who had attended Hole in the Wall camps over the years. Field commented that the actress was very much a mother earth. On the set of *Sybil* they didn't have junk food—they had crudités, sliced fruit, whole wheat bread and sunflower seeds from a health food store. The crew asked where the jelly donuts were but then they fell in love with her because everybody did. Field reported that the Newmans took their work and the condition of the world very seriously but not themselves. Behind their beautiful faces there were beautiful souls and profound talent, and Field was honored to call them her friends.

On February 21, 1993, Woodward was among the performers at a benefit for the project of the Eleanor Roosevelt Monument Fund titled "First Ladies of Song" at New York's Alice Tully Hall. Proceeds helped pay for an eight-foot-high bronze sculpture by Penelope Jenks and for the landscaping of the two surrounding acres in Riverside Park.

Woodward was considered for the role of Anna Madrigal in the mystery television miniseries *Tales of the City*, based on the book by Armistead Maupin. Olympia Dukakis was cast. On March 15, the Newmans had dinner at Galileo, an Italian restaurant in Washington, with President Bill Clinton, his daughter Chelsea and others.

She returned to television for the TNT movie *Foreign Affairs* (1993), broadcast on March 17. It had a teleplay by Chris Bryant based on the novel by Alison Lurie and was directed by Jim O'Brien. Woodward stars as Vinnie Miner, a divorced Corinth University English professor and author who on sabbatical in London finds love with Chuck Mumpson (Brian Dennehy), a married American sanitary engineer. Clothes by Amy Roberts include a repeated short-sleeved knee-length purple-blue belted dress, with hair by Tracy Smith worn in a short straight blonde style with bangs. The role sees the actress naked in bed and on the floor, though discreetly covered. There is a laugh from the plot point of having Vinnie be critical of women who do needlepoint in light of Woodward's real-life passion for it. She is funny, especially in her moaning when seduced by Chuck. The actress' best scene is perhaps when Vinnie gets angry at Chuck for feeling sorry for himself and then immediately regrets what she has done.

Rick Marin of *Variety* wrote that Woodward was sensational, and John J. O'Connor in the *Times* said she confidently demonstrated what professional grace she had.

She co-produced the made-for-TV movie *Blind Spot* which was shot in Pittsburgh and broadcast on May 2 on CBS. The teleplay was by Nina Shengold based on a story by Michael McTaggart and Ellen M. Violett. and the director was Michael Toshiyuki Uno. Woodward stars as Congresswoman Nell Harrington and Laura Linney plays her daughter Phoebe Ryan, whose cocaine addiction is revealed after the car crash death of Nell's Head of Staff and son-in-law Charlie (Reed Diamond). Costumes by Hope Hanafin include a beautiful low-cut blue jacket with matching floor-length skirt. Hair by Vera Mitchell is worn in a short graying-blonde wavy style with bangs. The role sees Woodward in ballet class, which perhaps explains why she looks physically thinner. The actress makes Nell funny in her anger and the treatment presents the real rumpled woman as well as the professional poised one. Her best scene is perhaps when she berates Phoebe for abandoning her newborn baby Olivia (Ashley Palmer), with Woodward mixing crying and emotionalism in her anger.

The show was praised by Todd Everett in *Variety* and John J. O'Connor in the *Times*, who wrote that she held the project together, managing to keep Nell decent and intelligent even while she was being just about impossible. The actress was nominated for the Outstanding Lead Actress in a Miniseries or a Special Emmy Award.

For Woodward, the show's subject of drugs took on obvious personal dimensions, after the 1978 death of Scott Newman and her work with the Scott Newman Center. Linney commented that Woodward mentored her.

On May 10, Woodward was the host of New York's City Center 50th Anniversary Gala, a celebration of the Center's history. Presiding over the proceedings, the actress commented, "If these walls could just talk."

On July 10, there was a fantasy auction at the Bay Street Theater, whose prizes included an evening at the opera with Woodward. On November 17, she attended the fifth annual Power Lunch in the Rainbow Room atop New York's Rockefeller Center to benefit Citymeals-on-Wheels. On December 21, she and Jonathan Demme hosted a benefit screening of *Philadelphia* to raise money for Gay Men's Health Crisis. The screening at New York's Gemini Twin Theater was followed by a cocktail reception at the Spanish Institute, with an exhibition of paintings by Juan Suarez Botas, who had died of AIDS.

Woodward in the made-for-TV *Blind Spot* **(1993).**

Woodward voiced the role of Margaret Sanger in the biographical made-for-TV movie *The Roots of Roe* (1993). The show, written by Jeremy Brecher and Andie Hass and directed by Hass, revealed the story of abortion and contraception in America from the first surgical abortion in 1742 to the struggles over *Roe v. Wade*.

On January 17, 1994, she was on hand to celebrate the 70th birthday of her singing coach Andy Anselmo at the Roundabout Theater in an event called "A Superstar Salute to Andy Anselmo." It started with a 7 p.m. cocktail party at the Roundabout Cafe followed by a performance and a supper party back at the café. The show benefited scholarship and community programs of the Singer's Forum Foundation, which provided singing, speech and performance lessons.

Woodward did the CBS-TV movie *Breathing Lessons* which was shot on location in Pittsburgh and broadcast February 6. The teleplay was by Robert W. Lenski based upon the book by Anne Tyler and the director was John Erman. It depicted a day in the life of a Baltimore married couple, Sam's Frame Shop framer Ira Moran (James Garner) and his wife Maggie (Woodward), who works at the Golden Willows nursing home. Costumes by Helen Butler-Barbon include hair curlers and clips, a slip and a patterned purple short-sleeved and belted knee-length dress. Hair by Vera Mitchell is worn in a short straight graying-blonde style with bangs, and notable flattering makeup is by Charlene Roberson. The role sees Woodward comb the hair of Katherine Erbe, who plays Fiona. She gets a funny line when Maggie tells Ira, "You and reality ought to go steady." The actress is very funny. Her best scene is perhaps when she sings "Love Is a Many Splendored Thing" at the funeral memorial service with Durwood (John Considine). The scene reunites the actors from *See How She Runs*. John J. O'Connor in *The New York Times* wrote that Woodward gave a deliciously on-target performance.

Photographs of her on location are seen in the DVD featurette *"Breathing Lessons*: Behind the Scenes Look." She reported that there were rehearsals, two days with Garner and Erbe, and a brief rehearsal with Eileen Heckart who played Mabel. The scene with Heckart in Nell's Café was hard even though the actors knew each other, because it was done on the first day of shooting. They were a mess for a while, with both going up on their lines. Woodward loved Anne Tyler's work, loved the character of Maggie, and the whole ambience of the piece. Though Maggie was someone she had played variations on many times, she liked the sweetness and the humanity. She used a complicated knitting pattern as a prop, curl clips on the side of her head, and a purse that had packets of crackers she had taken from various restaurants. The latter was something Woodward's mother used to do. Since Maggie was a friendly person, the actress found it was all right to be chatty with people on the set.

Garner commented that the pair hit it off in rehearsals and did things that were not in the script, like Maggie attempting to straighten out the car's fender after her accident rather than just sit in the car. The cast and crew had trouble not laughing in the singing scene. He said Woodward was just wonderful, and very brave. She was firstly a professional: a good actress who knew the material and exactly what she wanted to do. Secondly, as a person, Woodward was a sweet lady—a good person who treated everyone beautifully, feeling for people and caring about things.

Paul Winfield, who played Mr. Otis, said the couple had a natural chemistry, and his jaw just slackened when he sat and watched them having a wonderful time. Winfield compared their pairing to other great acting partnerships, like Tracy and Hepburn and Hume Cronyn and Jessica Tandy. There was something magical that had resonance beyond the script, like a hidden treasure.

The Newmans were among the signers of an advertisement suggesting that the Clinton Administration had adopted a racist policy toward Haitian refugees. Woodward was a supporter of Hillary Clinton, however, and defended her against attacks and partisan assault arising from her participation in the Whitewater land deal. The actress helped pay for a full-page *Times* ad (March 29) that likened Clinton to Eleanor Roosevelt and disputed several accusations central to the Whitewater inquiry.

At Sarah Lawrence College's 65th commencement on May 20, 1994, Woodward presented an honorary doctorate to Sidney Poitier. Laura Linney reported that when she was in a production of *Hedda Gabler* on Broadway from July 10 to August 7 and having a miserable time, she called Woodward for help. The actress saw the show and took Linney back to the Newmans' New York apartment, where Linney was expecting to hear a pearl of wisdom. But Woodward just told her that there was nothing to do and she just had to get through it.

The *Times* of July 17 reported that Woodward was one of the celebrity members of the Carriage Horse Action Committee, a group that fought what it called carriage-horse abuse. On August 22, she read poetry at New York's Mitzi Newhouse Theater as a benefit for Doctors Without Borders, a medical relief organization whose volunteers were then working in Rwanda and Zaire. Woodward read a poem by Lucille Clifton. The *Times* said that while waiting to go on stage, she sighed in frustration at the ways of the world. The actress believed the United States could be in those countries if Congressmen would stop fighting among themselves. For her, it was about what the country had become and how the world was going in the wrong direction. People were identifying with tribes and religions and regions and nations instead of with individuals.

On September 17, a silent auction at the Hole in the Wall Gang camp included a driving lesson from Woodward. On September 19, she attended a screening of the documentary *Women of Substance* at New York's Time & Life Building. She narrated the film, which was a portrait of the legal, moral and health care battles being waged to improve treatment opportunities for pregnant addicts and women with children.

On October 21, the Newmans were among those who received plaques acknowledging their lifetime achievements in drama at the Westport Arts Center's first annual arts awards. When Newman was the subject of an episode of Bravo Cable's talk show *Inside the Actors Studio,* he called her the only person he could dance with, and spoke of her organic approach to character before she rounded it out intellectually. The actor presumably joked when he said his relationship was impossible in the beginning, impossible halfway through, and still impossible.

The *Times* of October 30 reported that since the previous spring, Woodward had been a member of Pegasus, a non-profit group that taught horseback riding as therapy for disabled youngsters. On December 6, she hosted a memorial tribute to Arthur B. Krim at New York's Alice Tully Hall. He was an entertainment lawyer and a former chairman of Orion Pictures and United Artists who died in September at age 84. On December 14, the Newmans attended the New York premiere of his comedy *Nobody's Fool* at the Paris Theater. On January 11, 1995, there was a party at New York's Tiffany which included "An Antebellum Repast" table by the actress, as a piece from the Winter Antiques Show.

She returned to the stage in Joseph Kesselring's comedy *Arsenic and Old Lace*, which ran at New Haven's Long Wharf Theater from January 25 to February 26. Woodward played Abby Brewster, one of the murderous geriatric sisters, in the show directed by Joey Tillinger. Ben Brantley in the *Times* wrote that she didn't avoid the pitfalls of preciousness that came with her character but unwaveringly found the self-contained logic of her homespun brand of insanity.

The actress said Abby was an interesting character to daydream about. She reported that Joyce Ebert, who played her sister Martha, laughed at her theory that they should be twins and dress alike, and designer David Murin gave them similar costumes. Woodward believed Abby was stuck in a time warp, where she was really about 16 with a suitor who had been killed in World War I, which perhaps had pushed her over the edge. Murin's fanciful and garish clothes reflected the character's girlishness. The show was the first time the actress worked with Tillinger and she said he must have been shocked after the play's read-through, where Woodward didn't seem to do much work for the next few days but then started to pull it together. It took her several weeks into the run of the play to get the first scene. She kept forgetting lines, which was unusual for her, and thought there was something wrong until she finally found an overall intention for the scene.

On January 20, she attended the preview party for the 41st Winter Antiques Show at New York's Seventh Regiment Armory, a money-raising event for the East Side House

Settlement in the Bronx. In January, Newman became the owner of the journal *The Nation*. Editor-in-chief Victor Navasky had requested a business dinner with him, and he brought his wife. When the actor was asked by Navasky for $1 million, he said that was pretty rich, and she replied, "Yes, but you're pretty rich, dear."

On March 7, the couple attended the premiere of the Mikhail Baryshnikov Dance Solo "Tongue & Groove" at the Joyce Theater in New York. On April 3, she was co-host of an evening of show tunes for the benefit of City Center at New York's Plaza Hotel.

Four mannequins modeling dresses were Woodward's donation to the Westport Historical Society's costume exhibition "Westport Life Styles Past: How We Dressed, How We Lived," on display from May to June at Wheeler House. The four white batiste and linen dresses had been worn by the actress and her three daughters when the Newmans renewed their vows in 1983 at their Westport home on their 25th wedding anniversary.

Woodward and Wendy Wasserstein wrote a letter dated July 19 to the editor of the *Times* that was published on July 23. It was in response to the editorial of the 19th concerning Legislators Against the Arts: The women agreed on the importance of the National Endowment for the Arts. They had been working with the Literary Network, a federation of literary and writers' organizations, through the Congressional session on saving the Endowment, and also supported Representative Amo Houghton in his role as a leader in the fight to keep federal support.

Woodward appeared in A&E's television biographical documentary *Golden Anniversary*, broadcast on November 11. The show, written by Nick Clooney and directed by Richie Namm, celebrated the golden wedding anniversary of Queen Elizabeth II and Prince Philip, and charted all the happy and sad goings-on in their family.

Footage and photographs of the actress appeared in "Hollywood's Charming Rebel," the November 13 episode of the documentary series *Biography*, which was devoted to Newman. She also participated in it, making comments about her husband's career and sense of humor. Woodward said that in *The Silver Chalice* he looked like a girl in a skirt, and his late '70s character roles that were unsuccessful had Hollywood deny the enormous talent that he was. She described his humor as irascible, irreverent, sly and extremely bawdy, and reported that he broke up worse than her when doing a film take.

She directed a revival of *Golden Boy* for the Blue Light Theater Company's at New York's 45th Street Theater (November 27 to December 16). Reviving the play had been her idea after having staged it at the Williamstown Theater Festival eight years prior. Woodward was also on the board of advisers of the Blue Light Theater Company. Michael Ritchie replaced Peter Hunt as the producer of the Williamstown Festival on January 2, 1996. Ritchie had known the actress after being the stage manager for the Kenyon College and off-Broadway productions of *Candida*. On January 3, Woodward telephoned him to say she was there for him, for whatever he needed or wanted. Ritchie approved her directing the Clifford Odets play *Rocket to the Moon* later in the year.

The actress narrated director Melissa Hacker's documentary *My Knees Were Jumping: Remembering the Kindertransports*. It told the story of how, on the eve of World War II, Jewish children boarded trains taking them to refuge in London, many never to see their parents again. It was screened in January 1996 at the Sundance Film Festival. In March, the Newmans were driving back home from a dinner party when an oncoming car swerved into their lane and collided with their Volvo station wagon. Newman's hand swelled up and an x-ray revealed that it was broken.

On April 1, Woodward was the host of a dinner and cabaret show at New York's

Pierre Hotel to benefit the City Center. The evening honored Gerald Schoenfeld and Bernard B. Jacobs of the Shubert Organization. Also attending the event was Rupert Murdoch, owner of *The Post*. Woodward reportedly stopped her husband from attacking him. She was the host of the June 3 episode of *Great Performances*, "Dance in America: A Renaissance Revisited." The show was written by Holly Brubach and directed by Judy Kinberg.

The *Times* of July 14 reported that Woodward had persuaded Newman to give up auto racing. He said she told him to get out of the party while it was still cooking, and he thought that made sense. In a same-day *Times* article about Michael Ritchie, Woodward commented that her dream was that he would stay on as producing director of the Williamstown Theater Festival. She had joined the Williamstown board that year and said Ritchie had done everything imaginable to make it a successful season.

The actress returned to the Berkshire Theater Festival in Stockbridge to appear as Judith Bliss in *Hay Fever*. Sources differ as to the season dates, one claiming it was from July 30 to August 10, and another July 9 to 27. She directed *Rocket to the Moon* (August 14 to 24) at Williamstown's Other Stage.

On September 17, Woodward appeared in a gala Carnegie Hall concert celebration of the 35-year collaboration of Ismail Merchant and James Ivory. It benefitted AIDS research. Sponsored by Merchant Ivory Productions, the event included a dinner after the show.

In a December 22 *Times* interview, Allison Janney reported that Woodward had suggested she study at the Neighborhood Playhouse after graduating from Kenyon College. Woodward said that there was no doubt that Janney was a major talent who seemed to be able to do anything. Janney described Woodward as an inspiration and a mentor.

In 1996, Woodward was the host of director Joel. L. Freedman's short *Even If a Hundred Ogres....* That year the actress reported that she had taken her husband and actress Marisa Tomei to see Eve Ensler's *The Vagina Monologues*. Newman at first seemed taken aback by its frankness. Woodward said she glanced to the left and saw him stony-faced and bemused, while Tomei was sobbing.

Woodward narrated the documentary *Gun Control in Connecticut: Women Call the Shots*, broadcast on cable access television stations on January 12, 1997. Made by Third Wave Television, it tracked the gun control movement, showing how ordinary women and men took on the National Rifle Association lobby and won. Producer Amy Butkus Mooney reported that Woodward signed on with much enthusiasm from the start because she was a woman who cared about a lot of issues.

On March 14, the Newmans attended a meeting of the Westport Board of Finance where the officials recommended appropriating $3.7 million to purchase 30 acres of open land in the Coleytown area known as the "Poses Property." As part of the purchase, the board also endorsed the town's plan to accept a gift of 7.5 acres of land adjoining the property belonging to the couple, which would be used as a buffer for the Newman land.

On the April 16 episode of the news talk show *Charlie Rose,* Woodward spoke on directing Clifford Odets' *Waiting for Lefty*, about taxi drivers summoning the collective will to strike. The *Times* of April 27 had her interviewed about doing the play for Blue Light, on whose board of advisers she served. Woodward had a special affection for Odets, and reported that when she told people of her desire to direct *Golden Boy* they rolled their eyes and complained that his dramas often fell victim to messages. But the actress found the grittiness contemporary and believed he was one of the finest American playwrights. She had been introduced to the play as a student at the Neighborhood

Playhouse where some of her teachers, like Sanford Meisner, were former members of the Group Theatre. Set in the Depression era, the play made her recall how her father, a math teacher–baseball coach, picked peaches and played semi-pro ball in the summer to support the family. This tenacity in the face of hardship is what made the play still work, and it was about changing people's minds, which is what theater was for.

Woodward donated a check to a baby shower held on April 27 at New York's La Belle Epoque restaurant and jazz club. The eight-months-pregnant Roisin McAliskey was held in Holloway Prison in London in connection with a mortar attack on an unoccupied British Army barracks in June. No formal charges had been filed against her, and she denied any involvement in the attack. On May 27 the actress was the host for a dinner at New York's Pierre hotel benefiting Women in Need, which provided housing and services to women and children.

She returned to the Williamstown Theater Festival to direct *La Ronde* in a season from August 13 to 24. On September 13, Woodward participated in a benefit for the Hole in the Wall Gang Camp held in Ashford, Connecticut. The show at the camp's theater was a musical by A.E. Hotchner that was inspired by Cinderella and set in Hollywood.

The Newmans contributed a glowing tribute to Christopher Reeve in a 30-minute infomercial appearing on New York television stations and cable networks. Entitled "Circle of Friends," it asked for donations to help find a cure for spinal cord injuries and other causes of paralysis. On October 28, the couple were judges for the final round of a national competition conducted by Newman's Own and *Good Housekeeping* magazine for recipes using a Newman's Own company's food product. The event took place at the Pegasus Suite of New York's Rainbow Room, with the winner to receive $50,000 to be given to a worthy cause. Before the tasting began, the actor said it would be the perfect opportunity to fight in public. Woodward agreed it would be impossible since, like everything else in life, they had never chosen the same thing. He picked Towering Inferno Creole Posole submitted by Alexendria Sanchez of Albuquerque, New Mexico, while she voted for Franklin County, Florida's Own Frankly Fantastic Seafood Gumbo made by Jackie Gay of Carrabelle, Florida. The result was that two grand prizes of $50,000 were given.

On November 16, she was the chairwoman for a dinner at New York's Laura Belle restaurant which included an auction and a cabaret show to benefit the Williamstown Theater Festival. Woodward also spoke at the event and offered an evening at the ballet, accompanied by her, as one of the auction items. She attended *The Kennedy Center Honors: A Celebration of the Performing Arts* that took place on December 8. It was televised on December 26. The actress was there to speak for Edward Villella, one of the honorees. She appeared in the A&E *Biography* episode on Joan Collins, "A Personal Dynasty," broadcast on December 18. She also appeared in an episode of the biographical documentary TV series *The Directors*, "The Films of James Ivory," broadcast in 1997 on the Encore Movie Channel.

Woodward wrote the foreword for Sandy Dennis' 1997 book *A Personal Memoir*, which was published by Papier-Mache Press. She described Dennis' writing as having an almost Emily Dickenson sensibility with an elegant and dainty sense of humor. When the Newmans celebrated their 40th marriage anniversary on January 29, 1998, he commented that ultimately the couple delighted in watching their progression, and they both laughed a lot. The actor reported she was a mercurial lady and he never knew what he was going to wake up to the next morning, which made for some fascinating experiences.

Woodward said there were times when they both had to hang in when it felt like the marriage wouldn't last another day. The couple had to step outside themselves and become aware that three things were operating: her ego, his ego and "*our* ego." For the relationship to survive, they had to put the his-and-hers on hold and go for the *our*.

They were interviewed for an article in the *Times* of March 1 which said the couple lived on the 15th floor of a Manhattan apartment above Central Park when they were in New York. Newman reported there had been long, really difficult times, but they had enough lust and respect: The Newmans were lustily respectful and respectfully lustful.

The actress appeared in the television biographical documentary *James Dean: A Portrait*, broadcast on April 6. The show was written by Gary Legon and David Dalton and directed by Legon. She paid tribute to the late costume designer Edith Head at a benefit for the Design Industries Foundation Fighting AIDS on April 23 in the lobby of the New York Cipriani Hotel.

From April 27 to May 18, 1998, the Actors Studio marked its 50th anniversary with discussions and readings looking back at the legendary Group Theater and its productions. Woodward appeared in the opening night discussion.

They joined the organizational committee for a gala benefit on October 1 by the Westchester Holocaust Commission. Entitled "Portraits in Courage," it told the story of one of the rare rescues of Jews by Jews in Poland during World War II. On October 28, the couple judged seven dishes made from recipes that called for products made by Newman's Own food company at a lunch held at the Rainbow Room in New York's G.E. Building. The winner: a dish made with salsa and salad dressing, which was entered by Dianne Reilly, a fourth- and fifth-grade teacher from St. Albans, Vermont.

Woodward was interviewed for the *Times* of November 9. She was currently directing a workshop of the Howard Richardson–William Berney drama *Dark of the Moon*, a Broadway hit in 1945. Woodward reported that her favorite book was Willa Cather's *Lucy Gayheart*, which she reread at least once a year. It struck a very deep chord with her because it was so intensely romantic and had a sense of longing to go someplace else, which was a part of the actress as a child. It was also highly sensual, as the young main character Lucy was involved with the older singer Sebastian. Lucy reminded Woodward of a classmate at Louisiana State University, who was crowned queen of the school in both her freshman and sophomore years. She had the most radiant smile and a light somehow glimmered around her, and the actress was a member of the queen's court. There was also a Sebastian in her past: Ezio Pinza. She dreamed about turning the book into a movie, with Placido Domingo as Sebastian. As a first step in bringing it to a wider public, Woodward read the entire thing aloud for an audience at New York's Symphony Space. This was part of a series entitled "Singular Women," held over two evenings (November 8 and 9). She had taken a tentative step onstage at Symphony Space in May with a short story. Regarding making movies, the actress likened it to brain surgery: It was scary and maybe it worked and maybe it didn't. Among those she believed worked were *The Three Faces of Eve, Rachel, Rachel* and *Mr. & Mrs. Bridge*. In recent years, the actress had turned down movie offers. She kept getting scripts to play grandmas and didn't want to play one as she was already somebody's grandma.

On November 23, Woodward attended the 26th International Emmy Awards held at the Hilton Hotel in New York. She participated in "Selected Shorts: A Celebration of the Short Story" at Symphony Space, a ten-program series of readings that ran from January 27 to June 2, 1999.

The *Times* of June 27, 1999, reported that wax replicas of the couple were part of Madame Tussaud's Las Vegas, to open on July 8. The Newmans had married in a Las Vegas hotel and their replicas now welcomed guests to a wedding chapel furnished with memorabilia and photographs of celebrities who had tied the knot in Vegas. On August 9, they spoke at a memorial service for Sylvia Sidney, who had died on July 1 at New York's National Arts Club. Woodward returned to the Williamstown Theater Festival to fill in for an ailing Eileen Heckart in the part of Gladys Green in the Kenneth Lonergan play *The Waverly Gallery*. The show was a memory play about the mental decline of Lonergan's grandmother. Directed by Ellis Scott, it ran August 11–22 on the Nikos Stage. The Newmans went to see Heckart in the play on the weekend of the last week, but she withdrew from the production with a panic over forgetting her lines. The theater's artistic director Michael Ritchie asked Woodward if she would read the part for the last five performances. She agreed and went on after one rehearsal. The rest of the company helped, leading her about the stage or pointing to where the actress was to move next. She had some of the pages on a sofa and some on a kitchen table. Woodward said it was no wonder her 81-year-old friend Heckart had gotten sick, because the part was exhausting. Heckart had only had two weeks of rehearsal, and no actress could have learned the role in that time. Woodward sent her a large basket of white orchids with a note saying they were from her loving understudy, to get well soon, and that the Newmans loved her. Heckart managed to recover and joined the play when it transferred to the off-Broadway Promenade Theatre for a run that lasted from March 22 to May 21, 2000.

The Newmans bought one of the hand-crafted bas relief picture tiles on the Westport Public Library wall. Their tile was Max Shulman's 1957 novel *Rally 'Round the Flag, Boys!*, a fictional account of Westport's battle to prevent a missile base from being built there. The couple had moved to the town after starring in the movie version of the book. On September 21, they co-hosted a reception for First Lady Hillary Clinton at the Beachside home of Harvey Weinstein to raise funds for her New York Senatorial campaign.

11

Westport Country Playhouse

Woodward reported that in 1999, she was invited to lunch by Bill Haber, a Westport Country Playhouse committee board member. The theater was in danger of being torn down and the space made into a mall with parking lot, and her assistance was requested. The actress later commented she would have lain down in front of a truck if anyone ever thought of demolishing the space. She had gone to the Playhouse as a young woman to see *Anastasia* and had long been a donor and appeared in benefits there but never a proper play. Woodward believed its wonderful tradition was so important to all that it had to be preserved, and her efforts helped it to be. The January 2, 2000, *New York Times* reported that she was now head of the advisory council, replacing the retired Jim McKenzie, who had been the artistic director for 40 years. She said that a few years before, people had talked to McKenzie about appointing a new artistic director, and her name came up, but he wasn't quite ready to give it over. Woodward now agreed to take over some of McKenzie's functions on a part-time volunteer basis and to direct a play each season as able.

The January 16 *Times* reported that the personal involvement of the Newmans had helped preserve Trout Brook Valley, about 700 acres straddling the boundary of Weston and Easton, Connecticut. In January, she wrote the foreword for Woody Klein's book *Westport, Connecticut: The Story of a New England Town's Rise to Prominence*, which was released by Greenwood Press and the Westport Historical Society. The actress described the town as eclectic and cosmopolitan, and a Mecca for those who were traditionally untraditional.

The Westport County Playhouse declared her one of a new female triumvirate, breaking its patriarchal structure. Woodward joined with chief executive and executive director Elissa Getto and artistic manager Janice Muirhead, with the actress as the artistic catalyst. Getto and Muirhead cited her as their inspiration and primary motivation for coming to the playhouse. Woodward also enlisted Anne Keefe, one of the top stage managers in the world, feeling her involvement was mandatory. The actress later wondered what she had gotten herself into, as it was like jumping off the high diving board when you didn't know how to swim. Woodward preferred to call the advisory council an artistic committee, and their plan of action was to renovate the theater so it could operate all year rather than just do summer stock, and keep it close to its traditional appearance. But before renovations could begin, a season for the summer had to be put together, for the sake of continuity. Her total commitment to the Playhouse meant sacrificing the Williamstown Theater Festival this year.

On February 13, in Valentine's Day Week, the Newmans gave a single performance of A.R. Gurney's *Love Letters* at the Westport Country Playhouse as a benefit for the theater's regeneration. For the top ticket price, the bearer got to break bread with them before the show.

The couple were reported to be one of the quiet instigators and financial backers of a Broadway run for the Encores! concert series' production of *Wonderful Town* which had had a brief run at City Center two weeks prior. Woodward was on the board of both City Center and Encores! The show would not make it to Broadway until 2003. The June 4 *Times* said the actress had a sandwich named for her at Williamstown's Pappa Charlie's Deli. The Joanne Woodward consisted of peanut butter, jam, bananas and raisins on whole wheat.

Her title at the Westport Country Playhouse was now artistic advisory council co-chairwoman. She also directed the season's opener, W. Somerset Maugham's *The Constant Wife*, and acted in A. R. Gurney's *Ancestral Voices*. The latter was a *Love Letters*–style reading for five actors instead of two, with an entire cast change each week of a two-week run (July 10 to 22). The actress appeared in the second week with Newman in the comedy about a young man coming to terms with the divorce of his grandparents. Woodward said she had no trouble persuading her husband, saying the best way for him to be on stage was with a script in his hand.

She allowed that her name value had been helpful in increasing subscriptions to the Playhouse and helped in getting their plans to coalesce. Woodward also brought in actors and then had to find places for them to stay, giving over her barn and having them sleep on sofas. She said her home was now a boarding house.

On August 15, the Newmans went to New York's Tribeca Grill for a briefing on the three-month-old strike against the advertising industry. The main issue in the strike, which involved 135,000 members of the Screen Actors Guild and the American Federation of Television and Radio Artists, was how to pay actors for appearing in commercials.

Woodward commented to the *Times* of September 24 that her work at the Westport Country Playhouse was an extraordinary learning process and she was totally pleased with the season. Even though a new play done in collaboration with Williamstown Theater was problematic, it was an experiment that succeeded and the alliance would go on. They would also continue to do at least one play a year that reflected the history of the theater.

On November 11, the actress participated in a reading of *Arsenic and Old Lace* at New York's City Center. This was the inaugural production of the Center's new "Voices!" series: staged readings of great American plays of the last 100 years. The cast had one day of rehearsal prior to the performance.

The *Times* of February 23, 2001, reported that the couple had attended Pamela Gien's Off Broadway one-woman show *The Syringa Tree* which had opened on September 14, 2000, at the Playhouse 91 theater. The March 25 *Times* said that they donated birdhouses each year to be auctioned in an event entitled "In Celebration of Homes: The Art of the Birdhouse," held at Greens Farms Academy in Westport. The proceeds provided shelter and support to troubled adolescent girls in Westport's Project Return, a program that offered a family environment to a group of girls who conducted everyday lives in a farmhouse setting. Woodward was interviewed for the May 14 episode of the biographical documentary TV series *Intimate Portrait* on Allison Janney. The show was written by Gary Ponticeillo but the director is unknown.

On June 3, Woodward read from the works of Calvin Trillin for the annual cele-bratory find-raiser at the Westport Public Library Award. In the *Times* of June 17, she was called the new artistic director of the Westport Country Playhouse. She said she accepted the position, owing it to the Langners (Lawrence Langner in 1931 turned the red barn into a summer theater). The Playhouse had given both Newmans their first the-ater jobs, and it had become one of the most famous summer playhouses in the country. If you looked at a list of all the people who ever played there, you would see the names of every great performer from the past 75 years. In addition, Woodward felt she owed it to the town of Westport, which had been a home for their family for decades.

The *Times* of June 24 reported that the Newmans were volunteers and contributors to the college program of Bedford Hills Correctional Facility, a maximum security women's prison. On September 12, the couple was said to have dined at a restaurant near Westport when Newman began singing "The Star Spangled Banner" in response to the news of the 9/11 attack of the previous day. The entire house reportedly joined him. The idea for a revival of *Our Town* at the Westport Country Playhouse was also said to have come from the Newman's response to 9/11.

On October 28, Woodward participated in "For the Children," a benefit program for families affected by the 9/11 attacks, at the Playhouse. Proceeds were distributed to families in need by the Children's Aid Society in New York.

On November 2, WENN reported that the actress amusingly confirmed that her husband was still very much in control of his facilities after he had scared his Connecticut neighbors when spotted walking around talking to himself. Newman was in the process of recording his memoirs as a legacy for his five children.

On November 19, she was in a concert performance of *The World of Nick Adams*, A.E. Hotchner's stage adaptation of Ernest Hemingway's Nick Adams stories, at Avery Fisher Hall. The show was directed by Frank Corsaro. Woodward played Nick's difficult mother. Proceeds went to the Association of Hole in the Wall Gang Camps.

The Newmans did another performance of *Ancestral Voices* on April 6, 2002, at the Westport Country Playhouse as a benefit reading for the theater. It was directed by Arvin Brown. The couple went to see the play *Mornings at Seven* during the end of its Broadway run at the Lyceum Theatre to support their friends Piper Laurie, Estelle Parsons and stage manager Roy Harris. Laurie reported that the couple seemed genuinely surprised at how much fun the production was and were very pleased. After the show, they all left together and Laurie said that Woodward trailed behind her and Newman as he walked to find her a cab, thoughtfully letting the old friends have a moment. The couple went to New York's Café Carlyle on April 30 to hear James Naughton sing deep-voiced cabaret songs. Naughton was to direct Newman in *Our Town* at the Westport Country Playhouse, to open in May, and she was heard to say that it would be fine as her husband was not hard to direct. Naughton said he and the actress had been scheming for 15 years to get Newman back on stage.

She was the narrator of *Pale Male*, a documentary about a red-tailed hawk who lived on the side of a New York Fifth Avenue building. It was written by Janet Hess, based on the novel by Marie Winn, and directed by Frederic Lilien. The film premiered at the Brooklyn International Film Festival on June 1, 2002. The Newmans attended the New York premiere of his crime drama thriller *Road to Perdition* (2002) and the after party held at Grand Central Station.

The *Times* of October 11 reported that Woodward was the narrator of the birding video *World of Raptors*. Nothing else is known about it. On November 4, she participated in another performance of *The World of Nick Adams* at the Kodak Theatre in Hollywood to benefit the Hole in the Wall Gang Camps for Children. She was interviewed for the November 12 episode of the Canadian Broadcasting Corporation's biographical documentary TV series *Life and Times*, "A Man for All Stages: The Life and Times of Christopher Plummer."

The Newmans were interviewed for the *Times* of December 1 about the transfer of the Westport Country Playhouse production of *Our Town* to Broadway (June 5 to 22). They had been interviewed in the autumn on *The Today Show*. It had taken place at the grounds of the Playhouse, and the couple responded to questions they were notoriously weary of, like, "What's the secret to your long marriage?" Woodward wore a long skirt and boots and ate a tuna salad and an oatmeal cookie. The actress was at first surprised that her husband wanted to move *Our Town* to Broadway, with a season to run at the Booth Theatre (from December 4 to January 26, 2003). Although it once was a tryout theater, this is not what she had intended to use the Playhouse for. Her programming tried to find the balance between light summer fare and serious work that people might walk out of, as they did during last season's *Orson's Shadow* by Austin Pendleton. The meditation on fame and art used a semi-fictional encounter between Orson Welles and Laurence Olivier and was considered too heavy for some. After the summer season, the $17 million renovations were to begin, scheduled to be completed by the theater's 75th birthday in 2005.

Woodward appeared in the biographical documentary *The Education of Gore Vidal*, which premiered at the Sundance Film Festival on January 20, 2003. Written and directed by Deborah Dickson, it explored Vidal's extraordinary life and work, joining him at his cliffside villa in Ravello, Italy. She attended the closing night performance of *Our Town* on January 26, which was also Newman's birthday. The actress joined him on stage for the show's final curtain call.

She was interviewed for the documentary *The John Garfield Story*, broadcast on Turner Classic Movies on February 3. Woodward said that there wasn't a film of the actor's she didn't see. The actress spoke of his testifying at the House Un-American Activities Committee. She believed Garfield was in Hollywood at a time when an actor was not encouraged to have a range, yet within that framework, he made it work so that no two parts were exactly alike.

Woodward urged the Encores! advisory committee to present a semi-staged concert of the musical *House of Flowers* at New York's City Center. She had seen the original production, which ran on Broadway from December 30, 1954, to May 1955, about ten times and was enthralled by Truman Capote's poetic, witty lyrics. The actress said it was the essence of the kind of show that Encores! should do because it had truly disappeared without a trace. But she had no idea how difficult it would be. The Newmans donated most of the $135,000 cost of the new arrangements, and the concert took place on February 13. It was reported in the April edition of the *National Enquirer* that Woodward had covered her husband's beer refrigerator with photographs of car wrecks, in an effort to get him to stop racing, but he continued. Another source claims that by this time, he had given up the sport.

Woodward was interviewed in the August 24 *New York Times* about her plans for the Playhouse. She wanted to add new plays and celebrity names to the seasons, beef up its development division and rebuild for the future. The barn probably wouldn't have lasted another year and they were using a lot of the existing materials, pulling boards up and replacing them, and giving the audience more room—going from 707 seats to about 580. The actress acknowledged that the lost seats would affect the box office but their shows never had full houses anyway, except when Newman did *Our Town*. She wanted to present dance and children's theater and was cautiously optimistic that, after the renovations, they could do new work and have more productions move to Broadway. The *Our Town* transfer had been a wonderful experience, despite her husband's schedule limiting it to a short run.

In September 2003, the Newmans began work on the HBO miniseries *Empire Falls*, shot in Skowhegan and other Maine locations and broadcast on May 28, 2005. The teleplay was by Richard Russo, based on his novel. A decaying Maine town was the backdrop and Ed Harris starred as unassuming Empire Grill restaurant manager Miles Roby. Woodward played the supporting role of Francine Whiting, owner of the Grill and the town's textile mill. Director Fred Schepisi commented that this was Woodward's first film in ten years and it was great to have her back. He loved the malevolence the actress brought to Francine and how she enjoyed torturing Miles. Her costumes are by Donna Zakowska and her hair by Suzy Mazzarese Allison, Rose Chatterton and Jennifer Santiago (a shoulder-length straight silver style with a side part mostly worn in a ponytail). She gets a funny line in "Passionate decisions are seldom sound." Virginia Heffernan in the *Times* wrote that the actress exhibited haughty cordiality as a villainess. Emmy nominations were received for Woodward for Outstanding Supporting Actress in a Miniseries or a Movie, as well as Newman for Outstanding Supporting Actor. He won, she didn't.

In 2003, she voiced the character of Anne Martin in "Safe for Democracy," an episode of PBS's historical documentary series *Freedom: A History of Us*. The show was written by Joy Hakim, Philip Kunhardt III, Peter W. Kunhardt and Nancy Steiner, based on a story by Hakim, and the directors were Kunhardt III, Kunhardt and Steiner.

On March 9, 2004, the couple attended a production of *Sweeney Todd* at New York's Lincoln Center, which was part of the New York City Opera's spring gala. Woodward said they had seen the original Broadway production with Angela Lansbury which ran from March 1, 1979, to June 29, 1980. In July, the couple attended "A Change Is Going to Come: The Concert for John Kerry" at New York's Radio City Music Hall. It was to benefit Kerry Victory 2004, Kerry's 2004 Democratic presidential campaign.

On September 2 she was among those that read the United States Constitution at Cooper Union in New York's Great Hall as part of "Constitution Night." The *Times* of October 10 reported the Newmans had given $8,000 to the campaign for Diane Goss Farrell, the Democratic candidate for the Fourth Congressional District in Connecticut. They also had "Farrell for Congress" bumper stickers on their cars.

The Playhouse was scheduled to reopen in June 2005. Woodward said she hoped to have raised $30.6 million by then, for construction, an endowment, winter activities, a children's theater and a children's workshop. The original playhouse was to be preserved within a larger edifice that would accommodate an orchestra pit, offstage space, a shop to build sets, two lobbies, an elevator and more comfortable seating. She was astounded by the progress, saying it looked like an art form, which made the actress cry.

She was interviewed on November 5 by Linda Winer, the theater critic for *Newsday*, for the League of Professional Theatre Women's program "Women in Theatre: Dialogues with Notable Women in American Theatre." The show was directed by Audra D. Malone and broadcast on CUNY TV. Woodward spoke about how she became the artistic director of the Westport Country Playhouse, the renovations, her marriage to Newman in Vegas, signing her Fox Hollywood contract, directing, why she was not happy doing films, sponsoring dance and theater companies, acting on stage vs. film, her love of Clifford Odets' work, her children and grandchildren and Newman's enormous integrity.

For her husband's 80th birthday, on January 26, 2005, she had a party with 75 of their friends and family members and the Emerson String Quartet at their Westport home. Woodward was interviewed in the Turner Classic Movies documentary *The Adventures of Errol Flynn*, broadcast on April 5, 2005. It was written by Robert J. Jordan, Joan Kramer and David Heely, and directed by Heeley. The film presented the life of Flynn, with recollections from friends and family. She said that the actor was like Peck's bad boy because you could forgive him anything when he smiled. The actress recalled seeing his films as a child and appreciating Flynn's charm. He was gorgeous, fun and totally comfortable in what he did even in the most bizarre outfits. She also commented on Flynn's performances in the war drama *The Dawn Patrol* (1938), the romance *That Forsyte Woman* (1949) and the biographical romance *Too Much, Too Soon* (1958).

The *Times* of May 22 reported that the Westport Country Playhouse was about $3 million short of its goal of a $30.6 million refurbishment drive, but the renovations were almost complete with the space set to open its new doors for the summer season on June 16. After a tour of the theater, Woodward came to fully understand her own thoughts and emotions about it. Everything was new again and yet the Playhouse still seemed like a dear old friend. Her goal nearly realized, she would step down as the artistic director after the summer's season, becoming artistic director emeritus and a member of the board of directors. On June 21, the Playhouse announced that Tazewell Thompson, a director of stage and opera and a playwright himself, would become its new artistic director, taking over on January 1, 2006. He credited Woodward, whom he called his guardian angel. She had brought him to Westport, hiring him in 2003 to direct a production of *The Old Settler*. He became friendly with her, so when the call came to audition to lead the Playhouse, he was not surprised. Thompson met alone with Woodward, and realized they had a lot of the same ideas and thoughts and tastes and plans. She commented that he had wit and humor and a real sense of the need for education, outreach and being part of the community.

Richard Somerset-Ward's book *An American Theatre: The Story of Westport Country Playhouse, 1931–2005* was published by Yale University Press on June 11. The Newmans provided the foreword, and a chapter was devoted to Woodward's position as artistic leader from 2000 to 2005.

She directed a production of Carson McCullers's *Member of the Wedding* for the Playhouse; it ran from July 28 to August 14. Anita Gates in the *Times* commented that because Woodward and McCullers were both born in Georgia, it was disappointing that some of the accents on stage sounded generically, British-movie-star Southern.

Woodward chose Giles Havergal's adaptation of Charles Dickens's *David Copperfield* as her swan song at the Westport Country Playhouse, and co-directed with Anne Keefe. The show ran from December 11 to 17 and told the story of one young Englishman's encounters with scoundrels and clowns. It was praised by Anita Gates in the *Times*.

On September 25, the couple hosted a benefit dinner and musical tribute to Stephen Sondheim at the Westport Country Playhouse. She commented on her husband's new restaurant behind the Playhouse, Dressing Room: A Homegrown Restaurant. He made the best hamburger, and although Woodward recalled making some fine cakes for her daughters and proofing bread in the sauna, Newman was the cook in the family. The idea for the restaurant apparently came to him after they had recently eaten at a pricey one which had bad service and bad food. On February 10, 2007, the couple read love poems at the Playhouse in an event titled "Come Be My Love...Love Spoken Here." On May 21 she attended the Gala Salute To Director Wynn Handman at The Hudson Theater in New York.

In mid-year, Newman began experiencing symptoms of a heart attack. His wife insisted they call a doctor and after an examination, he was given a clean bill of health.

She was the narrator of the American-Ecuadoran documentary *Keepers of Eden* which screened at the Everglades International Film Festival on September 27. It was written by Douglas K. Dempsey and Matt Mazer, and directed by Yoram Porath, Christopher Gambale and Steven Meyer. The film presented the story of the Huarani tribe which had inhabited the rain forests of Ecuador for thousands of years, and were now in danger of being erased by the fallout caused by major oil companies.

In January 2008, Woodward and Anne Keefe returned as interim co–artistic directors of the Westport Country Playhouse, succeeding Tazewell Thompson, whose departure after two years was attributed to artistic and professional differences. The women were interviewed in the January 19 *Times*. They were described as looking like two former sorority sisters who had kept in touch, both with white hair now, and both dressed like affluent country ladies in pants outfits with good-looking jewelry. Woodward declined to comment on Thompson's leaving, as she had not been at the theater when it had happened. They were rethinking the season's schedule after the two plays that Thompson was going to direct were cancelled as a courtesy to him, with casting yet to be finalized for Morris Panych's comedy *Vigil*, due to go into rehearsals by the end of the month. The actress reported that that her two grandsons were taking acting classes, and she fantasized about doing big-cast shows (like *Liliom*) that were often too costly for regional theaters. On February 4, the women announced the new Playhouse schedule.

12

Paul Newman Dies

In early 2008, Newman was diagnosed with lung cancer. As the couple were preparing to celebrate their 50th wedding anniversary on January 29, *The National Enquirer* broke the story despite the fact that people had only been told on a need-to-know basis. He had undergone surgery and the prognosis was poor. The Newmans carried on with their party, he toasting her before their children and dearest friends. The actor said he felt privileged to love his wife and that being married to her was the joy of his life.

WENN via *The New York Post* reported on March 17 that the couple was seen at an oncologist's office. Woodward was said to have been very sweet with the staff while waiting for her husband to finish treatment. In late March, they were spotted dining at Café des Artistes in New York. In April came news that Newman had reportedly written a new will, cementing plans to leave the majority of his estate to Woodward.

On June 8, she attended the Alice Tully Hall after party for the celebration of Newman's Hole in the Wall camps. On June 11, the actor issued a statement after claims were published by tabloids that he only had six months to live and was under hospital supervision. Newman laughed off the rumors, insisting the treatment he was receiving was for nothing more than athlete's foot and hair loss. But now the *Los Angeles Times* picked up the story, saying the actor had terminal lung cancer and was having outpatient treatment at New York's Sloan-Kettering Center. His business partner, A.E. Hotchner, initially confirmed that Newman had been diagnosed 18 months prior. Hotchner then denied the story, claiming to be misquoted in an Associated Press article, and said he had no knowledge of any diagnosis or of the actor being treated for any illness.

In August, Newman was photographed leaving Memorial Sloan-Kettering in a wheelchair, and had reportedly told his doctors and his family that he wanted no more chemotherapy. He preferred to go home to Westport and see out his illness. On August 13, the Newmans went to Lime Rock Park so that he could gun around it in his Corvette, with Woodward and the girls riding behind him in the Volvo station wagon. Later in the month, the couple visited the original Hole in the Wall Camp in Ashford one more time. They toured the grounds in a golf cart and then ate sandwiches at a table beside the pond. Back in Westport, Woodward kept up her scheduled tasks with the Playhouse and the daily chores of the household. She also drove him around; Newman would sit in the car while she ran errands or bought corn from a roadside vegetable stand. The actor said that in the past when he drove her, his wife would say that they were not in a hurry, which is something Newman now said to her. On August 23, they dined at the Dressing Room restaurant in Westport.

In September 15, Woodward co-chaired a fundraising gala at the Playhouse; Newman had been forced to bow out of because of his health. A source told the *National Enquirer* that Woodward had dearly hoped he could attend because she knew there were words Newman wanted to say publicly. One source claimed that the couple attended an antiques–and-car show at a nearby country club, though the *Enquirer* said she went alone because he was too ill. The tabloid also said the actress came close to collapsing both physically and emotionally due to the toll her husband's illness had taken on her, but she continued to support him at home. In the last two weeks, the actor was unable to speak but Woodward put him on the phone to listen to Sidney Poitier when he called. On September 25, a doctor was summoned to the house as Newman was having trouble breathing; Newman refused the oxygen he had been using. The actor asked for some time alone with his wife, and they were behind closed doors for more than 20 minutes. He died at 6:45 p.m., sources differing on whether it was the same day or the next. She was reportedly devastated and told the family that Newman was now at peace, with no more suffering.

According to his wishes, he was cremated and the ashes scattered over his favorite racetrack. There was a private memorial service, followed by a gathering at the Newman restaurant, the Dressing Room. His will left the farmhouse in Westport, significant real estate holdings, and personal effects to his wife Joanne Woodward Newman.

She was said to have spent most of her time crying and in seclusion, refusing to see close friends. The actress also couldn't sleep and suffered from vagueness and confusion, forgetting names and reportedly nearly walking into traffic outside her Fifth Avenue apartment. It was said her condition was a sign of senile dementia. Friends noted that Newman had been concerned how she would carry on without him, since they were soulmates. He thought Woodward should return to what she did best besides being his life partner—acting—as a way of dealing with her loneliness and grief. According to *The National Enquirer*, the actress struggled with grief until her husband visited in a dream and told Woodward to get back to work. Perhaps granting his final wish would help to heal her broken heart.

On November 10, she directed a staged reading of the Sidney Howard play *They Knew What They Wanted* for the Westport Country Playhouse. The actress then appeared in the Playhouse holiday production of *A Holiday Garland* with performances on December 13 and 19, 20 and 21. Director John Tillinger commented that it was tricky because of her recent loss but everybody said it would be good for Woodward.

On January 13, 2009, Mark Lamos was named as the new artistic director of the Playhouse, succeeding Woodward and Anne Keefe. Lamos commented that the Newmans were the spirit of the Playhouse, and she still was.

On June 10, WENN reported that Julia Roberts had turned to Woodward to help calm her nerves before stepping on stage at a New York benefit on June 8. Roberts celebrated Newman's memory at Manhattan's Lincoln Center in aid of the Hole in the Wall Camps. At the podium, she admitted calling Woodward earlier in the day to ask if there was anything specific she should mention in her speech. The older actress was the host of the event and reportedly keen for the Camps to continue. She asked that Roberts talk of the fun that they all had and to say that the actor really enjoyed his life.

On November 2, the Westport Country Playhouse's Gala 2009 featured a salute to Woodward. The event's proceeds in part were to support the Woodward Intern and Apprentice program, recently named in recognition of her interest in training the next generation of theater artists. On November 11, WENN reported that the actress suffered a cancer scare in October. She had undergone a biopsy after a medical test showed a growth on her lung. A source told *The National Enquirer* that there were fears that Woodward was going to be diagnosed with lung cancer—just like Newman had been—perhaps because both had been heavy smokers for much of their lives. She was said to have lived with the passing of her husband every hour of every single day, and this scare brought back the vivid nightmares of when he was diagnosed and the long battle the actor endured. Woodward was relieved when the growth was ruled benign, but the stress of the situation had taken its toll on her. Pals feared for her health after she turned up at the Westport charity gala looking frail and pale, and her hair whiter and thinner. On November 18, Woodward presented Gore Vidal with the award for distinguished contribution to American letters at the National Book Awards. She described him as her dear friend and the second love of her life. The actress also told an anecdote about the christening of one of her daughters, with Vidal as godfather. He was holding the child gingerly and she got sprayed and cried and there was a moment's pause. Vidal then looked down and said, "Always a godfather, never a god."

The March 12, 2010, *New York Times* reported that she was on the honorary board of the non-profit Hudson Valley Writers' Center in Sleepy Hollow, New York, whose members come mostly from the Westchester area. The Center offered writing workshops for adults, children and social-service organizations.

A.E. Hotchner's book, *Paul and Me: 53 Years of Adventures and Misadventures with Paul Newman*, was published on March 23 by Nan A. Talese/Doubleday. It made several references to Woodward which included her battling with Newman when making *The Effect of Gamma Rays on Man-in-the-Moon Marigolds*, her reaction to Newman's race car driving, the couple's friendship with Jim Padula, their cemetery tours to find burial plots, Newman's 50th birthday party, and stage nights at the Hole in the Wall Camp.

Woodward provided the voice of Margaret Mitchell for "Change in the Wind," the July 15 episode of the TV documentary series *Andrew Young Presents*. Written by CB Hackworth and Young and directed by Hackworth, it told the story of the friendship between the writer and the legendary president of Morehouse College, Benjamin E. Mays.

On October 18, the actress attended the Elton John AIDS Foundation's ninth annual benefit at New York's Cipriani Wall Street. On October 21, she was at the celebration of Paul Newman's Hole in the Wall Camps at Avery Fisher Hall. On October 28, a photograph of her was placed in capsule at the Hollywood Walk of Fame Time Capsule press conference by Hollywood Chamber of Commerce president–CEO Leron Gubler. The photograph was of Woodward sitting on her own Walk of Fame star. In early November, she was co-chairperson for an evening entitled "Over the Moon Celebration" where Newman's Own Foundation awarded $1.4 million in 14 grants.

The *Times* of December 3 reported that the actress was on the lighting committee for the Fund for Park Avenue, which paid for the Park Avenue Christmas lights lit on the first Sunday of December. The trees and lights, which ran from 54th to 96th Street, remained a memorial to all who had lost their lives defending their country. Each of the 100 trees was adorned with 2500 little stringed lights, which were plugged into the bases of streetlamps, and they remained up through mid–January.

Woodward was the narrator of the animated video short *All the World*, written by Liz Garton Scanlon (based on her book) and directed by Galen Fott. It was released on DVD on June 20, 2011. The story centered on a circle of family and friends through the course of a day and affirmed the importance of all things great and small in the world.

Her voice was also heard in the romantic comedy *Gayby* (2012), as the uncredited New York–accented Jenn's Mother on an answering machine, with the actress' name listed in the film's end credit thanks. The film premiered at the South by Southwest Film Festival on March 12, 2012, and was then given a limited release on October 12 with the tagline "Sex with your best friend has never been this reproductive." It was written and directed by Jonathan Lisecki and based on the 2010 comedy short of the same title. The story centered on straight New York yoga instructor Jenn (Jenn Harris) and gay comic-book writer Matt (Matthew Wilkas) who were best friends from college and now in their thirties decide to have a child together.

On April 2, Woodward attended a Celebration of Paul Newman's Dream to benefit Hole in the Wall Camps at Avery Fisher Hall. On August 6, she was at an evening of fundraising at the Connecticut home of Harvey Weinstein. Also present was President Barack Obama, who paid tribute to her by saying that the Newmans were not only what he thought was best about American film but also just embodied the American spirit in many ways.

She was one of the executive producers and provided the voice of Doris for the drama *Lucky Them* (2013), which was in production from January 26, 2013, on location in Washington. The screenplay was by Huck Botko and Emily Wachtel, based on an idea by Caroline Sherman, and the director was Megan Griffiths. Toni Colette starred as Ellie Klug, a rock music critic for a Seattle magazine, who is assigned to track down her ex-boyfriend and missing musician Matthew Smith (Johnny Depp). Woodward is heard on Ellie's answering machine. She uses a Southern accent and identifies herself as Scarlett, reminding her tenant that her rent is overdue. The film premiered at the Toronto International Film Festival on September 6, 2013, before opening on May 30, 2014, with the tagline "Revisit your past. Rewrite your future." It was praised by Justin Chang in *Variety* and Peter Travers in *Rolling Stone* but received a mixed reaction from Rachel Saltz in the *Times*. The film was not a box office success.

The Newmans were family friends of *Lucky Them* co-writer Emily Wachtel, one source claiming she was their godchild but Wachtel saying they were only like godparents. Newman liked the script and, knowing how hard it was to get a film made, encouraged her by sending notes to people. One note, sent to several actors including Thomas Hayden Church, who played Charlie, was funny: "A quick read would keep a lot of people off the sauce." Newman also wrote to Johnny Depp, who was a fan of the Newmans. Newman continued to work on the film and hoped to make a cameo, but died before he was able. Woodward signed on to executive produce to help its cause.

Archival footage of Woodward appeared in the sports biographical documentary *Winning: The Racing Life of Paul Newman*, released on May 8, 2015. It was based on the book by Matt Stone and Preston Lerner, and directed by Adam Carolla. The film chronicled the 35-year car racing career of Newman. Woodward appears in a television interview with Sam Posey, on the set of *Mr. & Mrs. Bridge*, etc. The actress comments, perhaps comically, that she wasn't sure people in show business knew that her husband raced. Woodward believed acting was an enormously disciplined thing to do in terms of work and preparation and Newman's extreme preparation lent itself to the work that you had to do as a racer as you couldn't just leap into the car and start driving. He used to quote a saying that certainly applied to him: Winning wasn't everything, it was just all there was. She recalled an incident when a little boy identified the actor as the racer Paul Newman, which made him happy. At one point, she was seriously concerned that her husband's acting career was going to go down the drain because all he wanted to do was race.

It was reported in July 2017 that her health and memory were fading as she battled Alzheimer's. Most troubling was that Woodward had lost all memories of Newman, with her reportedly stating that she used to be married to someone handsome. For her wedding anniversary, Woodward believed that he was still alive and she put on a fancy dress and wanted to make him a candlelight dinner. Things continued to worsen. The actress needed nurses to care for her 24 hours a day, barely speaking or recognizing her children or grandchildren. She was treated during a drug trial at Yale University's Adler Geriatric Assessment Center but the family felt the disease had reached the point of no return and Woodward would soon be at the end. This came at a hard time when they were supposedly battling each other over Newman's estate. The daughters were also said to be worried about their mother's will, fearful she could leave them nothing and donate the money to charity.

The *Times* of October 27 reported that the Rolex watch Woodward had given to Newman had sold at auction for $17.8 million with a portion of the proceeds to benefit the Nell Newman Foundation and Newman's Own Foundation. She had given him the watch, engraved with the message "DRIVE CAREFULLY—ME" on the back, after the couple had starred together in *Winning*.

Allison Janney won the Best Supporting Actress Academy Award for the biography *I, Tonya* (2017), on March 5, 2018, and in her acceptance speech she thanked Woodward for the encouragement and generosity that gave the younger actress the confidence to think she could pursue a career in acting.

In September, *The National Enquirer* reported further on the progression of Woodward's illness. The Newman daughters are said to be steadfast in being there for their mother, with Melissa living in her parents' former Connecticut home next door.

Appendix: Career Credits

Theater

Picnic (February 19, 1953–April 10, 1954). Music Box Theatre, Broadway. Part: understudy for Madge and Millie.

The Lovers (May 10–May 12, 1956). Martin Beck Theatre, Broadway. Part: Douane.

Baby Want a Kiss (April 19 to August 22, 1964). Little Theatre, New York. Part: Mavis.

The Children's Hour (July 26, 1978, to unknown date). Berkshire Theater Festival, Stockbridge. Part: Martha Dobie.

Candida (June 5–21, 1981). Bolton Theatre, Kenyon College, Ohio. Part: Candida.

Candida (October 15, 1981–January 3, 1982). Circle in the Square Theater, off-Broadway. Part: Candida.

Hay Fever (dates unknown, 1982). Bolton Theatre, Kenyon College, Ohio. Part: Judith Bliss.

Handy, Dandy (October 14, 1984). Westport Country Playhouse, Connecticut. Part: unknown.

The Sea Gull (June 25 to July 21, 1985). Byrdcliffe Theater, Woodstock. Part: Arkadina.

The Glass Menagerie (August 20 to 25, 1985). Willamstown Theater Festival, Massachusetts. Part: Amanda Wingfield.

The Glass Menagerie (February 28 to April 13, 1986). The Long Wharf Theatre, New Haven, Connecticut. Part: Amanda Wingfield.

The Depot (October 1986). Westport Country Playhouse, Connecticut. Crew: Director.

The Depot (March 27, 1987). Interart Theater, New York. Crew: Director.

The Depot (March 28, 1987). Ethel Walker School, Simsbury. Crew: Director.

The Depot (April 12, 1987). Westport Country Playhouse, Connecticut. Crew: Director.

Golden Boy (August 4 to 15, 1987). Williamstown Theatre Festival. Crew: Director.

An Evening of Entertainment (October 26, 1987). Circle in the Square Theater, New York. Part: unknown.

Sweet Bird of Youth (April 22 to May 26, 1988). Royal Alexander Theatre, Toronto. Part: Alexandra Del Lago a.k.a. the Princess Kosmonopolis.

The Wall Breaks! (December 10, 1989). Marquis Theatre, New York. Part: Herself.

Ghosts (August 8 to 25, 1991). Woodstock River Arts, New York. Part: unknown.

Arsenic and Old Lace (January 25 to February 26, 1995) Long Wharf Theater, New Haven. Part: Abby Brewster.

Golden Boy (November 27 to December 16, 1995). Blue Light Theater Company, 45th Street Theater, New York. Crew: Director.

Hay Fever (July 9 to 27 or July 30 to August 10, 1996) Berkshire Theater Festival, Stockbridge. Part: Judith Bliss.

Rocket to the Moon (August 14 to 24, 1996) Other Stage, Williamstown Theater Festival, Massachusetts. Crew: Director.

Waiting for Lefty (April 19 to May 25, 1997) Blue Light Theater Company, Classic Stage Company Repertory, Off Broadway. Crew: Director.

La Ronde (August 13 to 24, 1997) Williamstown Theater Festival, Massachusetts. Crew: Director.

The Waverly Gallery (August 18 to 22, 1999) Williamstown Theater Festival, Massachusetts. Part: Gladys Green.

Ancestral Voices (July 17 to 22, 2000). Westport Country Playhouse. Part: unknown.

A Holiday Garland (December 13, 19 to 21, 2008). Westport Country Playhouse. Part: unknown.

Film

Count Three and Pray (1955). Part: Lissy.

A Kiss Before Dying (1956). Part: Dorothy "Dorie" Kingship.

The Three Faces of Eve (1957). Part: Eve "Evie" White/Eve Black/Jane a.k.a. Janey.

No Down Payment (1957). Part: Leola Boone.

The Long, Hot Summer (1958). Part: Clara Varner.

Rally 'Round the Flag, Boys! (1958). Part: Grace Bannerman.

The Sound and the Fury (1960). Part: Quentin Compson.

The Fugitive Kind (1960). Part: Carol Cutrere.

From the Terrace (1960). Part: Mary St. John.

Paris Blues (1961). Part: Lillian Corning.

The Stripper (1963). Part: Lila Green.

A New Kind of Love (1963). Part: Samantha "Sam" Blake.

Signpost to Murder (1965). Part: Molly Thomas.

A Fine Madness (1966). Part: Rhoda.

A Big Hand for the Little Lady (1966). Part: Mary.

Rachel, Rachel (1968). Part: Rachel Cameron.

Winning (1969). Part: Elora.

Ely Landau's King: A Filmed Record…. Montgomery to Memphis (1970). Part: Herself.

WUSA (1970). Part: Geraldine.

They Might Be Giants (1971). Part: Watson.

The Effect of Gamma Rays on Man-in-the-Moon Marigolds (1972). Part: Beatrice.

Summer Wishes, Winter Dreams (1973). Part: Rita.

The Drowning Pool (1975). Part: Iris.

The End (1978). Part: Jessica.

The Power to Change (1980). Part: Narrator.

Harry & Son (1984). Part: Lilly.

Strategic Trust: The Making of a Nuclear Free Palau (1984). Part: Narrator.

Women—for America, for the World (1986). Part: Herself.

The Glass Menagerie (1987). Part: Amanda.

Mr. & Mrs. Bridge (1990). Part: India Bridge.

The Age of Innocence (1993). Part: Narrator.

Philadelphia (1993). Part: Sarah Beckett.

Women of Substance (1994). Part: Narrator.

My Knees Were Jumping: Remembering the Kindertransports (1996). Part: Narrator.

Even If a Hundred Ogres … (1996). Part: Host.

Gun Control in Connecticut: Women Call the Shots (1997). Part: Narrator.

Pale Male (2002). Part: Narrator.

The Education of Gore Vidal (2003). Part: Herself.

Keepers of Eden (2007). Part: Narrator.

Gayby (2012). Part: Jenn's mother (voice). Uncredited.

Lucky Them (2013). Part: Doris (voice). Crew: Executive Producer.

Television

Robert Montgomery Presents: "Penny" (June 9, 1952). Part: Penny.

Omnibus: "Mr. Lincoln a.k.a. Abraham Lincoln, Part 2" and "Mr. Lincoln a.k.a. Abraham Lincoln Part 3" (November 30, 1952, and December 14, 1952, respectively). Part: Ann Rutledge.

Tales of Tomorrow: "The Bitter Storm" (December 26, 1952). Part: Pat.

Goodyear Television Playhouse: "The Young and the Fair" (July 26, 1953). Part: unknown.

Philco Television Playhouse: "A Young Lady of Property" (April 5, 1953). Part: Arabella Cuckenboo.

Danger: "In Line of Duty" a.k.a. "In the Line of Duty" (February 9, 1954). Part: unknown.

Philco Television Playhouse: "The Dancers" (March 7, 1954). Part: Emily.

Studio One: "Stir Mugs" (April 5, 1954). Part: Lisa Molloy.

Kraft Television Theatre: "Unequal Contest" (April 29, 1954). Part: unknown.

You Are There: "The Oklahoma Land Rush (April 22, 1889)" (September 12, 1954). Part: unknown.

The Web: "Welcome Home" (September 26, 1954). Part: unknown.

Singer Four Star Playhouse: "Interlude" (October 14, 1954). Part: Vicki.

Ford Theatre: "Segment" (October 21, 1954). Part: June Ledbetter.

The Elgin Hour: "High Man" (November 2, 1954). Part: Nancy.

Lux Video Theatre: "Five Star Final" (November 11, 1954). Part: Jenny Townsend.

Robert Montgomery Presents: "Homecoming" (November 22, 1954). Part: Elsie.

Armstrong Circle Theatre: "Brink of Disaster" (November 23, 1954). Part: unknown.

The Star and the Story: "Dark Stranger" (January 8, 1955). Part: Jill Andrews.

Star Tonight: "Death of a Stranger" (March 31, 1955). Part: unknown.

Kraft Television Theatre: "Cynara" (May 12, 1955). Part: unknown.

The 20th Century–Fox Hour: "The Late George Apley" (November 16, 1955). Part: Eleanor Apley.

The United States Steel Hour: "White Gloves" (December 21, 1955). Part: Rocky.

Kraft Television Theatre: "Eleven O'Clock Flight" (December 28, 1955). Part: unknown.

Studio One a.k.a. *Westinghouse Studio One*: "Family Protection" (May 28, 1956). Part: Daisy Gilmer.

Star Performance: "Watch the Sunset" (June 7, 1956). Part: Ann Benton.

Alfred Hitchcock Presents: "Momentum" (June 24, 1956). Part: Beth Paine.

Kraft Television Theatre: "Starfish" (June 27, 1956). Part: unknown.

The Alcoa Hour: "The Girl in Chapter One" (September 2, 1956). Part: unknown.

Person to Person (December 27, 1957). Part: Herself.

Playhouse 90: "The 80 Yard Run" (January 16, 1958). Part: Louise Darling.

The 30th Annual Academy Awards (March 26, 1958). Part: Herself.

Wide Wide World: "A Star's Story" (April 27, 1958). Part: Herself.

Person to Person (December 26, 1958). Part: Herself.

Toast of the Town (December 28, 1958). Part: Herself.

Tonight Starring Jack Paar (October 26, 1959). Part: Herself.

Here's Hollywood (February 14, 1961). Part: Herself.

At This Very Moment (April 1, 1962). Part: Herself.

The 34th Academy Awards (April 9, 1962). Part: Herself.

The Danny Kaye Show (March 2, 1966). Parts: Various.

Late Night with Johnny Carson (March 22, 1966). Part: Herself.

The 38th Annual Academy Awards (April 18, 1966). Part: Herself.

The Bell Telephone Hour: "Man Who Dances: Edward Villella" (March 8, 1968). Part: Herself.

The 22nd Annual Tony Awards (April 21, 1968). Part: Herself.

The Joey Bishop Show (October 1, 1968). Part: Herself.

The Joey Bishop Show (October 3, 1968). Part: Herself.

The Joey Bishop Show (October 11, 1968). Part: Herself.

Dee Time (October 19, 1968). Part: Herself.

Hubert Humphrey Telethon (November 5, 1968). Part: Herself.

Cinema: "Joanne Woodward" (November 14, 1968). Part: Herself.

The 41st Annual Academy Awards (April 14, 1969). Part: Herself.

The David Frost Show (October 10, 1969). Part: Herself.

Dee Time (October 18, 1969). Part: Herself.

The Mike Douglas Show (April 12, 1970). Part: Herself.

Dinah's Place (April 14, 1970). Part: Herself.

Parkinson (November 21, 1971). Part: Herself.

Eagle and the Hawk a.k.a. *The Eagle and the*

Hawk (November 26, 1971). Part: Narrator and herself.

All the Way Home (December 1, 1971). Part: Mary Follet.

The Dick Cavett Show (January 23, 1973). Part: Herself.

The Mike Douglas Show (December 17, 1973). Part: Herself.

The Fragile Mind (January 9, 1974). Part: Narrator.

The American Film Institute Salute to James Cagney (March 18, 1974). Part: Herself.

Dinah's Place (March 18, 1974). Part: Herself.

The 46th Annual Academy Awards (April 2, 1974). Part: Herself.

The Wild Places (December 2, 1974). Part: Herself.

The 1975 Annual Entertainment Hall of Fame Awards (February 22, 1975). Part: Herself.

Bicentennial Minutes (June 29, 1975). Part: Narrator.

The Carol Burnett Show (February 14, 1976). Part: Midge Gibson/Clarice Trickleson/Herself.

Dinah! (April 30, 1976). Part: Herself.

The Mike Douglas Show (September 22, 1976). Part: Herself.

Sybil (November 14 and 15, 1976). Part: Dr. Cornelia Wilbur/Narrator.

The John Denver Special (November 17, 1976). Part: Herself.

Little Women (November 17, 1976). Part: Marmee March/Narrator.

Circus of the Stars (January 10, 1977). Part: Herself.

The 1977 New Spirit Inaugural Concert (January 19, 1977). Part: Herself.

Dinah! (July 27, 1977). Part: Herself.

Good Morning America (November 16, 1977). Part: Herself.

All-Star Tribute to Elizabeth Taylor (December 1, 1977). Part: Herself.

Laurence Olivier Presents: "Best Play of the Year 1950: Come Back Little Sheba by William Inge." (December 31, 1977). Part: Lola.

See How She Runs (February 1, 1978). Part: Betty Quinn.

The Mike Douglas Show (February 9, 1978). Part: Herself.

The American Film Institute Salute to Henry Fonda (March 15, 1978). Part: Herself.

The Stars Salute Israel at 30 (May 7, 1978). Part: Herself.

The 30th Annual Primetime Emmy Awards (September 17, 1978). Part: Herself.

A Salute to American Imagination (October 5, 1978). Part: Herself.

A Christmas to Remember (December 20, 1978). Part: Mildred McCloud.

The Mike Douglas Show (May 23, 1979). Part: Herself.

The Mike Douglas Show (November 5, 1979). Part: Herself.

Today (November 12, 1979). Part: Herself.

Family: "Thanksgiving" (November 20, 1979). Crew: Director.

Angel Death (October 29, 1979). Part: Narrator.

The Streets of L.A. (November 13, 1979). Part: Carol Schramm.

Fred Astaire: Puttin' on His Top Hat (March 10, 1980). Part: Narrator.

The Shadow Box (December 28, 1980). Part: Beverly.

Crisis at Central High (February 4, 1981). Part: Elizabeth P. Huckaby and Narrator.

The Tomorrow Show with Tom Snyder (November 12, 1981). Part: Herself.

Come Along with Me (February 16, 1982). Crew: Director.

Night of 100 Stars (March 8, 1982). Part: Herself.

Candida (January 2, 1983). Part: Candida.

The 55th Annual Academy Awards (April 11, 1983). Part: Herself.

Hunger in the Promised Land (June 5, 1983). Part: Host.

The 41st Annual Golden Globe Awards (January 28, 1984). Part: Herself.

Bitte umblättern (May 28, 1984). Part: Herself.

Passions (October 1, 1984). Part: Catherine Kennerly.

An American Portrait (April 15, 1985). Part: Host.

Live from the Metropolitan Opera: "Tosca" (March 27, 1985). Part: Host.

Do You Remember Love (May 21, 1985). Part: Barbara Wyatt Hollis.

The Spencer Tracy Legacy: A Tribute by Katharine Hepburn (March 1986). Part: Herself.

America Masters: "Katherine Anne Porter: The Eye of Memory" (July 11, 1986). Part: Host.

American Masters: "Eugene O'Neill—A Glory of Ghosts" (September 8, 1986). Part: Host.

Live from the Metropolitan Opera: "Dialogues of the Carmelites" (April 4 and May 6, 1987). Part: Host.

Broadway's Dreamers: The Legacy of the Group Theatre (June 26, 1989). Part: Host, interviewer, director of *Golden Boy*.

The Metropolitan Opera Presents: "Turandot" (January 27, 1988). Part: Host.

The Metropolitan Opera Presents: "Tales from Hoffmann" (March 2, 1988). Part: Host.

De pelicula (April 24, 1989). Part: Herself.

American Masters: "Sanford Meisner: American Theater's Best Kept Secret" (August 27, 1990). Part: Herself.

The Home Front (November 20, 1990). Part: Herself.

American Masters: "Miracle on 44th Street: A Portrait of the Actors Studio" (July 8, 1991). Part: Herself.

Foreign Affairs (March 17, 1993). Part: Vinnie Miner.

Blind Spot (May 2, 1993). Part: Nell Harrington. Crew: Co-Producer.

The Kennedy Center Honors: A Celebration of the Performing Arts (December 30, 1993). Part: Herself.

The Roots of Roe (date unknown, 1993). Part: Voice of Margaret Sanger.

Breathing Lessons (February 6, 1994). Part: Maggie Moran.

Good Morning America (December 14, 1994). Part: Herself.

Golden Anniversary (November 11, 1995). Part: Herself.

Great Performances: "Dance in America: A Renaissance Revisited" (June 3, 1996). Part: Host.

Charlie Rose (April 16, 1997). Part: Herself.

Biography: "Joan Collins. A Personal Dynasty" (December 18, 1997). Part: Herself.

The Kennedy Center Honors: A Celebration of the Performing Arts (December 26, 1997). Part: Herself.

The Directors: "The Films of James Ivory" (date unknown, 1997). Part: Herself.

James Dean: A Portrait (April 6, 1998). Part: Herself.

Intimate Portrait: "Allison Janney" (May 14, 2001). Part: Herself.

Life and Times: "A Man for All Stages: The Life and Times of Christopher Plummer" (November 12, 2002). Part: Herself.

The John Garfield Story (February 3, 2003). Part: Herself.

Freedom: A History of Us: "Safe for Democracy" (date unknown, 2003). Part: Anne Martin (voice).

A&E Biography: "Paul Newman. Hollywood's Charming Rebel" a.k.a. "Hollywood' Cool Hand" (date unknown, 2003). Part: Herself.

The Adventures of Errol Flynn (April 5, 2005). Part: Herself.

Empire Falls (May 28, 2005). Part: Francine Whiting.

Change in the Wind (July 15, 2010). Part: Margaret Mitchell (voice).

Actors Hall of Fame Induction Ceremony (October 16, 2016). Part: Herself.

Bibliography

Adams, Val. "Union Bars 60 from Memorial for Miss Hansberry on WBAI." *New York Times*. January 9, 1967. Retrieved May 3, 2018 from http://www.nytimes.com.

Adler, Renata. "The Screen: 'Rachel, Rachel,' Portrait of a Spinster." *New York Times*. August 27, 1968. Retrieved May 5, 2018 from http://www.nytimes.com.

Alden, Robert. "Screen: Good Poker Tale." *New York Times*. June 9, 1966. Retrieved April 30, 2018 from http://www.nytimes.com.

Alexander, Ron. "The Evening Hours." *New York Times*. September 10, 1982. Retrieved July 20, 2018 from http://www.nytimes.com.

Anderson, Jack. "Review/Dance; City Center and Its Stars Celebrate 50 Years." *New York Times*. May 12, 1993. Retrieved August 27, 2018 from http://www.nytimes.com.

Apple, R.W. Jr. "100,000 Cheer Humphrey." *New York Times*. November 4, 1968. Retrieved May 12, 2018 from http://www.nytimes.com.

Archer, Eugene. "Fitzgerald Story Planned for Film." *New York Times*. February 10, 1961. Retrieved April 18, 2018 from http://www.nytimes.com.

_____. "New York Lures Movie Producer …" *New York Times*. August 19, 1961. Retrieved April 18, 2018 from http://www.nytimes.com.

_____. "Newman to Team with Miss Taylor." *New York Times*. July 20, 1960. Retrieved April 16, 2018 from http://www.nytimes.com.

_____. "… Roles for Paul Newman." *New York Times*. September 7, 1962. Retrieved April 24, 2018 from http://www.nytimes.com.

_____. "'Terror' in Transit." *New York Times*. August 30, 1964. Retrieved April 25, 2018 from http://www.nytimes.com.

Archerd, Army. "Paul Newman: TV Stories Better Than Film." *Variety*. December 5, 1974. Retrieved June 8, 2018 from http://www.variety.com.

Ash, Agnes. "Film Queens Win 'Oscars' for Fashions." *New York Times*. March 27, 1958. Retrieved March 26, 2018 from http://www.nytimes.com.

Atkinson, Brooks. "At the Theatre." *New York Times*. February 20, 1953. Retrieved February 6, 2018 from http://www.nytimes.com.

_____. "Theatre: 'The Lovers.'" *New York Times*. May 11, 1956. Retrieved February 17, 2018 from http://www.nytimes.com.

A.W. "Sharp Scalpel Used in 'No Down Payment.'" *New York Times*. October 31, 1957. Retrieved March 14, 2018 from http://www.nytimes.com.

Baldwin. Alec. "Theater; the Joy of the Stage, Even if Only for a Night." *New York Times*. November 5, 2000. Retrieved September 12, 2018 from http://www.nytimes.com.

Barbanel, Josh. "Bottle Bill: Why Governor Signed It." *New York Times*. June 27, 1982. Retrieved July 20, 2018 from http://www.nytimes.com.

Barnes, Clive. "'A New Spirit' Is a National Celebration of Togetherness in TV Inaugural Concert." *New York Times*. January 19, 1977. Retrieved June 18, 2018 from http://www.nytimes.com.

Barron, James. "Public Lives." *New York Times*. August 17, 2000. Retrieved September 12, 2018 from http://www.nytimes.com.

_____. "Boldface Names." *New York Times*. August 17, 2001. Retrieved September 13, 2018 from http://www.nytimes.com.

_____, with Steinhauer, Jennifer. "Boldface Names." *New York Times*. May 2, 2002. Retrieved September 14, 2018 from http://www.nytimes.com.

_____, _____ et al. "Public Lives." *New York Times*. October 28, 1998. Retrieved September 7, 2018 from http://www.nytimes.com.

Bart, Peter. "Movies; a Newman Non-Interview." *New York Times*. October 9, 1966. Retrieved May 2, 2018 from http://www.nytimes.com.

Bell, Arthur. "Sylvia's Souvenirs." *New York Times*. December 17, 1972. Retrieved May 22, 2018 from http://www.nytimes.com.

Bellison, Lillian. "… Gut Yontif." *New York Times*. April 8, 1979. Retrieved July 1, 2018 from http://www.nytimes.com.

Bender, Marilyn. "The Day of the Professional Amateur." *New York Times*. May 3, 1966. Retrieved May 2, 2018 from http://www.nytimes.com.

Bergan, Ronald. the *United Artists Story*. London: Octopus Books, 1986.

Bisport. Alan. "Preserving Towns, a Chapter at a Time." *New York Times*. December 23, 2001. Retrieved September 14, 2018 from http://www.nytimes.com.

Blau, Eleanor. "Weekender Guide." *New York Times*. April 13, 1984. Retrieved July 28, 2018 from http://www.nytimes.com.

Bloom, Julie. "Casting Announcements for LCT's

'Happiness' and More Theater News." *New York Times*. January 13, 2009. Retrieved October 1, 2018 from http://www.nytimes.com.

Bonderoff, Jason. *Sally Field*. New York: St. Martin's Press, 1987.

Branagh, Kenneth. *Sleuth*. Paramount Pictures/Castle Rock Entertainment/A RiffRaff Production/Timnick Films, 2007.

_____, and Caine, Michael. Sleuth DVD Audio Commentary. Sony Pictures Home Entertainment, 2008.

Brantley, Ben. "The Annotated Calender; Theater." the *New York Time*. September 11, 1994. Retrieved August 29, 2018 from http://www.nytimes.com.

_____. "Theater Review; Joanne Woodward as a Lethal Old Lady." *New York Times*. January 28, 1995. Retrieved August 30, 2018 from http://www.nytimes.com.

Brantley, Robin. "The Uneasy Odyssey of 'The Shadow Box.'" *New York Times*. December 28, 1980. Retrieved July 11, 2018 from http://www.nytimes.com.

Brenson, Michael. "Art People." *New York Times*. November 25, 1983. Retrieved July 27, 2018 from http://www.nytimes.com.

Brooks, Andree. "Joanne Woodward Accepts a Role in Saving Old House." *New York Times*. August 10, 1980. Retrieved July 11, 2018 from http://www.nytimes.com.

_____. "New Enthusiasm Surprises Feminists." *New York Times*. January 10, 1982. Retrieved July 19, 2018 from http://www.nytimes.com.

_____. "Portraits of Homes Win Popularity. " *New York Times*. December 19, 1982. Retrieved July 20, 2018 from http://www.nytimes.com.

Brown, Emma. "Last Goodbye." *Interview Magazine*. April 24, 2014. Retrieved June 21, 2018 from http://www.interviewmagazine.com.

Brown, Les. "Professor at Yale Will Make Westerns for Television." *New York Times*. April 6, 1976. Retrieved June 11, 2018 from http://www.nytimes.com.

Brown Miller, Susan. "Eleven Months After Chicago." *New York Times*. July 20, 1969. Retrieved May 15, 2018 from http://www.nytimes.com.

Brozan, Nadine. "Chronicle." *New York Times*. October 2, 1991. Retrieved August 24, 2018 fro http://www.nytimes.com.

_____. "Chronicle." *New York Times*. November 15, 1991. Retrieved August 24, 2018 from http://www.nytimes.com.

_____. "Chronicle." *New York Times*. April 4, 1992. Retrieved August 25, 2018 from http://www.nytimes.com.

_____. "Chronicle." *New York Times*. February 12, 1993. Retrieved August 26, 2018 from http://www.nytimes.com.

_____. "Chronicle." *New York Times*. January 10, 1994. Retrieved August 27, 2018 from http://www.nytimes.com.

_____. "Chronicle." *New York Times*. January 27, 1995. Retrieved August 29, 2018 from http://www.nytimes.com.

_____. "Chronicle." *New York Times*. April 30, 1997. Retrieved September 4, 2018 from http://www.nytimes.com.

_____. "Chronicle." *New York Times*. October 29, 1997. Retrieved September 4, 2018 from http://www.nytimes.com.

_____. "The Evening Hours." *New York Times*. October 10, 1986. Retrieved August 4, 2018 from http://www.nytimes.com.

Buckley, Tom. "At the Movies." *New York Times*. January 18, 1980. Retrieved July 7, 2018 from http://www.nytimes.com.

_____. "TV: On a Deadly Drug." *New York Times*. October 29, 1979. Retrieved July 3, 2018 from http://www.nytimes.com.

Calta, Louis. "Entertainers Join Cast of Political Hopefuls." *New York Times*. April 6, 1968. Retrieved May 5, 2018 from http://www.nytimes.com.

_____. "'The Lovers' Set for March Debut." *New York Times*. December 17, 1955. Retrieved February 15, 2018 from http://www.nytimes.com.

Canby, Vincent. "For 'Gamma Rays,' Another Opening..." *New York Times*. December 21, 1972. Retrieved May 27, 2018 from http://www.nytimes.com.

_____. "The Importance of Being Oscar." *New York Times*. April 20, 1969. Retrieved May 15, 2018 from http://www.nytimes.com.

_____. "Movie: 'The End' with Burt Reynolds." *New York Times*. May 10, 1978. Retrieved July 2, 2018 from http://www.nytimes.com.

_____. "Screen: 'Harry and Son,' with Paul Newman." *New York Times*. March 2, 1984. Retrieved July 23, 2018 from http://www.nytimes.com.

_____. "A Placid Marriage, and Undercurrents." *New York Times*. November 23, 1990. Retrieved August 19, 2018 from http://www.nytimes.com.

_____. "Screen." *New York Times*. June 10, 1971. Retrieved May 21, 2018 from http://www.nytimes.com.

_____. "The Talk of Cannes." *New York Times*. May 14, 1987. Retrieved August 10, 2018 from http://www.nytimes.com.

_____. "Theater Review; Sacrifice of Hands, Heart and Soul." *New York Times*. November 28, 1995. Retrieved August 31, 2018 from http://www.nytimes.com.

Capua, Michelangelo. *Yul Brynner: A Biography*. Jefferson, NC: McFarland, 2013.

Carolla, Adam. *Winning: The Racing Life of Paul Newman*. Sontalia Pictures/TrueCar, 2015.

Carroll, Diahann, with Firestone, Ross. *Diahann! An Autobiography*. New York: Ivy Books, 1986.

Chambers, Andrea. "That's No Gift Horse Joanne Woodward Is Looking in the Face: She's Paying Plenty." *People*. November 30, 1981. Retrieved July 16, 2018 from http://www.people.com.

Chang, Justin. "Toronto Film Review: 'Lucky Them.'" *Variety*. September 12, 2013. Retrieved June 21, 2018 from http://www.variety.com.

Charles, Eleanor. "Connecticut Guide." *New York Times*. May 16, 1982. Retrieved July 20, 2018 from http://www.nytimes.com.

_____. "Connecticut Guide." *New York Times*. July 11, 1982. Retrieved July 20, 2018 from http://www.nytimes.com.

_____. "Connecticut Guide." *New York Times*. October 16, 1994. Retrieved August 29, 2018 from http://www.nytimes.com.

_____. "The Guide." *New York Times*. August 2, 1998. Retrieved September 7, 2018 from http://www.nytimes.com.

_____. "The Guide." *New York Times*. February 6, 2000. Retrieved September 10, 2018 from http://www.nytimes.com.

_____. "The Guide …" *New York Times*. March 25, 2001. Retrieved September 13, 2018 from http://www.nytimes.com.

_____. "The Guide …" *New York Times*. June 3, 2001. Retrieved September 13, 2018 from http://www.nytimes.com.

_____. "The Guide …" *New York Times*. October 28, 2001. Retrieved September 14, 2018 from http://www.nytimes.com.

_____. "The Guide …" *New York Times*. June 1, 2003. Retrieved September 18, 2018 from http://www.nytimes.com.

_____. "In the Region …" *New York Times*. September 20, 1987. Retrieved August 11, 2018 from http://www.nytimes.com.

_____. "In the Region; Connecticut…" *New York Times*. August 1, 2004. Retrieved September 22, 2018 from http://www.nytimes.com.

_____. "Westchester." *New York Times*. June 30, 1985. Retrieved August 1, 2018 from http://www.nytimes.com.

_____. "Westchester Guide." *New York Times*. July 21, 1985. Retrieved August 1, 2018 from http://www.nytimes.com.

Chase, Chris. "And the Winners, Very Possibly, Are …" *New York Times*. March 24, 1991. Retrieved August 22, 2018 from http://www.nytimes.com.

Cohen, Barney. "Burt Reynolds: Going Beyond Macho." *New York Times*. March 29, 1981. Retrieved July 12, 2018 from http://www.nytimes.com.

Cohen, Marcia. "How Do Prominent Parents Govern Their Children's TV Habits?" *New York Times*. March 30, 1980. Retrieved July 7, 2018 from http://www.nytimes.com.

Collins, Glenn. "No Ruse Is Too Rash to Get a Reservation." *New York Times*. April 24, 1998. Retrieved September 7, 2018 from http://www.nytimes.com.

Corry, John. "Broadway." *New York Times*. May 12, 1978. Retrieved June 28, 2018 from http://www.nytimes.com.

_____. "Broadway …" *New York Times*. June 19, 1981. Retrieved July 13, 2018 from http://www.nytimes.com.

_____. "'Nickelby' Closing Is as Spectacular and Star-Studded as Its Opening." *New York Times*. January 5, 1982. Retrieved July 15, 2018 from http://www.nytimes.com.

_____. "TV: An Occult Whimsy." *New York Times*. February 16, 1982. Retrieved July 19, 2018 from http://www.nytimes.com.

Cote, David. "Say Goodbye to the Old Barn." *New York Times*. August 24, 2003. Retrieved September 19, 2018 from http://www.nytimes.com.

Cowan, Alison Leigh. "Using Iraq …" *New York Times*. October 10, 2004. Retrieved September 22, 2018 from http://www.nytimes.com.

_____. "Paul Newman, Philanthropist, Does Hereby Leave…" *New York Times*. November 26, 2008.

Retrieved September 29, 2018 from http://www.nytimes.com.

Crowther, Bosley. "Linda or Tatum—Oscar Winners?" *New York Times*. March 3, 1974. Retrieved June 5, 2018 from http://www.nytimes.com.

_____. "'Paris Blues' Opens at Astor." *New York Times*. November 8, 1961. Retrieved April 19, 2018 from http://www.nytimes.com.

_____. "Screen: Adaptation of 'Loss of Roses.'" *New York Times*. June 20, 1963. Retrieved April 21, 2018 from http://www.nytimes.com.

_____. "Screen: Down South." *New York Times*. March 28, 1959. Retrieved April 13, 2018 from http://www.nytimes.com.

_____. "Screen: 'Fugitive Kind.' " *New York Times*. April 15, 1960. Retrieved April 10, 2018 from http://www.nytimes.com.

_____. "Screen: Suburban Farce; 'Rally Round the Flag, Boys!' at the Palace." *New York Times*. December 24, 1958. Retrieved April 4, 2018 from http://www.nytimes.com.

_____. "The Screen: 'The Long, Hot Summer.'" *New York Times*. April 4, 1958. Retrieved March 19, 2018 from http://www.nytimes.com.

_____. "Screen: '3 Faces of Eve'; Personalities Study Opens at Victoria the Cast." *New York Times*. September 27, 1957. Retrieved March 11, 2018 from http://www.nytimes.com.

_____. "Where Are the Women?" *New York Times*. January 23, 1966. Retrieved April 28, 2018 from http://www.nytimes.com.

Cruice, Valerie. "Local History Catches Up to the Video Generation." *New York Times*. September 23, 1990. Retrieved August 20, 2018 from http://www.nytimes.com.

Cummings, Judith, and Albin Krebs. "… an Alumni Gala for Sanford Meisner." *New York Times*. October 9, 1980. Retrieved July 11, 2018 from http://www.nytimes.com.

Curtis, Charlotte. "George Zee, Restaurateur." *New York Times*. January 15, 1985. Retrieved July 31, 2018 from http://www.nytimes.com.

Daniels, Robert L. *Laurence Olivier: Theatre and Cinema*. San Diego, New York: A.S. Barnes & Co., 1980.

Darnton, Nina. "At the Movies." *New York Times*. November 21, 1986. Retrieved August 4, 2018 from http://www.nytimes.com.

Davidson, Muriel. "Joanne Woodward Talks All about Paul Newman." *Good Housekeeping*. February, 1969: 72–75, 122, 124, 126.

Dawson, Nick. *Dennis Hopper: Interviews (Conversations with Filmmakers Series)*. University Press of Mississippi, 2012.

Dewey, Donald. *Lee J. Cobb: Characters of an Actor*. Plymouth, UK: Rowman & Littlefield, 2014.

_____. "Washington Pays Tribute to Performing Artists." *New York Times*. December 7, 1992. Retrieved August 24, 2018 fro http://www.nytimes.com.

De Witt, Karen. "Chronicle." *New York Times*. September 3, 1990. Retrieved August 20, 2018 from http://www.nytimes.com.

Dougherty, Philip H. "Advertising." *New York Times*. December 7, 1978. Retrieved June 29, 2018 from http://www.nytimes.com.

Dowd, Maureen. "Testing Himself." *New York Times.* September 28, 1986. Retrieved August 4, 2018 from http://www.nytimes.com.

Druxman, Michael B. *Miss Dinah Shore: A Biography.* Albany, GA: Bear Manor Media, 2015.

Dullea, Georgia. "The Evening Hours." *New York Times.* October 9, 1987. Retrieved August 12, 2018 from http://www.nytimes.com.

_____. "Silver Anniversary, in Black and White." *New York Times.* November 2, 1991. Retrieved August 24, 2018 from http://www.nytimes.com.

Dunn, Ron. *Sybil: The Screenwriter Speaks/The Casting/The Production.* Warner Bros. Entertainment, 2006.

Dunning, Jennifer. "Arts and Entertainment; Dance." *New York Times.* April 18, 1993. Retrieved August 26, 2018 from http://www.nytimes.com.

_____. "Tchaikovsky Opener: Chaos and Pizzazz." *New York Times.* June 5, 1981. Retrieved July 13, 2018 from http://www.nytimes.com.

Eames, John Douglas. *The MGM Story: The Complete History of Fifty Roaring Years.* London: Octopus, 1975.

_____. *The Paramount Story: The Complete History of the Studio and Its 2,805 Films.* London: Octopus Books, 1983.

Ebert, Roger. "The Drowning Pool." January 1, 1975. Retrieved June 7, 2018 from http://www.rogerebert.com.

_____. "The Effect of Gamma Rays on Man-in-the-Moon Marigolds." April 10, 1973. Retrieved May 27, 2018 from http://www.rogerebert.com.

_____. "Harry and Son." January 1, 1984. Retrieved July 23, 2018 from http://www.rogerebert.com.

_____. "Philadelphia." January 14, 1994. Retrieved August 30, 2018 from http://www.rogerebert.com.

_____. "Winning." May 20, 1969. Retrieved May 14, 2018 from http://www.rogerebert.com.

Eder, Richard. "'Children's Hour' Staged At the Berkshire Festival." *New York Times.* July 29, 1978. Retrieved June 28, 2018 from http://www.nytimes.com.

Edwards. Russell. "… Gazing and Nosegays." *New York Times.* June 1, 1975. Retrieved June 10, 2018 from http://www.nytimes.com.

_____. "… Rooms in Scale." *New York Times.* March 30, 1975. Retrieved June 8, 2018 from http://www.nytimes.com.

_____. "… Stars Over Connecticut." *New York Times.* October 21, 1973. Retrieved June 3, 2018 from http://www.nytimes.com.

_____. " … UN We Believe." *New York Times.* September 9, 1973. Retrieved May 30, 2018 from http://www.nytimes.com.

Egan, James. "A Trip Into History on the Westport Bus." *New York Times.* August 17, 1975. Retrieved June 10, 2018 from http://www.nytimes.com.

Ehrlich, Phyllis A. "Future Events." *New York Times.* November 8, 1981. Retrieved July 15, 2018 from http://www.nytimes.com.

Elliott, Stuart. "The Media Business; Advertising." *New York Times.* October 17, 1997. Retrieved September 4, 2018 from http://www.nytimes.com.

Emblen, M. L. "New Jersey Guide." *New York Times.* May 12, 1991. Retrieved August 23, 2018 from http://www.nytimes.com.

Ennis. Thomas W. "Social Events." *New York Times.* March 24, 1991. Retrieved August 22, 2018 from http://www.nytimes.com.

_____. "Social Events." *New York Times.* March 31, 1991. Retrieved August 22, 2018 from http://www.nytimes.com.

Everett, Todd. "Hallmark Hall of Fame Blind Spot." *Variety.* April 30, 1993. Retrieved August 27, 2018 from http://www.variety.com.

Faber, Harold. "Marshall and 4 Others Get Freedoms Medals." *New York Times.* October 13, 1991. Retrieved August 24, 2018 from http://www.nytimes.com.

Fabricant, Florence. "Guides to the Current American Cuisine." *New York Times.* January 11, 1984. Retrieved July 28, 2018 from http://www.nytimes.com.

Farber, Stephen. "Woodward in CBS Film on Alzheimer's Disease." *New York Times.* March 11, 1985. Retrieved July 31, 2018 from http://www.nytimes.com.

Farinola, Michele. *Backstory: The Long, Hot Summer.* Prometheus Entertainment/Van Ness Films, Inc/Foxstar Productions/Fox Television/American Movie Classics. 2001.

Feaster, Felicia. "Article: The Effect of Gamma Rays on Man-in-the-Moon Marigolds (1972)." *Turner Classic Movies.* Retrieved May 27, 2018 from http://www.tcm.com.

Feron, James. "… Connecticut." *New York Times.* April 18, 1975. Retrieved June 8, 2018 from http://www.nytimes.com.

Ferrara. Greg. "Article: Rally 'Round the Flag, Boys! (1959). "*Turner Classic Movies.* Retrieved April 4, 2018 from http://www.tcm.com.

Ferretti, Fred. "The Evening Hours." *New York Times.* November 9, 1984. Retrieved July 29, 2018 from http://www.nytimes.com.

Field, Elizabeth. "'Reproductive Rights' Is Focus of Daylong, Oct. 24 Workshop." *New York Times.* September 28, 1986. Retrieved August 3, 2018 from http://www.nytimes.com.

Field, Sally. *In Pieces.* New York: Grand Central Publishing, 2018.

Fife, Stephen. "Dedicated to the Religion of Acting." *New York Times.* April 7, 1985. Retrieved July 31, 2018 from http://www.nytimes.com.

Finn, Maria. "Journeys; Raptors at Rush Hour, Homeward Bound." *New York Times.* October 11, 2002. Retrieved September 14, 2018 from http://www.nytimes.com.

Finn, Robin. "Public Lives …" *New York Times.* February 23, 2001. Retrieved September 13, 2018 from http://www.nytimes.com.

Fitzpatrick, Jackie. "For 1994: Clean Up the Office, Shed Pounds, Acquire Patience." *New York Times.* December 26, 1993. Retrieved August 27, 2018 from http://www.nytimes.com.

_____. "When Women Raise Their Voices." *New York Times.* January 12, 1997. Retrieved September 3, 2018 from http://www.nytimes.com.

Franks, Lucinda. "… Serious in Conversation." *New York Times.* March 12, 1975. Retrieved June 8, 2018 from http://www.nytimes.com.

Fraser, C. Gerald. "Inaugural Eve TV: Stars from Aaron to Woodward Set." *New York Times.* January 17, 1977. Retrieved June 18, 2018 from http://www.nytimes.com.

_____. "Miss Woodward, Newman Feted." *New York Times.* May 6, 1975. Retrieved June 10, 2018 from http://www.nytimes.com.

_____. "… Woodward at the Wheel." *New York Times.* February 14, 1982. Retrieved July 19, 2018 from http://www.nytimes.com.

Fricke, John. *Judy: A Legendary Film Career.* Philadelphia: Running Press, 2010.

Fujiwara. Chris. The *World and Its Double: The Life and Work of Otto Preminger.* New York: Faber & Faber, 2008.

Funke, Lewis. "News and Gossip of the Rialto …" *New York Times.* May 11, 1958. Retrieved March 26, 2018 from http://www.nytimes.com.

Garamekian, Barbara. "The Calendar." *New York Times.* June 25, 1984. Retrieved July 28, 2018 from http://www.nytimes.com.

Gardner, Sandra. "New Jersey Journal." *New York Times.* March 28, 1981. Retrieved July 19, 2018 from http://www.nytimes.com.

Gates, Anita. "Dramatic Duo Take Reins Again at Westport." *New York Times.* January 20, 2008. Retrieved September 29, 2018 from http://www.nytimes.com.

_____. "For a Veteran Thespian, a Welcome Return to Regional Theater." *New York Times.* April 2, 2009. Retrieved October 1, 2018 from http://www.nytimes.com.

_____. "Paul Newman to Direct 'Of Mice and Men.'" *New York Times.* February 10, 2008. Retrieved September 29, 2018 from http://www.nytimes.com.

_____. "Setting the Stage for Christmas." *New York Times.* December 5, 2008. Retrieved September 30, 2018 from http://www.nytimes.com.

_____. "Theater; Coming Attractions." *New York Times.* September 11, 2005. Retrieved September 25, 2018 from http://www.nytimes.com.

_____. "Theater Review; 'Copperfield' as a Fond, Fine Farewell." *New York Times.* December 11, 2005. Retrieved September 25, 2018 from http://www.nytimes.com.

_____. "Theater Review; from 'Me' to 'We': Searching for Bliss." *New York Times.* August 7, 2005. Retrieved September 25, 2018 from http://www.nytimes.com.

Geist, Kenneth L. *Pictures Will Talk: The Life & Films of Joseph L. Mankiewicz.* New York: Da Capo, 1978.

Gennocchio, Benjamin. "At Sarah Lawrence, Visual Arts Center Breaks Barriers." *New York Times.* October 31, 2004. Retrieved September 24, 2018 from http://www.nytimes.com.

Gertner, John. "Business; Newman's Own: Two Friends and a Canoe Paddle." *New York Times.* November 16, 2003. Retrieved September 19, 2018 from http://www.nytimes.com.

Ginzburg, Ralph. "Show Business—A Real Zoo." *New York Times.* May 3, 1987. Retrieved August 10, 2018 from http://www.nytimes.com.

Godbout, Oscar. "'The Adultress' Will Be Filmed …" *New York Times.* June 29, 1956. Retrieved February 23, 2018 from http://www.nytimes.com.

_____. "… Joanne Woodward Cast." *New York Times.* March 13, 1958. Retrieved March 23, 2018 from http://www.nytimes.com.

_____. " Musicians Seen Near Film Pact …" *New York Times.* August 25, 1958. Retrieved April 3, 2018 from http://www.nytimes.com.

Gonzalez, David. "Film; Cousin Bobby May Kiss, but He Doesn't Tell." *New York Times.* January 16, 1994. Retrieved August 27, 2018 from http://www.nytimes.com.

Goodman, Walter. "Review/Television; Seeking the Road to Transcendence." *New York Times.* July 8, 1991. Retrieved August 24, 2018 from http://www.nytimes.com.

Gordon, Jane. "Theater; The Old Red Barn Gets Red Velvet Seats." *New York Times.* May 22, 2005. Retrieved September 25, 2018 from http://www.nytimes.com.

_____. "Westport Country Playhouse Gets Closer to Its Second Act." *New York Times.* October 10, 2004. Retrieved September 24, 2018 from http://www.nytimes.com.

Goudsouzian, Aram. *Sidney Poitier: Man, Actor, Icon.* University of North Carolina Press, 2011.

Gould, Jack. "… 'The Girl in Chapter 1.'" *New York Times.* September 3, 1956. Retrieved February 19, 2018 from http://www.nytimes.com.

Gow, Gordon. Hollywood in the Fifties. New York: A. S. Barnes & Co.; London: A. Zwemmer Limited, 1971.

Green, Jesse. "The Prop Fetcher of 1950, with Quite a Future Ahead." *New York Times.* September 24, 2006. Retrieved September 25, 2018 from http://www.nytimes.com.

_____. "This School Is Out." *New York Times.* October 13, 1991. Retrieved August 24, 2018 from http://www.nytimes.com.

_____. "The Way We Live Now …" *New York Times.* February 9, 2003. Retrieved September 15, 2018 from http://www.nytimes.com.

Greenspun, Roger. "Screen: Allusive 'WUSA.'" *New York Times.* November 2, 1970. Retrieved May 17, 2018 from http://www.nytimes.com.

_____. "Screen: The Pilgrimage of Martin Luther King, Jr." *New York Times.* March 24, 1970. Retrieved May 30, 2018 from http://www.nytimes.com.

Grimes, William. "… Footlights." *New York Times.* March 7, 1997. Retrieved September 3, 2018 from http://www.nytimes.com.

Grissom, James. *Follies of God: Tennessee Williams and the Women of the Fog.* Alfred A. Knopf, 2015.

Gross, Jane. "Paul Newman, Race Driver." *New York Times.* July 1, 1979. Retrieved July 1, 2018 from http://www.nytimes.com.

Gross, Michael Joseph. "New England; Weekend in Williamstown." *New York Times.* June 4, 2000. Retrieved September 10, 2018 from http://www.nytimes.com.

Gruen, John. "Feisty Young Dancer with a Company of His Own." *New York Times.* August 31, 1975. Retrieved June 10, 2018 from http://www.nytimes.com.

Gussow, Mel. "Circle in Square Takes Its Closing Notice Down." *New York Times.* April 30, 1974. Retrieved June 5, 2018 from http://www.nytimes.com.

_____. "The Newmans: 2 Lives in the Movies." *New*

York Times. April 28, 1975. Retrieved June 9, 2018 from http://www.nytimes.com.

_____. "Reading a Cather Book with a Director's Eye." *New York Times*. November 9, 1998. Retrieved March 3, 2018 from http://www.nytimes.com.

Hall, Christopher. "Travel Advisory…" *New York Times*. June 27, 1999. Retrieved September 8, 2018 from http://www.nytimes.com.

Hampton, Wilborn. "Love, from a Villa to a Dentist's Office." *New York Times*. August 21, 1996. Retrieved September 1, 2018 from http://www.nytimes.com.

Harmetz, Aljean. "Film; Partnerships Make a Movie." *New York Times*. February 18, 1990. Retrieved August 20, 2018 from http://www.nytimes.com.

_____. "For Actresses; Life Doesn't Begin at 40." *New York Times*. January 23, 1980. Retrieved July 7, 2018 from http://www.nytimes.com.

_____. "Hollywood: This Way In." *New York Times*. March 13, 1983. Retrieved July 27, 2018 from http://www.nytimes.com.

_____. "Paul Newman, a Magnetic Titan of Hollywood, Is Dead at 83." *New York Times*. September 27, 2008. Retrieved September 29, 2018 from http://www.nytimes.com.

_____. "Stage View: A Luminous 'Menagerie' Glows at the Long Warf." *New York Times*. March 23, 1986. Retrieved August 2, 2018 from http://www.nytimes.com.

Harris, Robert, and Harvey, Anthony. DVD Audio Commentary. They Might Be Giants. Starz/Anchor Bay, 2000.

Harris, Roy. *Eight Women of the American Stage Talking About Acting*. Portsmouth, NH: Heinemann, 1997.

Haskell, Molly. *From Reverence to Rape: The Treatment of Women in the Movies*. New York: Penguin, 1974.

Hawes, William. *Live Television Drama, 1946–1951*. Jefferson, NC: McFarland, 2001.

Heffernan, Virginia. "A Small Town Tangled in a New England Knot." *New York Times*. May 27, 2005. Retrieved September 23, 2018 from http://www.nytimes.com.

Heller-Anderson, Susan. "Chronicle." *New York Times*. May 16, 1990. Retrieved August 20, 2108 from http://www.nytimes.com.

_____. "Women Begin Observances." *New York Times*. March 9, 1982. Retrieved July 19, 2018 from http://www.nytimes.com.

Higham, Charles. "Television." *New York Times*. April 18, 1971. Retrieved May 22, 2018 from http://www.nytimes.com.

Hirschhorn, Clive. *The Columbia Story*. London: Pyramid Books, 1989.

_____. *The Warner Bros. Story: The Complete History of the Great Hollywood Studio*. London: Octopus, 1979.

_____. *The Universal Story: The Complete History of the Studio and Its 2,641 Films*. London: Octopus Books, 1983.

Hofmann, Deborah. "Fashion; Even for Wagner, Short Is In at the Opera." *New York Times*. October 14, 1990. Retrieved August 20, 2018 from http://www.nytimes.com.

Holland, Bernard. "Battling AIDS from the Stage." *New York Times*. November 3, 1987. Retrieved August 12, 2018 from http://www.nytimes.com.

_____. "Concert: 'Music for Life,' a Benefit." *New York Times*. November 9, 1987. Retrieved August 12, 2018 from http://www.nytimes.com.

_____. "Metropolitan Opera Opens Its Second Century with a Fanfare." *New York Times*. September 25, 1984. Retrieved July 29, 2018 from http://www.nytimes.com.

Holtz, Jeff. "In Brief: Artistic Director Named for Westport Playhouse." *New York Times*. June 26, 2005. Retrieved September 25, 2018 from http://www.nytimes.com.

Hotchner, A.E. *Paul and Me: Years of Adventures and Misadventures with Paul Newman*. Nan A. Talese/Doubleday, 2010.

Ifill, Gwen. "Women's Coalition Rallies to Defend Mrs. Clinton." *New York Times*. March 29, 1994. Retrieved August 28, 2018 from http://www.nytimes.com.

Jackson, Carlton. *Picking Up the Tab: The Life and Movies of Martin Ritt*. Bowling Green, OH: Bowling State University Popular Press, 1994.

Johnston, Laurie, and Robert Thomas, Jr. "Notes on People; Celebrating an 11-Year Battle to Help the Consumer." *New York Times*. April 29, 1981. Retrieved July 12, 2018 from http://www.nytimes.com.

Jordan, Rene. *Marlon Brando. Pyramid Illustrated History of the Movies*. New York: Pyramid Publications, 1973.

J.P. S. "TV: 'Eighty-Yard Run' …" *New York Times*. January 17, 1958. Retrieved March 22, 2018 from http://www.nytimes.com.

Kael, Pauline. *Deeper Into Movies*. New York: Warner Books, 1973.

_____. *5001 Nights at the Movies*. New York: Holt, Rinehart & Winston, 1984.

_____. *Reeling*. Boston; Toronto: Little, Brown & Co., 1976.

Kakutani, Michiko. "The New Writers Vs Hollywood." *New York Times*. April 25, 1982. Retrieved July 19, 2018 from http://www.nytimes.com.

_____. "The Public and Private Joe Papp." *New York Times*. June 23, 1985. Retrieved July 31, 2018 from http://www.nytimes.com.

Kandell, Leslie. "Music; Star Revival of Copland and Hemingway." *New York Times*. November 18, 2001. Retrieved September 14, 2018 from http://www.nytimes.com.

Kanfer, Stefan. "Cinema: Lunatic of Manhattan." *Time*. April 26, 1971. Retrieved May 21, 2018 from http://www.time.com.

_____. *Somebody: The Reckless Life and Remarkable Career of Marlon Brando*. Alfred A. Knopf, 2008.

Kaplan, Fred. *Gore Vidal*. London: Bloomsbury Publishing, 2012.

Kaufman, Joanne. "Havens…" *New York Times*. February 28, 2003. Retrieved September 15, 2018 from http://www.nytimes.com.

Kaufman, Michael T. "About New York: A Power Lunch to Feed the Hungry." *New York Times*. November 17, 1993. Retrieved August 27, 2018 from http://www.nytimes.com.

Kazan, Elia. *The Selected Letters of Elia Kazan*. New York: Vintage Books, 2014.

Kennedy, Shawn G. "Postings; New Hands on Old Salem Reins." *New York Times*. January 15, 1984. Retrieved July 28, 2018 from http://www.nytimes.com.

Kerbel, Michael. *Henry Fonda. Pyramid Illustrated History of the Movies*. New York: Pyramid Publications, 1973.

_____. *Paul Newman. Illustrated History of the Movies*. London: Star Books, 1973.

Keyser, Les. *Hollywood in the Seventies*. San Diego; New York: A.S. Barnes & Company, Inc., 1981.

Khoury. Peter. "All of Broadway's a Stage." *New York Times*. August 9, 2013. Retrieved October 8, 2018 from http://www.nytimes.com.

Kilgannon, Corey. "Chronicle of a Changing City." *New York Times*. December 3, 2010. Retrieved October 2, 2018 from http://www.nytimes.com.

King, A. "Hollywood Star Joanne Woodward Can't Remember Husband Paul Newman Anymore." *Blasting News*. July 24, 2017. Retrieved October 9, 2018 from http://www.blastingnews.com.

Kissellgof, Anna. "Dance: Taylor 'Images' Premiered." *New York Times*. June 1, 1977. Retrieved June 27, 2018 from http://www.nytimes.com.

_____. "Taylor Dancers Set a Season in Capital." *New York Times*. October 4, 1976. Retrieved June 13, 2018 from http://www.nytimes.com.

_____. "What a Troupe Called Dancers Is About." *New York Times*. November 18, 1977. Retrieved June 27, 2018 from http://www.nytimes.com.

Klein, Alvin. "Critic's Notebook: Pondering the Role of the Reviewer." *New York Times*. July 30, 2000. Retrieved September 11, 2018 from http://www.nytimes.com.

_____. "Island's Theaters Look to a Revitalized Season." *New York Times*. June 3, 1993. Retrieved August 27, 2018 from http://www.nytimes.com.

_____. "Seeing Another Age on Separate Stages." *New York Times*. June 17, 2001. Retrieved September 13, 2018 from http://www.nytimes.com.

_____. "Stellar Students Crowd a Teacher's Schedule." *New York Times*. May 30, 1993. Retrieved August 27, 2018 from http://www.nytimes.com.

_____. "Theater: A Woman's Decision, the Reverberations." *New York Times*. July 9, 2000. Retrieved September 11, 2018 from http://www.nytimes.com.

_____. "Theater: Actor as Overseer, Actors as Ensemble." *New York Times*. December 3, 1995. Retrieved August 31, 2018 from http://www.nytimes.com.

_____. "Theater: Critic's Notebook: Taking to the Stage for Sustenance." *New York Times*. August 29, 1999. Retrieved September 8, 2018 from http://www.nytimes.com.

_____. "Theater: Critic's Notebook: Uncertain Season." *New York Times*. June 25, 2000. Retrieved September 11, 2018 from http://www.nytimes.com.

_____. "Theater: Dreaming Big Dreams in Westport." *New York Times*. January 30, 2000. Retrieved September 10, 2018 from http://www.nytimes.com.

_____. "Theater: In 'The Depot' Politics Is the Point." *New York Times*. March 15, 1987. Retrieved August 9, 2018 from http://www.nytimes.com.

_____. "Theater: On the Trail of the Audacious." *New York Times*. January 2, 2000. Retrieved September 9, 2018 from http://www.nytimes.com.

_____. "Theatre: Westport Sets Fall Season." *New York Times*. September 8, 1985. Retrieved August 1, 2018 from http://www.nytimes.com.

_____. "Theater Review: The Contagion of Hate." *New York Times*. July 6, 2003. Retrieved September 18, 2018 from http://www.nytimes.com.

_____. "Westport Playhouse Facing More Change." *New York Times*. September 24, 2000. Retrieved September 12, 2018 from http://www.nytimes.com.

Klein, Woody. *Westport, Connecticut: The Story of a New England Town's Rise to Prominence*. Westport, CT: Greenwood, 2002.

Klemesrud, Judy. "Awards Bring Out Actors Studio Alumni." *New York Times*. November 6, 1980. Retrieved July 11, 2018 from http://www.nytimes.com.

_____. "In the Running for the E.R.A." *New York Times*. September 3, 1979. Retrieved July 1, 2018 from http://www.nytimes.com.

_____. "Movies." *New York Times*. August 8, 1971. Retrieved May 22, 2018 from http://www.nytimes.com.

_____. "Neigborhood Playhouse Turns 50, and the Stars Turn Out." *New York Times*. December 5, 1978. Retrieved June 28, 2018 from http://www.nytimes.com.

_____. "Rallying Women on Nuclear War Issues." *New York Times*. September 9, 1984. Retrieved July 28, 2018 from http://www.nytimes.com.

Knickerbocker, Paine. "San Francisco Fete in Retrospect." *New York Times*. November 16, 1958. Retrieved April 5, 2018 from http://www.nytimes.com.

Knopf, Alfred A. "Sidney Lumet on 'The Fugitive Kind': Delighted and Challenged." *James Grissom*. December 9, 2012. Retrieved April 11, 2018 from http://www.jamesgrissom.blogspot.com.au.

Krampner, Jon. *Female Brando: The Legend of Kim Stanley*. New York: Backstage Books, 2006.

Kratofil, Colleen. "Paul Newman's Famous Rolex from Joanne Woodward Sells for $17.8 Million." *People*. October 27, 2017. Retrieved October 9, 2018 from http://www.people.com.

Krebs, Albin. "... Actors Studio Awards." *New York Times*. September 13, 1980. Retrieved July 11, 2018 from http://www.nytimes.com.

_____. "... for an Opera Buff, a 'Dream Come True.'" *New York Times*. October 4, 1980. Retrieved July 11, 2018 from http://www.nytimes.com.

Krebs, Albin, and Robert Thomas, Jr. "Notes on People: Sylvia Sydney Learns Isaac Stern Isn't Forbidding at All." *New York Times*. January 22, 1981. Retrieved July 12, 2018 from http://www.nytimes.com.

Kresh, Paul. "From 1917 to 1984, Musicals Offer Plenty to Sing About." *New York Times*. August 12, 1984. Retrieved July 28, 2018 from http://www.nytimes.com.

Kuby, Michael. "Summer Festival; Theater ..." *New York Times*. May 19, 1991. Retrieved August 24, 2018 from http://www.nytimes.com.

La Gorce, Tammy. "A Chrysalis for Writers in an Old Train Stop." *New York Times*. March 12, 2010. Retrieved October 2, 2018 from http://www.nytimes.com.

Landazuri, Margarita. "Article: A Fine Madness (1966). " *Turner Classic Movies*. Retrieved May 2, 2018 from http://www.tcm.com.

Latham, Aaron. "Paul Newman: The Real Thing." *Rolling Stone*, No. 387., January 20, 1983: 14–15, 19–21, 62.

Laurie, Piper. *Learning to Live Out Loud: A Memoir*. Crown/Archtype, 2011.

Law, Jude. Sleuth DVD Audio Commentary. Sony Pictures Home Entertainment, 2008.

Lawson, Carol. "Actors Pay Homage to O'Neill, Strindberg." *New York Times*. November 12, 1982. Retrieved July 20, 2018 from http://www.nytimes.com.

_____. "Broadway." *New York Times*. October 23, 1981. Retrieved July 15, 2018 fro http://www.nytimes.com.

_____. "Broadway Celebrates Eugene O'Neill's Birthday." *New York Times*. October 20, 1981. Retrieved July 15, 2018 from http://www.nytimes.com.

_____. "Broadway: Joanne Woodward Returns in Fall in Shaw's 'Candida.'" *New York Times*. July 10, 1981. Retrieved July 13, 2018 from http://www.nytimes.com.

_____. "Chronicle." *New York Times*. September 12, 1997. Retrieved September 4, 2018 from http://www.nytimes.com.

_____. "City's Stage Heritage Shown." *New York Times*. March 20, 1984. Retrieved July 28, 2018 from http://www.nytimes.com.

_____. "… Joanne Woodward." *New York Times*. June 27, 1976. Retrieved June 11, 2018 from http://www.nytimes.com.

_____. "Joanne Woodward Had 'A Movie-Star Dream.'" *New York Times*. September 17, 1981. Retrieved July 14, 2018 from http://www.nytimes.com.

_____. "Met Opening Revives Glitter." *New York Times*. September 24, 1985. Retrieved August 1, 2018 from http://www.nytimes.com.

Lax, Eric. *Newman. Paul Newman: A Celebration*. London: Pavilion, 1996.

Levy, Shawn. *Paul Newman: A Life*. New York: Three Rivers Press, 2009.

Lewis, Grover. "The Redoubtable Mr. Newman." *Rolling Stone*. July 5, 1973. Retrieved June 1, 2018 from http://www.rollingstone.com.

Lewis, Richard Warren. "Waiting for a Horse Paul Newman Makes a Western." *New York Times*. November 6, 1966. Retrieved May 2, 2018 from http://www.nytimes.com.

Leydon, Joe. "Gayby." *Variety*. March 28, 2012. Retrieved October 5, 2018 from http://www.variety.com.

Liebenson, Bess. "In Decades Past in Westport, the Way They Were." *New York Times*. May 14, 1995. Retrieved August 31, 2018 from http://www.nytimes.com.

Linney, Laura. Celebrity Podcast. Episode 22. *Little Known Facts*. Retrieved August 27, 2018 from http://www.littleknownfactspodcast.com.

Lipton, James. *Inside Inside*. New York: Dutton, 2007.

LoBianco, Lorraine. "Articles: Count Three and Pray (1955)." *Turner Classic Movies*. Retrieved March 3, 2018 from http://www.nytimes.com.

Long, Robert Emmet. *The Films of Merchant Ivory*. New York: Harry N. Abrams, 1997.

_____. *James Ivory in Conversation: How Merchant Ivory Makes Its Movies*. University of California Press, 2006.

Lovinger, Caitlin and Urso, Steve. "Straw Hats Off, Please, Curtain Going Up." *New York Times*. May 11, 1997. Retrieved September 4, 2018 from http://www.nytimes.com.

Lowry, Brian. "Empire Falls." *Variety*. May 25, 2005. Retrieved September 23, 2018 from http://variety.com.

Lyman, Rick. "The Lives They Lived: Sanford Meisner; the Proof Is in the Protégé." *New York Times*. January 4, 1998. Retrieved February 2, 2018 from http://www.nytimes.com.

_____. "A Wind of Gratitude Blows Through the Performing Arts." *New York Times*. December 8, 1997. Retrieved September 7, 2018 from http://www.nytimes.com.

Maker, Elizabeth. "A Renaissance in Full Bloom for Aging Theaters." *New York Times*. March 11, 2007. Retrieved September 26, 2018 from http://www.nytimes.com.

Malden, Karl. *When Do I Start? A Memoir*. New York: Limelight Editions, 2004.

Malone, Audra D. "Women in Theatre: Linda Winer in Conversation with Joanne Woodward." The League of Professional Theatre Women/CUNY TV, 2005.

Marin, Rick. "Foreign Affairs." *Variety*. March 16, 1993. Retrieved August 23, 2018 from http://www.variety.com.

Marks, Peter. "Looking Back at a Rebellious Spirit." *New York Times*. April 29, 1997. Retrieved September 4, 2018 from http://www.nytimes.com.

_____. "On Stage, and Off …" *New York Times*. September 15, 1995. Retrieved August 31, 2018 from http://www.nytimes.com.

Maslin, Janet. "Film: Paul Newman Directs 'Glass Menagerie.'" *New York Times*. October 23, 1987. Retrieved August 5, 2018 from http://www.nytimes.com.

_____. "Review/Film: Philadelphia; Tom Hanks as an AIDS Victim Who Fights the Establishment." *New York Times*. December 22, 1993. Retrieved August 28, 2018 from http://www.nytimes.com.

McCarthy, Todd. "Philadelphia." *Variety*. December 6, 1993. Retrieved August 30, 2018 from http://www.variety.com.

McFadden, Robert D. "Delegates from World Are Doing the Town." *New York Times*. September 29, 1990. Retrieved August 20, 2018 from http://www.nytimes.com.

McKinley, Jessie. "On Stage and Off…" *New York Times*. May 19, 2000. Retrieved September 10, 2018 from http://www.nytimes.com.

_____. "On Stage and Off…" *New York Times*. September 29, 2000. Retrieved September 12, 2018 from http://www.nytimes.com.

_____. "Settling Down to Take Over Westport Theater." *New York Times*. August 28, 2005. Retrieved September 25, 2018 from http://www.nytimes.com.

Meisner, Sanford, and Dennis Longwell. *Sanford Meisner on Acting*. New York, Toronto: Vintage, 1987.

Merchant, Ismail. *Merchant-Ivory: Interviews*. University Press of Mississippi, 2012.

Miller, Bryan. "Diners Sitting Out 'Great Wine War.'" *New York Times*. March 24, 1984. Retrieved July 28, 2018 from http://www.nytimes.com.

Miller, Frank. "Article: The Fugitive Kind (1960)." *Turner Classic Movies*. Retrieve April 10, 2018 from http://www.tcm.com.

_____. "Film Article: The Three Faces of Eve." *Turner Classic Movies*. Retrieved February 25, 2018 from http://www.tcm.com.

Miller, Gabriel. *The Films of Martin Ritt: Fanfare for the Common Man*. Jackson: University Press of Mississippi, 2000.

Mitgang, Herbert. "'100 Stars' and More to Benefit Actor's Fund." *New York Times*. January 6, 1982. Retrieved July 15, 2018 from http://www.nytimes.com.

Mohr, Charles. "200 Women Turn Out for Parley to Seek Ways to Halt Arms Race." *New York Times*. September 13, 1984. Retrieved July 27, 2018 from http://www.nytimes.com.

Mooner, Wendy. "In with the New at the Winter Antiques Show." *New York Times*. January 12, 1995. Retrieved August 29, 2018 from http://www.nytimes.com.

Morella, Joe and Epstein, Edward Z. *Paul and Joanne: A Biography of Paul Newman and Joanne Woodward*. London: W.H. Allen, 1989.

Morris, Bob. "The Night …" *New York Times*. August 28, 1994. Retrieved August 28, 2018 from http://www.nytimes.com.

_____. "The Night …" *New York Times*. September 25, 1994. Retrieved August 30, 2018 from http://www.nytimes.com.

_____. "The Night …" *New York Times*. January 22, 1995. Retrieved August 29, 2018 from http://www.nytimes.com.

_____. "The Night …" *New York Times*. March 12, 1995. Retrieved August 30, 2018 from http://www.nytimes.com.

_____. "The Night …" *New York Times*. July 14, 1996. Retrieved September 2, 2018 from http://www.nytimes.com.

Morris, Bernandine. "… Four Years in Paris." *New York Times*. December 6, 1973. Retrieved June 3, 2018 from http://www.nytimes.com.

_____. "Shop Talk." *New York Times*. April 26, 1974. Retrieved June 5, 2018 from http://www.nytimes.com.

Musante, Fred. "Acre by Acre, Preserving the Character of the State." *New York Times*. January 16, 2000. Retrieved September 9, 2018 from http://www.nytimes.com.

Nason, Richard. "Fugitive' Is Shot." *New York Times*. July 5, 1959. Retrieved April 6, 2018 from http://www.nytimes.com.

Nathan, Jean. "A Performer Who Finally Grew Into Her Talent." *New York Times*. December 22, 1996. Retrieved September 1, 2018 from http://www.nytimes.com.

Navasky, Victor F. "… Golden Days." *New York Times*. May 5, 1974. Retrieved June 5, 2018 from http://www.nytimes.com.

Nemy, Edith. "Broadway." *New York Times*. September 28, 1984. Retrieved July 29, 2018 from http://www.nytimes.com.

_____. "Chronicle." *New York Times*. March 17, 1993. Retrieved August 26, 2018 from http://www.nytimes.com.

_____. "Starry 7 Dwarfs in Camp for Fun and a Good Cause…" *New York Times*. September 19, 1994. Retrieved August 29, 2018 fro http://www.nytimes.com.

_____. "Who's Who of Santa's Stockings." *New York Times*. December 13, 1977. Retrieved June 28, 2018 from http://www.nytimes.com.

Netter, Susan. *Paul Newman and Joanne Woodward: An Unauthorised Biography*. London: Piatkus, 1989.

Newman, Paul. "The 'G' in G.O.P. Is for 'Glitch.'" *New York Times*. February 27, 1986. Retrieved August 2, 2018 from http://www.nytimes.com.

Newman, Paul, and A. E. Hotchner. *Shameless Exploitation in Pursuit of the Common Good: The Madcap Business Adventure by the Truly Oddest Couple*. New York: Nan A. Talese, 2003.

Ney, Joanna. "'Dancers' Takes the Big Step—The New York Debut." *New York Times*. April 3, 1977. Retrieved June 18, 2018 from http://www.nytimes.com.

Nixon, Rob. "Article: From the Terrace (1960)." *Turner Classic Movies*. Retrieved April 16, 2018 from http://www.tcm.com.

_____. "Article: Paris Blues (1961)." *Turner Classic Movies*. Retrieved April 17, 2018 from http://www.tcm.com.

_____. "Article: The Sound and the Fury." *Turner Classic Movies*. Retrieved April 14, 2018 from http://www.tcm.com.

_____. "Articles: Winning (1969)." *Turner Classic Movies*. Retrieved May 14, 2018 from http://www.tcm.com.

Nordheimer, Jon. "Los Angeles Ballet Fights Uphill Battle." *New York Times*. August 14, 1975. Retrieved June 10, 2018 from http://www.nytimes.com.

O'Brien, Daniel. *Paul Newman*. London: Faber & Faber, 2004.

O'Brien, Scott. *Sylvia Sidney: Paid by the Tear*. Albany, GA: BearManor Media, 2016.

O'Connor, John J. "'Dialogues of Carmelites.'" *New York Times*. May 6, 1987. Retrieved August 10, 2018 from http://www.nytimes.com.

_____. "Joanne Woodward as an Alzheimer's Victim." *New York Times*. May 21, 1985. Retrieved July 31, 2018 from http://www.nytimes.com.

_____. "Review/Television: Group Theater and the Legacy of Its Great Dare." *New York Times*. June 26, 1989. Retrieved August 13, 2018 from http://www.nytimes.com.

_____. "Review/Television: Kennedy Center Awards' Glitter Is Blemished by Film-Clips Dispute." *New York Times*. December 30, 1992. Retrieved August 25, 2018 from http://www.nytimes.com.

_____. "Review/Television; Middle-Aged Romance Amid Dreaming Spires." *New York Times*. March 17, 1993. Retrieved August 23, 2018 from http://www.nytimes.com.

_____. "… Sunday." *New York Times*. November 12, 1976. Retrieved June 13, 2018 from http://www.nytimes.com.

_____. "Television Review: Two Decades of Dance: a Scrapbook of Favorites." *New York Times*. June 3, 1996. Retrieved September 1, 2018 from http://www.nytimes.com.

_____. "TV …." *New York Times*. December 14, 1976. Retrieved June 13, 2018 from http://www.nytimes.com.

_____. "TV…." *New York Times*. November 17, 2018. Retrieved June 13, 2018 from http://www.nytimes.com.

_____. "TV: Celebrating New Year's, 'Sheba.'" *New York Times*. December 30, 1977. Retrieved June 28, 2018 from http://www.nytimes.com.

_____. "TV Christmas Fare: Musical and a Drama." *New York Times*. December 19, 1978. Retrieved June 29, 2018 from http://www.nytimes.com.

_____. "TV: Joanne Woodward, 40, 'Sweet' and Running." *New York Times*. February 1, 1978. Retrieved June 28, 2018 from http://www.nytimes.com.

_____. "TV: Little Rock, 1957: 'Crisis at Central High.'" *New York Times*. February 4, 1981. Retrieved July 10, 2018 from http://www.nytimes.com.

_____. "TV: Love Was Link for Tuesday and Wednesday." *New York Times*. December 3, 1971. Retrieved May 24, 2018 from http://www.nytimes.com.

_____. "TV: 'Streets of L.A.,' with Joanne Woodward." *New York Times*. November 13, 1979. Retrieved July 5, 2018 from http://www.nytimes.com.

_____. "TV Review: The Met Opera's 'Tales of Hoffmann.'" *New York Times*. March 2, 1988. Retrieved August 16, 2018 from http://www.nytimes.com.

_____. "TV Review: Zeffirelli's Lavish 'Turandot' at the Met Opera." *New York Times*. January 27, 1988. Retrieved August 16, 2018 from http://www.nytimes.com.

_____. "TV Reviews …" *New York Times*. March 27, 1985. Retrieved July 31, 2018 from http://www.nytimes.com.

_____. "TV Reviews: 'Eugene O'Neill,'" Channel 13 Profile." *New York Times*. September 8, 1986. Retrieved August 3, 2018 from http://www.nytimes.com.

_____. "TV Reviews: 'Passions' and 'Booker' on Tonight." *New York Times*. October 1, 1984. Retrieved July 26, 2018 from http://www.nytimes.com.

_____. "TV Weekend: A Leisurely Tour of Anne Tyler's Small Miracles." *New York Times*. February 4, 1994. Retrieved August 28, 2018 from http://www.nytimes.com.

_____. "TV View." *New York Times*. December 1, 1974. Retrieved June 8, 2018 from http://www.nytimes.com.

_____. "TV View." *New York Times*. November 11, 1979. Retrieved July 5, 2018 from http://www.nytimes.com.

_____. "TV Weekend: A Politician's Awakening to Drugs in Her Family." *New York Times*. April 30, 1993. Retrieved August 27, 2018 from http://www.nytimes.com.

O'Neill, Laurie A. "Celebrity Recipes Aids Cancer Society." *New York Times*. November 14, 1982. Retrieved July 20, 2018 from http://www.nytimes.com.

Oumano, Elena. *Paul Newman*. London: Robert Hale, 1989.

Papazian, Rita. "Protecting What's Left of Open Space." *New York Times*. January 11, 1998. Retrieved September 7, 2018 from http://www.nytimes.com.

Passafiume, Andrea. "Article: Behind the Camera on the Long, Hot Summer." *Turner Classic Movies*. Retrieved March 20, 2018 from http://www.tcm.com.

_____. "Article: Rachel, Rachel (1968)." *Turner Classic Movies*. Retrieved May 7, 2018 from http://www.tcm.com.

_____. "Article: Rally 'Round the Flag, Boys! (1959)." *Turner Classic Movies*. Retrieved April 4, 2018 from http://www.tcm.com.

Paquette, Carole. "Under the Big Top: If It's Party Time It's Fun to Have a Tent." *New York Times*. May 17, 1998. Retrieved September 7, 2018 from http://www.nytimes.com.

Peck. Seymour. "Up-and-Coming in Movies." *New York Times*. January 26, 1958. Retrieved March 22, 2018 from http://www.nytimes.com.

Pogrebin, Robin. "Theater: An Evening of American Classics." *New York Times*. December 1, 2002. Retrieved September 15, 2018 from http://www.nytimes.com.

_____. "Theater: Pitching In for Paul Newman and Other American Icons." *New York Times*. November 18, 2001. Retrieved September 14, 2018 from http://www.nytimes.com.

Porter, Darwin. *Paul Newman: The Man Behind the Baby Blues: His Secret Life Exposed*. Blood Moon Productions, 2009.

Pryor, Thomas. M. "Actress Famine Hits Hollywood." *New York Times*. September 13, 1956. Retrieved February 24, 2018 from http://www.nytimes.com.

_____. "'Baby Doll' Star Gets a New Role … " *New York Times*. January 9, 1957. Retrieved February 23, 2018 from http://www.nytimes.com.

_____. "… Cast Additions Made." *New York Times*. April 2, 1957. Retrieved February 26, 2018 from http://www.nytimes.com.

_____. "… Child's Play." *New York Times*. July 6, 1958. Retrieved April 3, 2018 from http://www.nytimes.com.

_____. " Debbie Reynolds in Columbia Deal …" *New York Times*. March 8, 1959. Retrieved April 6, 2018 from http://www.nytimes.com.

_____. "Filming Planned of 'Adam and Eve' …" *New York Times*. November 11, 1956. Retrieved February 25, 2018 from http://www.nytimes.com.

_____. "… Fox Revises Comedy." *New York Times*. June 10, 1958. Retrieved March 26, 2018 from http://www.nytimes.com.

_____. "Fox to End Lull in Movie Output." *New York Times*. July 29, 1956. Retrieved February 24, 2018 from http://www.nytimes.com.

_____. "Grauman's Closes for Alterations …" *New York Times*. February 2, 1958. Retrieved March 23, 2018 from http://www.nytimes.com.

_____. "Hollywood's 'Oscar' Night …" *New York Times*. March 30, 1958. Retrieved March 26, 2018 from http://www.nytimes.com.

_____. "Jerry Wald Buys 'World of Crime.'" *New York Times*. September 18, 1957. Retrieved February 28, 2018 from http://www.nytimes.com.

_____. "… 'Joanne's 'Eves.'" *New York Times*. March

24, 1957. Retrieved February 24, 2018 from http://www.nytimes.com.

_____. "John Wayne Signs for Cavalry Film ..." *New York Times*. August 15, 1958. Retrieved April 3, 2018 from http://www.nytimes.com.

_____. "Music's the Thing in Movies' Plans." *New York Times*. May 23, 1955. Retrieved February 13, 2018 from http://www.nytimes.com.

_____. "... Odets Is Writing Script." *New York Times*. April 23, 1958. Retrieved March 26, 2018 from http://www.nytimes.com.

_____. "26 Stars Line Up for 'Oscar' Show ..." *New York Times*. January 30, 1958. Retrieved March 23, 2018 from http://www.nytimes.com.

_____. "... Trebled Personality." *New York Times*. May 18, 1956. Retrieved February 24, 2018 fro http://www.nytimes.com.

Quinn, Kathleen. "'Twas Method, Yet There Was Madness in It." *New York Times*. June 25, 1989. Retrieved August 17, 2018 from http://www.nytimes.com.

Quirk, Lawrence J. *Paul Newman a Life*. Plymouth, UK: Taylor Trade Publishing, 2009.

R.F.S. "Joan Blondell Appears in 'White Gloves.'" *New York Times*. December 22, 1955. Retrieved February 15, 2018 from http://www.nytimes.com.

Ramirez, Anthony. "Boldface Names. " *New York Times*. January 21, 2004. Retrieved September 19, 2018 from http://www.nytimes.com.

Ravo, Nick. "Who's Hustling Whom? a Paul Newman Court Drama." *New York Times*. June 16, 1988. Retrieved August 16, 2018 from http://www.nytimes.com.

Reed, Rex. "Movies: the Doug and Mary of the Jet Age." *New York Times*. September 1, 1968. Retrieved May 9, 2018 from http://www.nytimes.com.

Reif, Rita. "Christmas Trees Reflect Tastes of 22 Celebrities." *New York Times*. December 4, 1964. Retrieved April 25, 2018 from http://www.nytimes.com.

Resnick, Sylvia Safran. *Burt Reynolds: An Unauthorized Biography*. New York: St. Martin's Press, 1983.

Reynolds, Burt. *But Enough About Me*. London: Blink Publishing, 2015.

Reynolds, Simon. "Paul Newman 'Wants to Die at Home.'" *Digital Spy*. August 8, 2008. Retrieved October 3, 2018 from http://www.digitalspy.com.

Rich, Frank. "Stage: Shaw's 'Candida' with Miss Woodward." *New York Times*. October 16, 1981. Retrieved July 15, 2018 from http://www.nytimes.com.

Rich, Motoko. "Gore Vidal: Awardee, Storyteller, Godfather." *New York Times*. November 18, 2009. Retrieved October 1, 2018 from http://www.nytimes.com.

Ritt, Martin. *Martin Ritt: Interviews*. Jackson: University Press of Mississippi, 2003.

Roberts. Steven V. "Who (and What) Makes Oscar 'Possible'?" *New York Times*. April 13, 1969. Retrieved May 12, 2018 from http://www.nytimes.com.

Robertson, Campbell. "Boldface Names." *New York Times*. March 12, 2004. Retrieved September 19, 2018 from http://www.nytimes.com.

_____. "In Which We Are Envious of the Australians." *New York Times*. May 13, 2005. Retrieved September 24, 2018 from http://www.nytimes.com.

Robinson, Douglas. "Rising Southern Star." *New York Times*. October 6, 1957. Retrieved February 28, 2018 from http://www.nytimes.com.

Robinson, Ruth. " ... a Novel Party." *New York Times*. April 26, 1981. Retrieved July 12, 2018 from http://www.nytimes.com.

_____. "Future Events." *New York Times*. December 5, 1982. Retrieved July 20, 2018 from http://www.nytimes.com.

_____. "Future Events." *New York Times*. February 6, 1983. Retrieved July 27, 2018 from http://www.nytimes.com.

Rockwell, John. "Pop Life." *New York Times*. December 17, 1976. Retrieved June 13, 2018 from http://www.nytimes.com.

Rodriquez, Elena. *Dennis Hopper: A Madness to His Method*. New York: St. Martin's Press, 1988.

Rohter, Larry. "Film; Crossing the Bridges with the Newmans." *New York Times*. November 18, 1990. Retrieved August 21, 2018 from http://www.nytimes.com.

Rothstein, Mervin. "Memorial Tribute to Joshua Logan, in His Words." *New York Times*. November 15, 1988. Retrieved August 17, 2018 fro http://www.nytimes.com.

_____. "On Stage." *New York Times*. November 24, 1989. Retrieved August 19, 2018 from http://www.nytimes.com.

Rovin, Jeff. *Joan Collins: The Unauthorized Biography*. Toronto, New York, London, Sydney, Auckland: Bantam Books, 1984.

Russian, Ale. "... Allison Janney and More Oscar Nominees Reveal the Women Who Inspire Them Most." *People*. February 22, 2018. Retrieved October 9, 2018 from http://www.people.com.

Russo, Richard, and Fred Schepisi. *Empire Falls* DVD Audio Commentary. HBO Studios, 2007.

Saland, Ronald. *Harper Days Are Here Again*. Professional Films/Robbins Nest Production, Year unknown.

Saltz, Rachel. "Tracking Down a Rock God, Despite the Emotional Risk." *New York Times*. May 29, 2014. Retrieved June 21, 2018 from http://www.nytimes.com.

Saville, Victor. *The Silver Chalice*. Warner Bros./A Victor Saville Production, 1954.

Sayre, Nora. "The Screen." *New York Times*. October 22, 1973. Retrieved June 1, 2018 from http://www.nytimes.com.

Schechter, Scott. *Judy Garland: The Day-by-Day Chronicle of a Legend*. Taylor Trade Publishing, 2006.

Schiro, Anne-Marie. "Benefit Sale Gets Glamour Second Hand." *New York Times*. October 27, 1979. Retrieved July 3, 2018 from http://www.nytimes.com.

Schneider, Michel. *Marilyn's Last Sessions*. Edinburgh: Canongate Books, 2011.

Schumach, Murray. "Theatre Project to Bow on Coast." *New York Times*. July 31, 1960. Retrieved April 16, 2018 from http://www.nytimes.com.

_____. "Many Stars Join TV Cancer Show." *New York*

Times. March 29, 1962. Retrieved April 19, 2018 from http://www.nytimes.com.

_____. "Fox Carrying On in Spite of Crisis." *New York Times*. July 2, 1962. Retrieved April 19, 2018 from http://www.nytimes.com.

_____. "... Tarnished Warrior." *New York Times*. July 8, 1962. Retrieved April 19, 2018 from http://www.nytimes.com.

_____. " ... No Fanfare." *New York Times*. August 25, 1963. Retrieved April 24, 2018 from http://www.nytimes.com.

Schwartz, Paula, and Steve Urso. "Theater: On Stages Around the Nation." *New York Times*. May 12, 1996. Retrieved August 31, 2018 from http://www.nytimes.com.

Schwartz, Tony. "ABC-TV Will Replace 8 Shows in 6½ Prime-Time Hours in Fall." *New York Times*. April 30, 1981. Retrieved July 12, 2018 from http://www.nytimes.com.

_____. "Fanciful Men, More Realistic Women." *New York Times*. September 12, 1982. Retrieved July 20, 2018 from http://www.nytimes.com.

_____. "Television: It's Prime Time for Veteran Actors and Women At Work." *New York Times*. August 30, 1981. Retrieved July 14, 2018 from http://www.nytimes.com.

Sculthorpe, Dean. *Van Heflin: A Life in Film*. Jefferson, NC: McFarland, 2016.

Sellers, Robert. *Hollywood Hellraisers: The Wild Lives and Fast Times of Marlon Brando, Dennis Hopper, Warren Beatty, and Jack Nicholson*. New York: Skyhorse Publishing, 2010.

Senft, Bret. "If You're Thinking of Living in: Carnegie Hill." *New York Times*. August 23, 1992. Retrieved August 25, 2018 from http://www.nytimes.com.

Severson, Kim. "He's Got the Salad Covered. Can He Serve You Dinner?" *New York Times*. September 27, 2006. Retrieved September 26, 2018 from http://www.nytimes.com.

Sharkey, Betsy. "Maupin's 'Dream of the Future, Set in the Past.'" *New York Times*. February 28, 1993. Retrieved August 26, 2018 from http://www.nytimes.com.

Shattuck, Kathryn. "Burt Reynolds Has Made Mistakes, but He Regrets Nothing." *New York Times*. March 23, 2018. Retrieved October 9, 2018 from http://www.nytimes.com.

_____. "City Center Plans to Try to Catch Up with the Joneses." *New York Times*. February 5, 1999. Retrieved September 8, 2018 from http://www.nytimes.com.

Shaw, Dan. "Chronicle." *New York Times*. May 21, 1994. Retrieved August 28, 2018 from http://www.nytimes.com.

Shepard, Richard F. "'Katherine Anne Porter' on 13's 'Masters' Series. " *New York Times*. July 11, 1986. Retrieved August 2, 2018 from http://www.nytimes.com.

Sheraton, Mimi. "Newman's Salad Dressing: Oil, Vinegar, and Ballyhoo." *New York Times*. September 15, 1982. Retrieved July 20, 2018 from http://www.nytimes.com.

Sheward, David. *Rage and Glory: The Volatile Life and Career of George C. Scott*. Milwaukee, WI: Applause Theatre & Cinema Books, 2008.

Shewey, Don. "How to Be a Producer, in One Instant Lesson." *New York Times*. July 14, 1996. Retrieved September 1, 2018 from http://www.nytimes.com.

Shipler, David K. "Campaigners Lure Talented Women." *New York Times*. July 17, 1968. Retrieved May 5, 2018 from http://www.nytimes.com.

Shtier, Rachel. "Championing Odets, Unfashionable as That Is." *New York Times*. April 27, 1997. Retrieved September 4, 2018 from http://www.nytimes.com.

Simonson, Robert. "Theater; a Summer Veteran Gets New Life." *New York Times*. July 30, 2000. Retrieved September 11, 2018 from http://www.nytimes.com.

Singer, Penny. "Bob Detmer, a Visionary Video Maker." *New York Times*. October 30, 1994. Retrieved August 29, 2018 from http://www.nytimes.com.

Skow, John et al. "Verdict on a Superstar." *Time*. 1982, Vol. 120, No. 23: 68–72, 74–75, 77.

Smith, Dinitia. "A Star in Twilight Turns Reflective." *New York Times*. March 1, 1998. Retrieved September 7, 2018 from http://www.nytimes.com.

_____. "Theater: At Last, Playing Grandma, She Gets to Be the Star." *New York Times*. April 2, 2000. Retrieved September 10, 2018 from http://www.nytimes.com.

_____. "Theater: Today the Anatomy, Tomorrow the World." *New York Times*. September 26, 1999. Retrieved September 8, 2018 from http://www.nytimes.com.

Soares, Emily. "Article: Summer Wishes, Winter Dreams (1973)." *Turner Classic Movies*. Retrieved June 1, 2018 from http://www.tcm.com.

Solomon, Aubrey. *The Three Faces of Eve* DVD Audio Commentary. 20th Century Fox, 2013.

_____. Leo McCarey's *Rally 'Round the Flag, Boys!* DVD Audio Commentary. 20th Century Fox, 2007.

Somerset-Ward, Richard. *An American Theatre: The Story of Westport Country Playhouse, 1931–2005*. New Haven, CT: Yale University Press, 2005.

Sommer, Bob. "A Curtain Call for the Hyde Park Playhouse." *Chronogram*. May 27, 2008. Retrieved July 2, 2018 from http://www.chronogram.com.

Stafford, Jeff. "Articles: A Kiss Before Dying (1956)." *Turner Classic Movies*. Retrieved February 20, 2018 from http://www.tcm.com.

_____. "Articles: The Drowning Pool (1975)." *Turner Classic Movies*. Retrieved June 7, 2018 from http://www.tcm.com.

_____. "Articles: The End (1978)." *Turner Classic Movies*. Retrieved July 2, 2018 from http://www.tcm.com.

Stanko, Dieter. "Piece by Piece, History in a Tile Mural." *New York Times*. September 5, 1999. Retrieved September 8, 2018 from http://www.nytimes.com.

Stanley, Alessandra. "Film; Scorsese, from the Mean Street to Charm School." *New York Times*. June 28, 1992. Retrieved August 25, 2018 from http://www.nytimes.com.

Stern, Stewart. *No Tricks in My Pocket: Paul Newman Directs*. New York: Grove Press, 1989.

Stevens, Matt. "Paul Newman Rolex Sells at Auction

for Record $17.8 Million." *New York Times*. October 27, 2017. Retrieved October 8, 2018 from http://www.com.

Stone, Matt, and Lerner, Preston. *Winning. the Racing Life of Paul Newman*. Minneapolis, MI: MBI Publishing Company and Motor Books, 2009.

Strauss, Neil. "Lush Odes to the Art of Two Film Makers." *New York Times*. September 19, 1996. Retrieved September 1, 2018 from http://www. nytimes.com.

Sylbert, Richard, and Townsend, Sylvia. *Designing Movies: Portrait of a Hollywood Artist*. Westport, CT: Praeger Publishers, 2006.

Taubman, Howard. "Theater: 'Baby Want a Kiss' Opens." *New York Times*. April 20, 1964. Retrieved April 24, 2018 from http://www.nytimes.com.

Teltsch, Kathleen. "Chronicle." *New York Times*. August 25, 1992. Retrieved August 25, 2018 from http://www.nytimes.com.

_____. "Newman to Endow New Chair." *New York Times*. March 27, 1991. Retrieved August 22, 2018 from http://www.nytimes.com.

Terrace, Vincent. *Encyclopedia of Television Series, Pilots and Specials, Volume 2*. New York: New York Zoetrope, 1985.

Thames, Stephanie. "Article: A Big Hand for the Little Lady (1966)." *Turner Classic Movies*. Retrieved April 30, 2018 from http://www.tcm.com.

Thomas, Tony and Solomon, Aubrey. *The Films of 20th Century Fox*. Secaucus, N.J.: the Citadel Press, 1979.

Thompson, Howard. "… Fun and Names." *New York Times*. April 8, 1975. Retrieved June 8, 2018 from http://www.nytimes.com.

_____. " … Joanne Woodward to Star." *New York Times*. May 16, 1962. Retrieved April 19, 2018 from http://www.nytimes.com.

_____. "M-G-M Double Bill." *New York Times*. May 20, 1965. Retrieved April 29, 2018 from http://www.nytimes.com.

_____. "Movie 'Terrace' Under Local Construction." *New York Times*. January 3, 1960. Retrieved April 14, 2018 from http://www.nytimes.com.

_____. "Ritt for the Record on Direction." *New York Times*. June 1, 1958. Retrieved March 26, 2018 from http://www.nytimes.com.

_____. "Screen: 'From the Terrace' Opens." *New York Times*. July 16, 1960. Retrieved April 16, 2018 from http://www.nytimes.com.

_____. "Screen: Human Element at Speedway." *New York Times*. May 23, 1969. Retrieved May 14, 2018 from http://www.nytimes.com.

_____. "… Self-Analysis." *New York Times*. August 26, 1962. Retrieved April 19, 2018 from http://www. nytimes.com.

Thompson, Nathaniel. "Article: Signpost to Murder (1965). *Turner Classic Movies*. Retrieved April 29, 2018 from http://www.tcm.com.

Tierney. John. "The Big City; a Movie Star Who Favors Pigeon Meat." *New York Times*. May 31, 2002. Retrieved September 14, 2018 from http:// www.nytimes.com.

Tomasson, Robert E. "Social Events." *New York Times*. September 21, 1986. Retrieved August 3, 2018 from http://www.nytimes.com.

_____. "Social Events..." *New York Times*. March 22, 1987. Retrieved August 10, 2018 from http://www. nytimes.com.

_____. "Social Events." *New York Times*. October 11, 1987. Retrieved August 12, 2018 from http://www. nytimes.com.

_____. "Social Events." *New York Times*. October 25, 1987. Retrieved August 12, 2018 from http://www. nytimes.com.

_____. "Social Events." *New York Times*. November 1, 1987. Retrieved August 12, 2018 from http:// www.nytimes.com.

_____. "Social Events." *New York Times*. February 5, 1989. Retrieved August 17, 2018 from http://www. nytimes.com.

_____. "Social Events." *New York Times*. May 6, 1990. Retrieved August 20, 2018 from http://www. nytimes.com.

_____. "Social Events." *New York Times*. May 13, 1990. Retrieved August 20, 2018 from http://www. nytimes.com.

Travers, Peter. "Arts, Briefly." *New York Times*. January 4, 2008. Retrieved September 26, 2018 from http://www.nytimes.com.

_____. "At the Movies." *New York Times*. January 20, 1989. Retrieved August 17, 2018 from http://www. nytimes.com.

_____. "At the Movies." *New York Times*. September 22, 1989. Retrieved August 19, 2018 from http:// www.nytimes.com.

_____. "At the Movies." *New York Times*. January 26, 1990. Retrieved August 19, 2018 from http://www. nytimes.com.

_____. "Footlights." *New York Times*. January 27, 1999. Retrieved September 8, 2018 from http:// www.nytimes.com.

_____. "Lucky Them." *Rolling Stone*. May 29, 2014. Retrieved June 21, 2018 from http://www. rollingstone.com.

_____. "Mr. and Mrs. Bridge." *Rolling Stone*. January 16, 1991. Retrieved August 19, 2018 from http:// www.rollingstone.com.

_____. "This Week." *New York Times*. April 27, 1998. Retrieved September 7, 2018 from http://www. nytimes.com.

Van Gelder, Lawrence. "At the Movies." *New York Times*. October 30, 1987. Retrieved August 12, 2018 from http://www.nytimes.com.

Vidal, Gore. *Palimpsest: a Memoir*. New York: Penguin Books, 1995.

Vogel, Carol. "Chelsea Dawning …" *New York Times*. November 17, 1995. Retrieved August 31, 2018 from http://www.nytimes.com.

Wadler, Joyce. "Boldface Names." *New York Times*. May 22, 2003. Retrieved September 18, 2018 from http://www.nytimes.com.

_____. "Boldface Names." *New York Times*. December 9, 2004. Retrieved September 24, 2018 from http:// www.nytimes.com.

Wagner, Robert, and Eyman, Scott. *I Loved Her in the Movies: Memories of Hollywood's Legendary Actresses*. New York: Penguin, 2016.

Wanger, Walter, and Hyams, Joe. *My Life with Cleopatra: The Making of a Hollywood Classic*. New York: Vintage, 2013.

Weber, Bruce. "Richard Russo, Happily at Home in

Winesburg East." *New York Times*. July 2, 2004. Retrieved September 20, 2018 from http://www.nytimes.com.

———. "Theater ..." *New York Times*. January 9, 2000. Retrieved September 9, 2018 from http://www.nytimes.com.

Weiler, A.H. "'... a New Kind of Love.'" *New York Times*. October 31, 1963. Retrieved April 25, 2018 from http://www.nytimes.com.

———. "Critics Name 'Lion in Winter' Best Film by 13–11." *New York Times*. December 31, 1968. Retrieved May 12, 2018 from http://www.nytimes.com.

———. "'Day for Night' Wins Film Critics.'" *New York Times*. January 9, 1974. Retrieved June 5, 2018 from http://www.nytimes.com.

———. "Film: Newman as Harper." *New York Times*. June 26, 1975. Retrieved June 7, 2018 from http://www.nytimes.com.

———. "Joanne Woodward, Lady Shrink." *New York Times*. November 2, 1969. Retrieved May 15, 2018 from http://www.nytimes.com.

———. "Movies." *New York Times*. January 24, 1971. Retrieved May 22, 2018 from http://www.nytimes.com.

———. "Newmans in Deal for 'Gamma Rays.'" *New York Times*. July 7, 1970. Retrieved May 22, 2018 from http://www.nytimes.com.

———. "... Off Broadway." *New York Times*. July 21, 1957. Retrieved February 28, 2018 from http://www.nytimes.com.

———. "... on Locations." *New York Times*. May 10, 1959. Retrieved April 6, 2018 from http://www.nytimes.com.

———. "Passing Picture Scene." *New York Times*. November 8, 1959. Retrieved April 13, 2018 from http://www.nytimes.com.

———. "... Selected Shorts." *New York Times*. October 15, 1972. Retrieved May 22, 2018 from http://www.nytimes.com.

Weinraub, Bernard. "On Stage and Off With: Steve Lawrence and Eydie Gorme." *New York Times*. September 10, 1992. Retrieved March 24, 2018 from http://www.nytimes.com.

———. "...Planners Are Embarrassed." *New York Times*. January 12, 1977. Retrieved June 18, 2018 from http://www.nytimes.com.

———. "Recalling John Garfield, Rugged Star KO'd by Fate." *New York Times*. January 30, 2003. Retrieved September 15, 2018 from http://www.nytimes.com.

Widdicome, Ben. "On This Night, Everyone's a Singer." *New York Times*. October 20, 2010.

Retrieved October 2, 2018 from http://www.nytimes.com.

Wilson, John S. "On the Fine Art of Singing with Style." *New York Times*. May 15, 1965. Retrieved April 28, 2018 from http://www.nytimes.com.

Worth, Robert. "Bringing College Back to Bedford Hills." *New York Times*. June 24, 2001. Retrieved September 13, 2018 from http://www.nytimes.com.

Wrathall, Nicholas. *Gore Vidal: The United States of Amnesia*. Bull Frog Films/Amnesia Productions/SuperFilms!/audax Films, 2013.

Wyatt, Edward. "Dennis Hopper, 74, Hollywood Rebel, Dies." *New York Times*. May 29, 2010. Retrieved October 2, 2018 from http://www.nytimes.com.

Yamato, Jen. "Toni Collette Filming Paul Newman's Final Pic 'Lucky Them.'" *Deadline*. January 29, 2013. Retrieved June 21, 2018 from http://www.deadline.com.

Yankee, Luke. *Just Outside the Spotlight: Growing Up with Eileen Heckart*. New York: Back Stage Books, 2006.

Yarrow, Andrew L. "Astoria Expands on Its Movie Heritage." *New York Times*. September 28, 1986. Retrieved August 4, 2018 from http://www.nytimes.com.

Yazigi, Monique P. "Neighborhood Report; Upper East Side ..." *New York Times*. July 17, 1994. Retrieved August 28, 2018 from http://www.nytimes.com.

Zacky, Brent and Burns, Kevin. *Cleopatra: The Film That Changed Hollywood*. Prometheus Entertainment/Van Ness Films/Foxstar Productions/Fox Television Studios/American Movie Classics, 2001.

Zindel, Paul. "What's a Nice Boy from Staten Island Doing in Hollywood?" *New York Times*. August 1, 1971. Retrieved May 22, 2018 from http://www.nytimes.com.

Zolotow, Sam. "... Fund Sponsors 'Othello.'" *New York Times*. February 19, 1964. Retrieved April 25, 2018 from http://www.nytimes.com.

———. "'Lovers' Puts Off Arrival by a Day." *New York Times*. April 27, 1956. Retrieved February 17, 2018 from http://www.nytimes.com.

———. "Newmans to Star on Broadway Bill." *New York Times*. April 4, 1963. Retrieved April 24, 2018 from http://www.nytimes.com.

———. "Costigan Expands Play." *New York Times*. February 25, 1964. Retrieved April 25, 2018 from http://www.nytimes.com.

———. " ... Revival Planned." *New York Times*. September 9, 1966. Retrieved May 2, 2018 from http://www.nytimes.com.

Index

Numbers in *bold italics* indicate pages with illustrations